This book has power. It's honest, o   national shifts that every leader need   'ine
insights from a life lived with intention, depth, and distinction. I've long admired the resilience, resolve, and potent impact of her leadership. *Metamorph* helps me understand how I can lead with transformational reciprocity. Everyone who longs for integrity and impact needs to read this book.

DANIELLE STRICKLAND, kingdom entrepreneur; founder, Boundless Enterprise; author, *The Other Side of Hope, Better Together, The Ultimate Exodus, The Liberating Truth, A Beautiful Mess, The Zombie Gospel*, and *Just Imagine*

Kate Coleman's *Metamorph* is a game changer! This dynamic read blends timeless biblical wisdom with relatable stories of everyday heroes, igniting your potential for transformation. Coleman's insights challenge you to rethink leadership and personal growth, making it accessible and inspiring. With her engaging style, you'll feel empowered to embrace change and lead with purpose. This book isn't just a read; it's a call to action. Dive in and unlock the extraordinary within you—your journey to transformation starts here!

BEN LINDSAY, founder and CEO, Power the Fight; author, *We Need To Talk About Race: Understanding the Black Experience in White Majority Churches*

Kate Coleman's latest book is a masterpiece for those who find they are hungry for wise, just, emotionally intelligent, and godly leadership. Moreover, it is firmly rooted in her own life so well-lived for God. With the increasing diversity and complexity of societies in all parts of the world, Coleman's profound insights into biblical principles of leadership interspersed with real stories and practical applications brings a deeply refreshing and much-needed vision of leadership. Coleman speaks into our lives from a broad and prophetic mindset calling the church to Christlike leadership with hope in the power of the Spirit to transform the mind and the heart. This book is not only for leaders or those aspiring to leadership but also brings a powerful message of healing and hope for the whole church.

LUCY PEPPIATT, theologian; Principal, Westminster Theological Centre; author, *The Imago Dei: Humanity Made in the Image of God*

I found myself shouting "Yes! Yes! Yes!" while reading Kate Coleman's book—agreeing that allowing God to change our personal and leadership mindsets leads to greater transformation in our ministries, organizations, and mission. Our societies are becoming increasingly diverse, and if we do not pay attention to the important paradigms she outlines—which are the principles of effective intercultural ministry—we risk falling behind and growing leaders who are unable to cope with our world today.

JESSIE TANG, intercultural ministry director, Diocese of Leicester; ethnomusicologist; UK network leader and trainer, Songs2Serve; strategic team, Intercultural Churches

Stand still for a moment. Be quiet. Can you feel it? The tremor coming up through your feet? The whole of the planet and life is shifting and moving beneath and around us. If you have eyes, you see it everywhere. Coleman sees and feels it. She paints a brilliant, vivid reflection of the internal and external journey leaders must navigate as new world(s) begin to emerge. I am indebted and thankful for the wisdom, prophetic voice, and call to be a metamorph. Thank you.

TIM LEA, white, over fifty, male, educated Christian and networks facilitator and animator, Fresh Expressions UK Ltd

If, like me, you have been waiting for a provocative leadership book that interweaves ancient spiritual wisdom with everyday lived experiences, this is it! *Metamorph* is a refreshing, thoughtful, decolonized, holistic curriculum for leaders from all walks of life, backgrounds, and cultures. For practitioners it is a much-needed example for the next level in global leadership development research, models, sources, and practices. Read it (multiple times), be transformed, and let's transform our world!

GRACE OWEN, founder and CEO, Greater Flourishing; spiritual director, life writer, retreat leader, and former board director, CAMFED International

Our minds were confronted and our hearts animated by reading Kate Coleman's words of seemingly ordinary people navigating the emerging story in front of them in extraordinary ways. We stopped, turned to each other and said, "This is our story!" Coleman eloquently and in her beautifully gentle but firm way unpacks the reality facing leaders in today's world. As a couple who have never really fit into the established mindsets and structures of the inherited church, it was like a mic drop moment! As pioneer disrupters we commend this book to you, but be warned—it may even disrupt your own thinking and ideas!

ANDREA AND ANDREW VERTIGAN, national pioneer leaders, UK Salvation Army

Metamorph is a transformative journey for Christian leaders seeking to become more like Jesus and make a lasting impact in the world. Kate Coleman challenges us to first embody the change we want to see in others, recognizing that personal transformation precedes collective transformation. Drawing on the lives of biblical figures, Coleman offers practical insights for cultivating authentic leadership. By learning from their mistakes and successes, we can deepen our own leadership journey and empower those we lead more effectively. Pick up this book, read it, and most importantly, apply its important lessons.

RICH ROBINSON, cofounder, Movement Leaders Collective, Creo, and Catalyse Change; author, *All Change*

Biased? Yes, I am! What can I say about *Metamorph* without personally commenting on my best friend, Kate Coleman? Every page embodies years of wisdom, insight, personal growth, learning, and lived experience. Coleman has a rare and unique gift that manages to balance theological rigor with practical down to earth, "uncommon common sense." All are invited to take a journey of growth and development from the inside out. Go slow, go steady … this is a book you'll need to reflect on, discuss with others, and return to time and time again.

REV. CHAM KAUR-MANN, codirector, Next Leadership

I've had the privilege of accessing Kate Coleman's wisdom through personal coaching during key moments of my leadership transformation journey. This book dares us to look beneath the surface, to uncover what we don't know about ourselves, and to allow God to reveal those things only he knows about us. Through biblical stories, Kate shares powerful insights and asks important questions that help us glimpse a new personal vision. I recommend this book to leaders and aspiring leaders who desire to fulfill their divine assignment and discover their own personal transformation story.

ANGIE RUSBRIDGE, chief finance officer, YMCA Norfolk, UK

Metamorph is a vital read for those striving to be transformative leaders in today's ever-changing world. Kate Coleman doesn't just offer wisdom; she shares her heart and unique journey, guiding us to rethink leadership. Her wise—often prophetic—perspective is both refreshing and urgently needed. Through her honest and insightful writing, Coleman shows us that leadership starts with inner transformation. The old models of charisma over character no longer serve anyone. Coleman challenges readers to grow (up) and to become better leaders and people. This book is a must-read for anyone who wants to lead others and lead themselves well now and in the future.

WENDY BEECH-WARD, strategic consultant,
The Drummer Agency; former event director, Spring Harvest;
former creative director, Compassion International

Metamorph is a leadership book whose time has come. Kate Coleman's clear and prophetic voice combines fresh insights from biblical stories with wisdom gleaned from the challenges of being the UK's first Black woman Baptist minister. She invites us to transform our sense of ourselves as leaders en route to becoming catalysts of transformation in our communities. Coleman challenges us to become and to multiply disrupted disruptors, preparing God's people for a much-needed move of the Spirit across the Western church. If you are a Christian leader seeking to walk in step with the Spirit today, *Metamorph* is a must-read.

ADRIAN S. LOCK, teaching fellow (Leadership),
Spurgeon's College; founder, Deeper Leaders and
White Allies Network; cofounder, Enabled Leaders

In *Metamorph,* Rev. Dr. Kate Coleman brings both wisdom and wit to expertly guide anyone who loves Jesus to make the biggest difference in the world. Coleman's faithfulness to God and honoring of the majority world ensure that this book is both a challenge and an encouragement. Theologically robust while being deeply practical, *Metamorph* invites each of us to do the work needed to be change-makers in whatever arena we find ourselves.

NATALIE COLLINS, CEO, Own My Life; author, *Out Of Control: Couples, Conflict and the Capacity for Change, Abuse Is A Verb: How to Talk and Write About Abuse,* and *Gender-Aware Youth Work: Confronting Gender-Based Injustice with Young People*

Metamorph is a deft blend of biblical truth, prophetic insight, and years of leadership experience, delivered with a striking mix of humor and vulnerability. Good as it is, be warned: Only read it if your transformation is more important to you than your comfort. While the path that unfolds in its pages is costly, there is compelling reassurance in knowing its author has walked and still walks this way herself.

DAMILOLA MAKINDE, formation team, KXC (King's Cross Church); advocacy engagement lead, Evangelical Alliance

I encourage you to read this book slowly and prayerfully, with notebook and pen to hand and an open heart. If you allow it, *Metamorph* will not only challenge you; it will also change you. Coleman has written another excellent contribution not only to the leadership world but also to kingdom leadership, where the reader is invited to embrace a journey of personal transformation with the goal of progressing God's purposes in this world. If you're looking for inspiration and insight to become an agent of change, *Metamorph* is a must-read!

SHIRENE AGBELUSI, associate pastor, Coventry Elim, UK

A work of inestimable significance, Coleman's *Metamorph* gets at the heart of why most leadership initiatives fail and how to fix them. As she asserts, "We expect leaders to enact a kind of positive change they have never personally experienced for themselves." Through Coleman's wisdom, we can instead embrace personal transformation and, in turn, transform the world around us. This is a book I will be rereading and recommending for years to come.

ONEYA OKUWOBI, assistant professor of Sociology, University of Cincinnati; author, *Who Pays for Diversity?* (forthcoming)

As I have sought to pioneer access to palliative care in the Kingdom of Lesotho, the principles highlighted in *Metamorph* have significantly shaped my own leadership development. I've had the honor and privilege of tapping into Coleman's wisdom, knowledge, and insight, and I love the fact that they are firmly founded on biblical narratives. *Metamorph* will empower twenty-first-century leaders globally with the necessary skills to navigate personal and professional terrains in a quest to address the multidimensional service gaps in our communities both near and far.

TEBELLO MALICHABA LEPHEANE, CEO, Starlight Oasis of Hope Hospice, Kingdom of Lesotho

This book is not just for our traditional understanding of a "leader" but is actually for everyone. *Metamorph* offers insightful and wise perspectives and reflections for our journeys of trying to be authentic, integrous humans. Written in a style that is refreshingly honest and easy to engage with, it brings humor and heartfelt stories alongside the most profound wisdom that stops you in your tracks! Weaving in her own experiences, a host of other sources, and a rich Bible narrative, Coleman speaks to our hearts and will move the reader to reflection and enable transformation … or metamorphosis!

ELLIE GAGE, CEO, Kintsugi Hope

This book will establish a hunger for growth and development where complacency has set in. Experience the joy of your salvation while challenged to morph into all God intends you to be. Growth often pivots around challenge, struggle, and glorious mistakes. *Metamorph* will help you to look in the mirror without being overwhelmed by the flaws you see or the successes you have already experienced. If you want to see things change, you must be the change you want to see. God says, "See, I am doing a new thing!" (Isa. 43:19). It is in our kingdom DNA to do likewise. This book shows you how. Happy morphing!

HELEN YOUSAF, creative arts pioneer; prophetic artist; collaborator; trustee, United Christian Broadcasters

If you're merely looking to set leadership goals and broaden your knowledge, this book isn't for you. If, however, you're seeking to become more Christlike in every way, recognize the ongoing work of the Holy Spirit, and are committed to serving God and his people until the day you leave this planet … *Metamorph* will equip you to give all you are to the transformation of yourself and those you serve. Coleman has done more than write a book or create a tool; she has poured herself into the transformative work of the Holy Spirit.

USHA REIFSNIDER, PhD, British Gujarati Christ follower; regional codirector, Lausanne Europe; director, CMMW (Centre for Missionaries from Majority World); missionary, ECM (European Christian Mission)

We need a new kind of leader. Kate Coleman's book *Metamorph* will go a long way to helping us grapple with what those leaders might look like. Coleman is unafraid to delve into areas usually swept under the carpet and dares to go where others fear to tread. She brings a prophetic voice with practical solutions all deeply grounded in the Scriptures she clearly loves. Her use of stories, many from her own life, make this book accessible yet deeply profound. An important book for all "leaders" who actually lead—don't miss it!

STEVE AND ANGIE CAMPBELL, senior pastors, The C3 Church; national directors, Global Leadership Network, UK and Ireland

META MORPH

KATE COLEMAN

META MORPH

Transforming Your Life and Leadership

Inspired Wisdom from the Extraordinary,
Ordinary People of the Bible

100 MOVEMENTS
PUBLISHING

First published in 2024 by 100 Movements Publishing
www.100Mpublishing.com
Copyright © 2024 by Kate Coleman

All rights reserved. No portion of this book may be reproduced or transmitted in any form or by any means, electronic or mechanical, including photocopying, recording, or by any information storage and retrieval system, without permission in writing from the author. The only exception is brief quotations in printed reviews.

The author has no responsibility for the persistence or accuracy of URLs for external or third-party internet websites referred to in this book and does not guarantee that any content on such websites is, or will remain, accurate or appropriate.

Some names have been changed to protect the privacy of individuals.

Library of Congress Control Number: 2024945887

All Scripture quotations, unless otherwise indicated, are from Holy Bible, New International Version®, NIV®. Copyright © 1973, 1978, 1984, 2011 by Biblica, Inc.™ Used by permission of Zondervan. All rights reserved worldwide. www.zondervan.com. The "NIV" and "New International Version" are trademarks registered in the United States Patent and Trademark Office by Biblica, Inc.™

Scripture quotations marked ESV are from the ESV® Bible (The Holy Bible, English Standard Version®), © 2001 by Crossway, a publishing ministry of Good News Publishers. Used by permission. All rights reserved.

Scripture quotations marked MSG are taken from *The Message*, copyright © 1993, 2002, 2018 by Eugene H. Peterson. Used by permission of NavPress. All rights reserved. Represented by Tyndale House Publishers.

Scripture quotations marked NET are taken from *The NET Bible*®. Copyright ©1996–2017 by Biblical Studies Press, L.L.C. All rights reserved.

Scripture quotations marked NKJV are taken from the New King James Version®. Copyright © 1982 by Thomas Nelson. Used by permission. All rights reserved.

Scripture quotations marked NLT are taken from the *Holy Bible*, New Living Translation, copyright ©1996, 2004, 2015 by Tyndale House Foundation. Used by permission of Tyndale House Publishers, Carol Stream, Illinois 60188. All rights reserved.

Scripture quotations marked NRSV are taken from the *New Revised Standard Version Bible*, copyright © 1989, 1995 by the Division of Christian Education of the National Council of the Churches of Christ in the United States of America. Used by permission. All rights reserved.

ISBN 978-1-955142-60-1 (print)
ISBN 978-1-955142-61-8 (eBook)

Cover design and interior artwork: Jude May
Cover image © mycelia | iStock

100 Movements Publishing
An imprint of Movement Leaders Collective
Richmond, Virginia
www.movementleaderscollective.com

*To Mohinder Kaur: We don't share the same language,
yet you know me like a mother.
To all you metamorphs: Seen and unseen, near and far ...*

CONTENTS

Foreword by Christine Caine — xvii
Foreword by Alan Hirsch — xxi
Preface — xxiii

PART ONE: INTRODUCING METAMORPHOSIS — 1

1 METAMORPHIC LEADERSHIP
Changing Leaders, Changing Leading — 3

2 TRANSFORMING WISDOM
Living Parables, Leading through Story — 25

PART TWO: TRANSFORMING IDENTITY — 47

3 MOSES: A PATH TO SELF-DISCOVERY
Nurturing Curiosity from the Inside Out — 49

4 THE WOMAN AT THE WELL: THE ART OF BECOMING
Defeating Self-Limiting Mindsets — 77

PART THREE: TRANSFORMING COMMUNITY — 103

5 MARY AND ELIZABETH: TOGETHER IS BETTER
Leveraging the Power of Friendship — 105

6 THE APOSTLES: JUST LEADERSHIP
Developing Radical Empathy to Break Systemic Strongholds — 131

PART FOUR: TRANSFORMING MISSION   **161**

  7 **ESTHER: LEADING ON PURPOSE**
       Discerning Your "Whys"   163

  8 **THE 120: MULTIPLYING DISRUPTED DISRUPTORS**
       Embedding a Strategic Mission Mindset   191

The Metamorphic Journey Continues   *221*
Acknowledgments   *223*
Notes   *225*
About the Author   *249*

FOREWORD

Christine Caine

I believe that *Metamorph* is the most important leadership book you will read. Kate Coleman has given us a prophetic, personal, profound, and practical gift in this book. It is obvious to anyone paying attention that our world has fundamentally changed in every way over the past two decades, and if we are going to be the leaders God has called us to be, we must radically reimagine what Christian leadership actually is. Clearly, what we have been doing is not working, and as someone smart once said, "The definition of insanity is doing the same thing over and over again and expecting different results."[1]

Like many people, I stumbled into a ministry leadership role almost by accident. The problem was, I not only brought my academic qualifications and gifts to that job in 1990, but I also brought my brokenness, wounds, and baggage. I was a devoted and committed Jesus-follower, but years of abuse, marginalization, and abandonment had caused deep trauma; and, because I did not deal with it, let's just say it dealt with me. I am grateful that, as difficult as the lesson was, it happened very early on in my leadership journey and forced me to deal with the pain and trauma of my past. It was obvious the disparity between my inner life and my external practices would eventually lead to my collapse.

If I wanted to change the world for the glory of God, I had to let God change me from the inside out. I did not need to hide behind a position, title, or system where I could feign behavior modification. Instead, I needed to embrace personal transformation. My gifts and talents were taking me to a place that my character could not keep me, and I have no doubt that, had I not committed to the process of ongoing personal transformation, I would today be another one of the failed leadership stories that are sadly all too common in the ministry world.

This is why I believe *Metamorph* is such an important book. Kate masterfully unpacks how Jesus himself gives us the power of positive growth and change and that "if we participate with God in renewing our minds and transforming our practices, habits, and behaviors, we can become the powerful change agents God intends."[2] In order to do this we have to be willing to reconsider everything we think we know about leadership. God is doing a new thing in a new way in our times, and we must be willing to get on board with his methods instead of trying to hold on to our old paradigms, frameworks, and expectations.

In my early days of leadership, I was often the only woman at whatever table I was sitting at and the first woman to do almost everything I was called to do. I was also the daughter of Greek immigrants, and the whole white, Anglo-Saxon Protestant world was an odd minefield to navigate for someone with my background and life experience. If I had not had a deep sense of the call of God and an utter dependence on the power of the Holy Spirit to help me become who I needed to be to do what I was called to do, I would not have made it. The systems, structures, pipelines, and pathways for leadership development and opportunities were not designed for people like me.

Today, I have the opportunity to work alongside some of the most amazing leaders in the fight against human trafficking. The quarterly Zoom gathering with our global team is my favorite meeting. On each call, around two hundred staff represent twenty offices in fifteen nations. For 58 percent of our team, English is their second or third language. Women represent 75 percent of our global team, which ranges from nineteen to seventy-eight years old. I marvel at the wonderful and diverse people God has brought together from around the globe to help abolish slavery everywhere forever. When I started out on my leadership journey, this kind of co-laboring was unheard of, but for the younger generation, it is the air they breathe. If we are to fulfill the mission of God and reflect how God is at work in our world to our world then we need a leadership transformation—a metamorphosis.

We have the opportunity and responsibility to do things differently, and this book shows us how. The hour is urgent, and the mission is vital. We must feed "internal transformational mindsets," which will help us cultivate "observable actions, practices, and behaviors that ultimately shape and transform metamorphs."[3] If you internalize and implement the insights of this book, you will not only become the leader you were designed to be, but you will also raise up and unleash a generation to be the leaders God has made them to be.

Let's do this!

FOREWORD

Alan Hirsch

Much of my work over the last thirty years has been about calling the church in the West to respond to the challenges of our times by recentering our lives on Christ, renewing our minds to his ways, and sparking movements that allow our churches and organizations to unleash kingdom transformation organically.

Yet, what is most required in this vital work is the presence of godly leaders—men and women who don't just hold the necessary skills to maintain the status quo or evoke a sense of "success" based on our outdated forms of Christendom but who are ready to respond to ongoing metanoia. Metanoia is a paradigm shift and conversion that changes the heart. Jesus initiated his public ministry with a call to metanoia: "The kingdom of God has come near. Repent [*metanoia*] and believe the good news!" (Mark 1:15). Metanoia is the gateway for seeing through a different, Jesus-shaped lens and is the way of life Jesus invited all who follow him to embrace.

This book is a guide for leaders to live out this call. *Metamorph* offers an enlightening journey, one that has the potential to profoundly impact anyone willing to engage deeply with its content. Kate's work stands out for its thoughtful integration of timeless wisdom, biblical understanding, and practical insights, making it both a theoretical exploration and a hands-on guide for transformational leadership.

Kate's ability to weave together biblical narratives—storied stories—with contemporary leadership challenges creates a rich tapestry that invites leaders to consider how they pursue ongoing transformation for themselves and for the sake of those they lead. This book urges readers to reflect deeply on their own leadership journeys and consider how they might embrace change and transformation in their own contexts.

Kate offers an inside-out approach, beginning with the inner life of the individual and expanding outwards. By progressively exploring identity, community, and mission, she provides a structured framework culminating in a compelling vision of metamorphic leadership.

In today's rapidly changing world, *Metamorph* is essential reading for those who want to address the complexities and challenges of modern leadership. Kate does this with refreshing honesty and clarity, refusing to shy away from the hard truths but instead encouraging leaders to confront these realities head-on with courage and faith. Although we may feel disheartened as we hear of so many leadership failures across the church, Kate's emphasis on personal transformation as a precursor to organizational and societal change is a powerful reminder of the ripple effect that authentic, Jesus-centered leadership can have.

In essence, *Metamorph* is a masterful work that combines scholarly insight with practical application. It is a must-read for anyone serious about leading with integrity and purpose in today's complex world. I truly hope that we will see many metamorphs rise up to the challenge of making a lasting impact through transformative leadership for kingdom change.

PREFACE

What I wanted to do for this world was to change it for the better, I was going to write a book that was going to show people a reflection of themselves. Then the world changed me, or at least it changed how I saw it.
HABULEMBE MWANAKALANGA

When I started writing this book, I was not in the best of places. Many factors contributed to this, including the usual suspects of health, circumstances, and people. Then again, none of us writes in a vacuum, so I can see now—with the benefit of hindsight, of course—how God used these challenges and other experiences to shape what you are now reading.

In 2022, I had two significant surgeries within a short period. My codirector and best friend, Cham, also had three more that same year—two minor surgeries because of a sudden decline in her eyesight, and ironically, her third major surgery was identical to one of mine. It would be an understatement to say it was a time of immense physical, mental, emotional, and spiritual strain! Neither of us had ever been hospitalized with any kind of major (or indeed minor) "anything." So we were taken completely by surprise to find ourselves fast-tracked, almost simultaneously, into emergency operations at what seemed to be the worst time imaginable ... amidst a global pandemic.

For some reason, we expected to bounce back into action as if nothing had happened, having somehow conveniently forgotten we were now a whole year older than the year before! But it soon became clear that our bodies had fewer cooperative plans for us anyway and, with weakened immune systems, we simply succumbed to one infection after another.

I'm grateful that despite having to work between and after each operation, as well as facing the prospect of being financially overstretched at the worst time imaginable (did I mention the pandemic?), the healing proceeded steadily. Some we met in hospital had been far less fortunate. However, eighteen months later, we were considerably worse for wear, exhausted, and bone weary in ways we'd never experienced before. Perhaps predictably, my hair fell out, and Cham developed a mysterious red, blotchy, and insanely itchy skin condition. Usually, we're great at keeping one another buoyed; but we were now both "down" at the same time, and things were not looking good.

Our organization was going through significant changes too, from rebranding to new opportunities and increased demands. We faced internal challenges, unexpected relational issues, and a continuous flow of distressing family news. The unexpected losses of dear friends due to COVID-19 and other illnesses during the pandemic only added to the weight of it all.

One British saying captures it well: "It never rains, but it pours." Let's just say … this was torrential! Yet we found ourselves under the protective umbrella of prayer. Months earlier, we'd sensed a prompting to intensify our weekly prayer and fasting routines. (This had to be divine, as I don't willingly forgo meals!) Simultaneously, our incredible friends and prayer partners offered us timely prophetic insights and prayers, often unaware of our specific circumstances. The storm that had stripped us back was a powerful reminder of our weaknesses and frailties, as well as of God's unwavering goodness and grace. Amazingly, our relationships with God were better than ever before … then again, there's nothing quite like multiple crises for improving one's prayer life.

Perhaps it was ironic that at the very same time I was having this mini-revival, I was also feeling particularly ambivalent about my relationship with the church. This wasn't a reflection on any one church in particular or even the church I attended. Instead, it arose from a combination of things, including my disappointment at the lukewarm responses of church leaders to the killing of George Floyd on May 25, 2020, a feeling compounded by a research project I'd just completed into the church's historical ties with slavery and the slave trade. Then, like everyone else, I also witnessed the record number of high-profile Christian leadership failures across the entire spectrum of the global church with very little evidence we'd learned anything from our previous mistakes. So, I was definitely out of love with the idea of church as I knew it. It seemed in stark contrast to the community Jesus had envisioned and initiated. I was sick, tired, weary, and frankly desperate not just for change but also for profound transformation.

So, I could hardly believe it when an incredible opportunity arose to collaborate with a diverse group of women leaders, both nationally and internationally, to envision a new path for Christian faith communities—a path that meant reimagining Christian leadership too. Shortly after this, I received an invitation to "chaplain" a three-day event celebrating exceptional Black professionals dedicated to exploring ways to safeguard young Black lives across the UK. The experience was mind-blowing and reignited a fire in me that I hadn't realized had gone out. Many attendees were significantly younger than me, and as I observed them, I wondered if I'd ever been quite as bold and self-assured as a younger leader myself. On my journey home, I found myself praying for them and smiling intermittently to myself at their incredible potential. It's anyone's guess what my fellow train passengers made of my alternating facial expressions.

Both these "interventions" were an undeniable Godsend. Both allowed me to explore "out loud" and to dream again. *What was God up to? How might the landscape change for Christian leaders and leadership in the future? And what might the past reveal about the leaders needed for the future ahead?*

In the land of my birth, Ghana, there is a symbolic language called *Adinkra*. One of its symbols is the Sankofa: It depicts a bird flying forward while looking back, carrying an egg in its beak. Sankofa urges us to retrieve wisdom from our past in order to fully realize our potential as we move ahead. It signifies that what may have been lost or forgotten can be reclaimed and reenergized. When I started writing about leaders, leadership, and transformation, I had already begun revisiting some old truths in fresh ways. I was convinced of the pressing need for those of us devoted to Jesus and leading in his name to embrace nothing less than transformation as an integral part of the journey of following him and as a fundamental element in progressing God's purposes.

As is often the case, the season had granted me a "gift." As my body compelled me to slow down, it also prompted me to reflect on what truly mattered. I knew that I had to be about the business of developing leaders whenever and wherever I could. I knew I would have to relinquish the many things I *could* do to focus on the few things I *should* do. I also realized there was a parallel between my writing journey and my personal and organizational journey. Cham and I often refer to these moments as "living parables" because, during these times, the Holy Spirit crafts what can only be described as bespoke curricula. In this instance, the curriculum for me faithfully mirrored each challenge and lesson I happened to be writing about at the time.

Cham and I also actively participate in the developmental journeys we design for others on our programs and learning experiences. For many years, our refrain has simply been, "We're on the program too." This has enabled us to stay attentive to what God might be saying or doing in and through us. This season, though emotionally demanding, felt just like those transformational journeys but on a far grander scale.

I am a huge believer in the power of God to transform difficulties, situations, and individuals (myself included) in ways that change the world around them for the better. In the following pages, you will find a written expression of my ongoing conviction and commitment to this truth. And, despite having more than thirty-five years' experience of local and national church leadership, as well as the privilege of having coached and mentored some truly outstanding women and men from all over the world, I am just as committed to being on this "program" of leadership transformation with you.

PART ONE

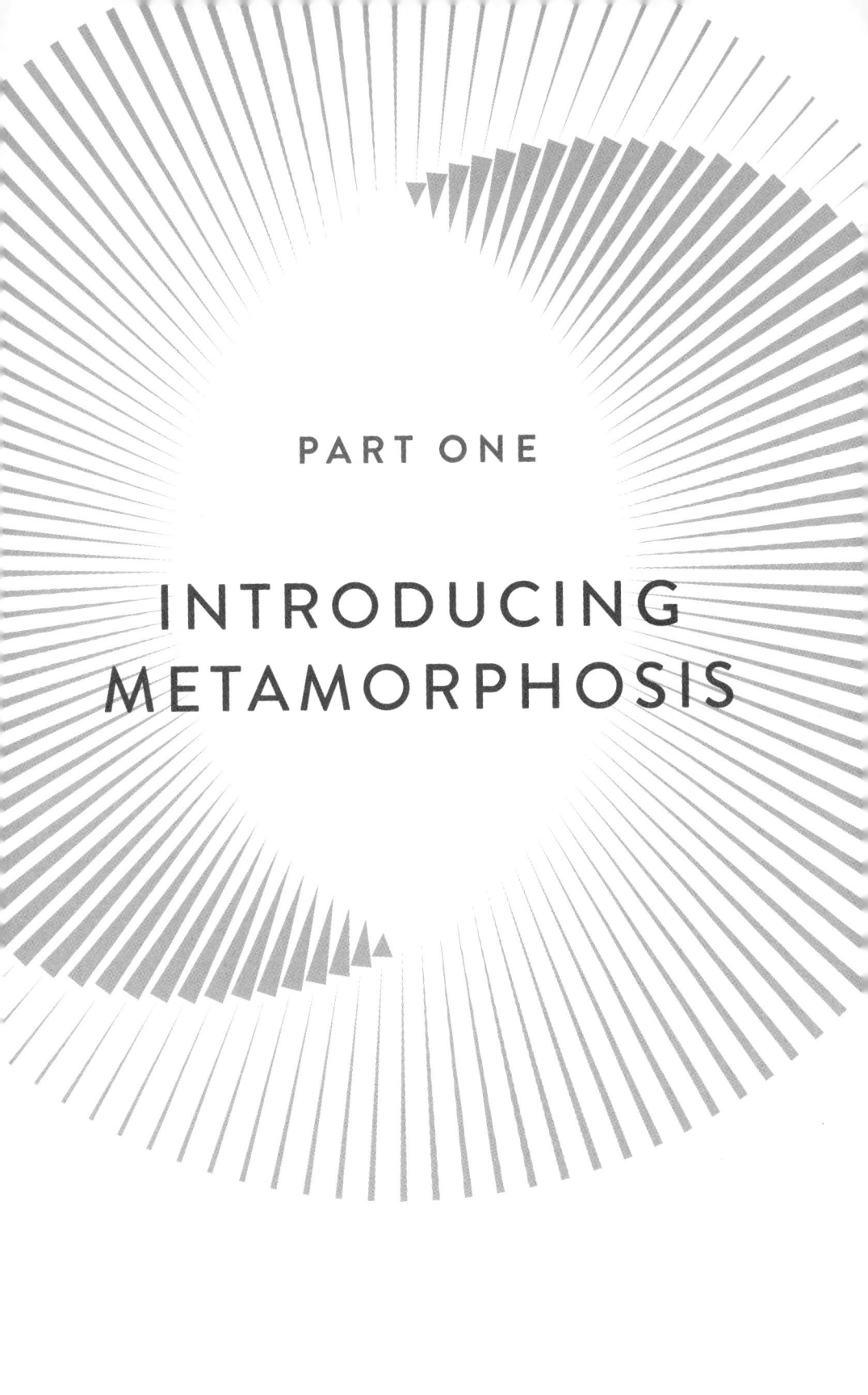

INTRODUCING METAMORPHOSIS

METAMORPHIC LEADERSHIP

Changing Leaders, Changing Leading

What you're supposed to do when you don't like a thing is change it. If you can't change it, change the way you think about it.
MAYA ANGELOU

The process of becoming a leader is much the same as the process of becoming an integrated human being.
WARREN BENNIS

And we all, who with unveiled faces contemplate the Lord's glory, are being transformed [metamorphoumetha] into his image with ever-increasing glory, which comes from the Lord, who is the Spirit.
THE APOSTLE PAUL

Years ago, I stumbled across a story about someone who wanted to change the world. They invested considerable effort but couldn't seem to achieve anything significant. They shifted their focus to their country, thinking they should start there, but again, they saw very little progress. Subsequently, they turned their attention to their city and even their neighborhood, yet success eluded them at every turn. Then they thought they could at least change their family, but that endeavor also fell short. Frustrated, they decided to focus on changing themselves. What happened next was entirely unexpected. As they transformed, their family followed suit. Their changed family influenced the neighborhood, which in turn impacted the city. The changed city affected their country and ultimately led to a transformation that rippled across the entire world.[1]

THE LEADERSHIP IMPERATIVE

This book is about how we bring about desperately needed change. But, according to our morality tale, we often begin the journey in precisely the wrong place. Our story suggests that it is one thing to recognize the need for change but quite another to identify what actually needs changing in the first place.

Leadership is often credited as the vital factor in driving positive change. So, given the degree of change needed in our wider society,[2] and even in our own households, ignoring the challenges, demands, or indeed pitfalls of leadership is a luxury we can ill afford.

For followers of Jesus, leadership occurs when an individual or group partners with God to advance his purposes in whatever shape or form this may take. This understanding of leadership establishes the supremacy of God, and it also always positions us as followers so that God alone occupies the leading edge, first chair, or primary catalyzing role in however we choose to think about leadership. Thankfully, God's leadership supremacy doesn't exclude us from participation; we are, after all, "co-workers" together with Christ (1 Cor. 3:9). Instead, God invites us to share in his governance, as seen in Genesis chapter 1, and makes us partners with him in a leadership journey that takes us through personal transformation to becoming agents of transformation in this world.[3]

All this should be welcome news to followers of Jesus, entrusted as we are with "works, which God prepared in advance for us to do" (Eph. 2:10). It implies, in theory at least, that by simply accepting and acting on God's invitation, any one of us, regardless of sex, ethnicity, personal history, educational attainment, or talents, can be "called" upon to lead.

Many Christians, myself included, view positive change as evidence of God at work. But as we shall see, no change comes without complication, pain, or struggle. Genuine change actually emerges from a multitude of endeavors taking place across diverse landscapes, involving different kinds of people, in different eras, that ultimately impact situations and individuals in uneven and often unpredictable ways. Although it may be clearly laid out from God's perspective and open to everyone, the path of leadership is, humanly speaking, far more complex, messy, and frustrating than many expect and in ways that are often hard to predict.

The Changing Nature of Leadership

The leadership journey, whether physical, geographical, behavioral, spiritual, or otherwise,[4] is increasingly complicated because leadership means different things to different people who, as it turns out, are living in ever closer proximity to one another. Sex, culture, age, and ethnicity can all influence what people consider valid leadership issues or appropriate leadership styles. Our background, history, social groups, and the conferences we choose to attend all say something about our leadership preferences. For Christians, even our view of the Holy Spirit's role in our day-to-day activities and our understanding of God as immanent or transcendent can impact *how* we believe leadership should be exercised and *who* we think should exercise it.[5]

Today, leadership success often depends on our capacity to navigate the increasingly diverse relational borders we encounter. These not only include diversity of experience and the distinct characteristics of organizations and departments but also ideology, gender, sex, ethnicity, and so on.[6]

As our relational borders have expanded, workplaces, organizations, and ministry environments have also evolved. The environment in which we exercise leadership is changing in increasingly complex ways. In the Western world, as people live longer, the different values and expectations of nearly five distinct generations are emerging in workspaces and ministry settings, heightening already existing tensions. Each generation has a unique perspective on what suitable leadership, approaches to work, and even dress codes should look and feel like. Even in other global contexts, what may have looked like effective leadership fifty, thirty, or even twenty years ago is very different from what effective leadership looks like today.

Influence based purely on institutional role, position, and permission—accompanied by hierarchical, top-down directives—is no longer universally acceptable. The pervasive presence of social media has made it far easier for ordinary people to influence decision-making by simply bypassing traditional gatekeepers altogether. Meanwhile, traditional leadership tasks are increasingly being delegated to artificial intelligence (AI).[7] There has also been a departure from leadership models that invite hubris, arrogance, and the "solo heroic journey" (which was never really appropriate in the first place!). Instead, there has been a necessary shift toward relational, cooperative models of leadership that invite participation and rely less on "telling" and more on "listening." These models also prioritize ethical, humble, and authentic leadership that cultivates shared vision, mutual goals, trust, loyalty, respect, and reliability. Overall, this has led to individuals in churches, communities, civil society, and businesses feeling less like cogs in a wheel and more like valued contributors with significant roles in making change happen.

Leadership thinking is also expanding beyond conventional Western frameworks that rely heavily on logic, data, algorithms, and (sometimes epic!) report writing. There's been a growing acknowledgment of the significance of spirituality and other types of knowledge and information. Franciscan priest and writer Father Richard Rohr describes how "Western models of development usually focus on the rational mind, which offers one way of knowing reality, but in fact, there are many other ways of perceiving and expressing human experience."[8] In her book *Our Unforming: De-Westernizing Spiritual Formation*, spiritual director Cindy S. Lee summarizes three major cultural orientations: linear to cyclical, cerebral to experienced, and individual to collective.[9] In the West, we imagine development as a straight line with a beginning, middle, and end, with measurable progress markers along the way. We focus on the accumulation of knowledge, and our leadership approaches tend toward excessive individualism. When we want to know how advanced a person, church, or organization is, we look to what they know and how much they've achieved rather than what kind of person or organization they are or even how wise they are. Eastern and Global-South thinkers see development as a cycle rather than a straight path. They value the quality of change and transformation more than just gaining information. They also tend to prioritize the well-being of the community and collective voices over individual desires and achievements. In this paradigm, increasing wisdom and experience are the main indicators of growth within individuals, communities, and organizations. Each of these orientations exists along a continuum, and each has its own strengths and weaknesses. Increasing global interaction and mixing means that few individuals and communities will truly live at the extremes of each continuum.

Western leaders, accustomed to authority, resources, and predictability, now face unfamiliar and morally charged challenges. They also increasingly have an opportunity to learn from non-Western leaders already familiar with navigating uncertainty, scarcity, and oppression and whose cultural orientation often better equips them for these realities.[10] But Western leaders must first recognize that these insights aren't always communicated through the Western models they are accustomed to. Indigenous traditions, for example, often draw leadership wisdom from community, nature, signs, and symbolism that speak deeply to the subconscious.[11] Those open to the ingenuity and resilience of these alternative paradigms must develop the skill of "interpreting other tongues" if they are to benefit from the invaluable insights into adaptability, spirituality, resilience, and community commitment often found in them. Those who raise the value of humility to a leadership non-negotiable,[12] and who are willing to learn from those they have traditionally believed needed to learn from them,[13] will grow the most as leaders.

It's ironic that some Christians embrace theologies that justify culturally bound expressions of leadership and support the notion that "real" power resides in certain individuals at the "top" of our organizations and churches. Followers of Jesus should readily grasp that we already have power within us and that the Holy Spirit actually offers us more! We should also be eager to imitate a Savior who uses power for the benefit of others rather than himself and advocates for others rather than at their expense. Even today, some Christian organizations and churches are stuck in outdated and toxic leadership models, even though the imagery of the body of Christ is a more fitting blueprint for leadership than the desire of some Christian communities for a "king to judge us like all the other nations have" (1 Sam. 8:5 NLT).

The COVID-19 pandemic, ongoing environmental crises, widespread migration, evolving global discussions on race and female leadership, and the emergence of artificial intelligence—known collectively as a polycrisis—continue to highlight the need for ongoing and substantial change.[14] However, this will not simply be about letting go of old paradigms, although this would be a good start; it will also be about adopting an entirely new playbook and redefining our approaches to leadership altogether. As US congresswoman Lois Frankel notes, with the continuous evolution of the external environment, followers evolve too.[15] This evolution necessitates a parallel shift in *how* people are led and *who* should be leading.

The Changing Faces of Leadership

I used to know when I was speaking to a group of leaders, at least in formal terms. They had titles, positions, and authorized roles. They engaged in certain types of activity and were invested with permissions and authority by their institutions, churches, movements, and organizations. These individuals were sanctioned representatives, almost like ambassadors, and I was struck by their uniformity, not just in appearance but also in their manner and approach to leadership. These individuals were frequently presented as the official and acceptable "faces" of leadership. Their outfits (whether suits, jackets, or trendy ripped jeans) or even their hairstyles were a kind of aesthetic signature. They also adopted an approach to leadership they presumed and promoted as universally applicable but, in reality, rarely applied to more than a select few.

Until recently, genuine collaboration within work or ministry spaces has been notably lacking (some would say it still is). Anyone considered remotely "different" was simply expected to erase every aspect of themselves deemed unnecessary and conform seamlessly to existing cultures, structures, systems, and processes with no questions asked or objections raised. Historically, and even now, they have been consciously and unconsciously pressured into reshaping their ways of thinking, speaking, acting, being, and dressing (and for Black people, even how they style their hair!) to be more like white men or women in their leadership looks, style, language, or approach. This expectation has also existed in many of our churches, even those self-identifying as multi-ethnic or intercultural. However, if we are to unveil the leadership potential of every individual, we must take a very different approach.

For many years, I was the only Black woman Baptist minister in the UK, navigating a context that scarcely acknowledged women or Black people in leadership roles. I remember one white male colleague telling me that as a Black, single female minister, all I now needed was a wheelchair! He thought he was being very funny. I did not laugh. I didn't look like anyone else or approach things like colleagues who were white church leaders, male or female. On one occasion, I was explicitly told that my approach to ministry was wrong because of what I prioritized, the way I preached, who I allowed into the pulpit, and how I dressed, which was unlike white Baptist ministers at the time, male or female. I even attempted to conform by wearing the then "uniform" of incredibly unflattering fuzzy woolly sweaters favored among UK Baptist ministers at the time (mainly blue and beige, as I recall). Let's just say they did nothing for me! Frustratingly, I have been subjected to similar sentiments on so many occasions I have simply lost count.

All this was compounded by the scarcity of women (of any hue) I could look to for advice or learn from. Nearly everywhere I turned—aside from a select few "havens"—the message echoed loud and clear: "You don't belong here as you are; to fit in, you must change and become more like us." It felt suffocating and profoundly distressing to be adrift in a church, seminary, and work culture that demanded such conformity and failed to recognize the existence, let alone the validity, of other ways of seeing and being. Einstein once said, "Everyone is a genius. But if you judge a fish on its ability to climb a tree, it will spend its whole life believing it's stupid."[16] I believe many "fish-like" leaders are being expected to climb trees in churches and organizations all over the world today.

The *Harvard Business Review* article from February 2021, titled "Stop Telling Women They Have Imposter Syndrome," by Ruchika Tulshyan and Jodi-Ann Burey, perceptively highlights a profound truth:

> We don't belong because we were never supposed to belong. Our presence in most of these spaces is a result of decades of grassroots activism and begrudgingly developed legislation. Academic institutions and corporations are still mired in the cultural inertia of the good ol' boys' clubs and white supremacy. Biased practices across institutions routinely stymie the ability of individuals from underrepresented groups to truly thrive. The answer to overcoming imposter syndrome is not to fix individuals but to create an environment that fosters a variety of leadership styles.[17]

I have known for years that existing leadership systems, processes, and cultures were never designed with women or people of color in mind. Leadership, traditionally, has been narrowly defined by standards tailored to suit white male norms (and occasionally white female norms). This has made it difficult for women and people of color to survive, let alone flourish, within many existing leadership landscapes. These environments only truly work for a limited range of predominantly white men who are rewarded and endorsed by a system that largely echoes their language, experiences, and perspectives, irrespective of their actual creativity, capabilities, or competence! Ironically, not even all white men (or white women, for that matter) reap the benefits of this arrangement.

I still encounter this traditional mold of leadership today but find myself increasingly interacting with a different kind of leader. I'll call these the less conventional "faces" of leadership. These leaders come in varied forms, some with titles and official recognition; others, however, operate without such formalities. They stand out because of their remarkable diversity, which goes beyond the usual organizational variety we've become accustomed to, such as education, sector, interests, skills, or expertise. They also now include broader demographic aspects, such as gender, race, ethnicity, culture, abilities, socioeconomic status, and generational differences that also shape the way people think and act. Interestingly, some of these new types of leaders do not even "think" of themselves as leaders in the traditional sense, nor do they adhere to the appearance, language, or preoccupations of the old-style leaders. Yet they are actively partnering with God, advancing his purposes, and transforming the very fabric of the world as they know it.

This new kind of leader shatters old paradigms, frameworks, and expectations. They dare to take fresh approaches and offer new possibilities for a transformed and transforming future, yet they are seldom "the usual suspects."

So the new kind of leader could be anyone. Perhaps, more to the point, it could be you! We could argue that this kind of leadership has always existed, but the difference now is its growing normalization. In other words, this new kind of leader isn't just growing in numbers; they are here to stay.

TRANSFORMING LEADERS, TRANSFORMING LEADERSHIP

Freed from the constraints of outdated leadership structures, we have an opportunity to construct healthier leadership cultures where individuals don't have to suppress large parts of themselves in order to make progress. It seems that anyone can be empowered to make a difference. Indeed, the future of successful organizations will partly depend on their ability to recognize that leadership can live everywhere in the organization and that everyone should be encouraged to take ownership and exercise responsibility in ways that make the best use of their abilities and passions.

Each of us is called to discern our vision and mission and embrace the fact that God entrusts us to make meaningful change in the world. Not everyone, of course, will have the same scale of influence. Some may even be individual contributors, but we will all have an opportunity to partner with God and enable something to happen that would not have happened without us. But to realize this, we will all need the kind of personal development that can transform us into leaders who actively contribute to the world we long to see.

Changed Leaders Make Change

Like the story of the person who wanted to change the world, those who aspire to bring about change should be willing to adapt their own mindset and behaviors *before* seeking meaningful change elsewhere. In other words, personal transformation must precede collective transformation, in much the same way as global transformation is said to begin with human transformation.[18] Far from a demand for perfection, we are invited to adopt a disposition perpetually open to personal change.

Leaders who embrace this perspective usually like to lead by example, and their willingness to engage in their own development seemingly inspires people to believe in transformation elsewhere. True leadership, rooted in the commitment to personal transformation, is distinct from the narrow, self-serving pursuit of popularity often mistaken for leadership.[19] For although popularity can lead to things *changing*, only transformed leaders *transform* the world for the better. Richard Rohr makes a helpful distinction between the two: "The word *change* normally refers to new beginnings. But the mystery of transformation more *often happens not when something new begins, but when something old falls apart.*"[20]

Before we can experience true transformation, we must be willing to let our old ways "fall apart." Leaders who have learned to "fall apart" also tend to nurture a mentality capable of creating what does not yet exist. Those who are committed to changing themselves for the better also tend to change the people, systems, and structures around them for the better. They simply can't seem to stop themselves and better still, seem disinclined to do so.

Without the essentials of personal transformation, self-leadership, and transformative influence, all that remains is mere aspiration, just as the morality tale at the beginning of this chapter implies. But when we and our plans "fall apart," it becomes possible to experience personal transformation and become transformative in ways that initiate the systemic changes we so desperately need in our world today.

The Origin of Metamorphs

The Greek word that encapsulates our much-needed leadership transformation is "metamorphosis" from the Greek prefix *meta*, which carries the meaning of "beyond," "after," or "with," indicating a change, and *morphe*, which denotes "form" or "shape." Unlike simple "change," which typically involves adjustments to an existing system, metamorphosis describes a far more comprehensive and radical developmental journey that leads to an altered form or sometimes even a higher or more developed state. In other words, as suggested earlier, "not every change amounts to a transformation but every transformation involves fundamental change."[21]

As a concept, metamorphosis is often linked to the growth stages of various insects and amphibians and typically involves the key phases of egg, larva, pupa (chrysalis), and imago (mature adult). A classic example is when a caterpillar transforms into a butterfly and progresses through a metamorphosis from the caterpillar to the pupa,[22] and from the pupa to the adult butterfly. As this happens, it undergoes such a profound alteration in its form, structure, habits, and appearance that the emerging butterfly bears little, if any, visible resemblance to its initial caterpillar form.

However, metamorphosis is not limited to insects and amphibians, as I discovered during a recent visit to the beautiful country of Sri Lanka. As part of our itinerary, my traveling companions and I were taken to a gemstone manufacturer by our tour guide. Now, anyone who knows me well knows I have little to no interest in precious stones. (Diamonds are definitely not this girl's best friend!) So, as I was attempting to navigate the shortest "escape" route across the showroom, I stumbled upon a glass case labeled "metamorphic rock." Having never studied geography I had no idea this was even a thing. Needless to say, despite being surrounded by rubies, emeralds, sapphires, and diamonds, it was here that I chose to pause and linger. Our tour guide looked suitably unimpressed that mere stones, of all things (and not even the expensive variety), had caught my attention. However, for our guide, at least, the worst was yet to come. I became even more animated when I discovered that Sri Lanka is well known for gemstones precisely because it is geologically composed of around 90 percent Precambrian metamorphic rock. As the name implies, they literally begin life as one type of rock and, with pressure, heat, and time, gradually change into another type of rock entirely. A few days after this already memorable experience, God topped it all when "out of the blue," I was gifted with my very own piece of metamorphic stone! (I'll leave the telling of that story to another day.)

Up to 80 percent of insects and over half of all vertebrates (animals with backbones like humans) are metamorphic and change from one form to another, just like metamorphic rock.[23] However, the concept of metamorphosis can also be applied to humans. In his blog post, "Transformation or Transfiguration?" episcopal priest Marshall Scott notes,

> Metamorphosis was a familiar concept from Ovid's play, "Metamorphosis." The play was completed about the same time Jesus was born. So, in the world around the earliest Christians this idea of metamorphosis was common. In it characters are changed, not only in form, but in substance, in essence. Narcissus really becomes a flower. Arachne really becomes a spider. Scylla really becomes a seabird. Niobe really becomes a rock. Metamorphosis didn't just change what you looked like, but changed what you are.[24]

Indeed, humans can be truly metamorphic, although not in quite the same way as insects, amphibians, and rocks.[25]

Jesus advocated metamorphosis when he used the Greek word *metanoia*, which we usually translate as "repent." The word literally means "to change one's mind" and points to the profound shift in mindset and heart that precedes a new way of living. In his book *Seven Ways to Change the World*, Jim Wallis describes it this way:

> Jesus proclaimed in the Gospel of Matthew, "Repent, for the kingdom of heaven is at hand." The word he used was *metanoia*, which in the Greek literally means transformation, from the root of the word *metamorphosis*. He is saying that a whole new order is about to enter history and, if you want to be part of it, you will need a change so fundamental that the Gospel of John would later refer to it as a new birth.[26]

So, it should come as no surprise that the exact same concept dominates the thoughts and writings of the apostle Paul. In Paul's thinking, metamorphosis involved fundamental and observable developmental changes. He believed in the potential for human beings to undergo a metamorphosis capable of profoundly and visibly altering their mindset, physicality, and behavior.

In 2 Corinthians 3:18, Paul insists that metamorphosing is the envisioned state for every genuine follower of Jesus and the avowed work of the Spirit. "And we all, who with unveiled faces contemplate the Lord's glory, are being transformed [metamorphosed] into his image with ever-increasing glory, which comes from the Lord, who is the Spirit."

Here, the Christian journey is portrayed as a progression where everything changes, including our disposition, practices, habits, and behaviors, from one level of glory to another (*metamorphoo* in Greek, literally "transfiguration"). Here, believers are to be the active and eager recipients of transformative change. Similarly, in Romans 12:2, believers are encouraged to proactively participate in metamorphosis: "Do not conform to the pattern of this world but be transformed [metamorphosed] by the renewing of your mind." According to Paul, only the profound change associated with metamorphosis allows for a departure from our old ways and facilitates a significant break from what would otherwise be the natural order of things. In other words, metamorphosis is presented as the sole means for bringing about a fundamental change to the present condition of our hearts, minds, habits, behaviors, and practices.

In this book, I am combining the abbreviated term "morph," meaning fundamental change or transformation, together with "meta," this time taken to mean a foundational idea that can help shape our identity and practices,[27] to describe the people, groups, and organizations who lead both from and for a fundamental transformation: "metamorphs."

According to 2 Corinthians 3:18, to be personally transformed and transformative as actively participating metamorphs, we are to uncover our faces, removing every barrier from before our eyes so that we can perceive our true state in the light of Jesus' nature. Far from evoking despair or hopelessness, we are encouraged to approach this unveiling with confidence in the knowledge that as we "fall apart," Jesus himself will guide, change, transform, and equip us in our transition into the next magnificent phase of our lives and leadership.

THE CHRISTIAN'S "META" VERSE

In an age captivated by a technologically driven "metaverse," Christians are called to navigate their own "meta" reality,[28] centered on the two vital Greek concepts mentioned earlier: metanoia and metamorphosis. Both are important as we explore the transformation of leaders and leadership. However, metanoia appears to emphasize the inward and subjective nature of transformation, while metamorphosis seems more oriented toward the outward, observable, and developmental aspects of the necessary transformation. Metanoia occurs when a current belief that motivates our actions, practices, and behaviors is superseded by another stronger, deeper truth. Effective leadership requires constant metanoia, constant transformation in thinking. However, only metamorphosis can reveal whether deeper truths have indeed been transformational and led to the observable external changes we'd expect in our actions, habits, and behaviors. In other words, when our beliefs truly change, our actions also change. It is therefore impossible to have the inward experience of metanoia without an outward expression of metamorphosis in the Christian life. However, once we have come to faith and are alive to God's new creation, the converse is also true: By changing our actions, our beliefs can also be changed. By inculcating practices and habits that best reflect who we want to be as leaders, we are able to cultivate a mindset that is increasingly aligned with God's will (Rom. 12:2, James 2:26 NLT).[29] Metanoia and metamorphosis act like a virtuous cycle where each promotes, reinforces, and supports the other.

While "metanoia" and "metamorphosis" are biblical ideas, the terms "leader" and "leadership" are not explicitly biblical. But writer Steven Croft reminds us that, "the Judeo-Christian tradition provides the longest continuous source of reflection on questions of leadership in the whole of human history."[30] However, we misconstrue this tradition when we treat leadership as a noun or an identity that can be possessed or attained. Leadership is never a mere mindset; it is always more than what we think or purport to believe or say. We come closer to biblical thinking when we regard leadership as a verb— as something we do, as in "leading"—rather than as something we are. The Bible also presents leadership as a dynamic rather than static activity that is just as much the result of metamorphosis as it is intended to be metamorphic. In other words, emphasizing metamorphosis and what is recognizable and observable is important to leadership because transformative practices, habits, and behaviors—although inevitably emerging from transformed hearts and minds—also support ongoing personal and societal transformation.

So, my intention throughout this book is to inspire those who lead to cultivate strategies that promote our "falling apart." These strategies predispose us to the transformative practices, habits, and behaviors that support our internal and external transformation. The strategies we will consider include nurturing curiosity, defeating self-limiting mindsets, leveraging friendship, developing radical empathy, discerning our "whys," and embedding a strategic mission mindset. These strategies *emerge from* and *lead to* the kind of transformative practices, habits, and behaviors you will find throughout this book. In leadership, it is important to avoid any confusion between our impact and our intentions. Some believe that because their hearts are in the right place, their leadership practices, habits, and behaviors will also be in the right place. In reality, even good people do terrible things, so leaders must intentionally cultivate strategies that facilitate the practices, habits, and behaviors that better express their leadership intentions. Our ability to "notice" and reflect on our development as leaders is also critical. Only by promoting *and* surrendering to the process of metamorphosis can we make metamorphic leadership possible. And only a conscious (metanoic) desire to be shaped and formed within God's purposes, both inwardly and outwardly, can give rise to the metamorphs so urgently needed in our world today.

The Metamorphic Is Everywhere

Since metanoia, metamorphosis, and leading are central to the Christian story, we would expect to see multiple examples of each throughout the Bible. And indeed, examples abound. However, this book is committed to feeding the internal transformational mindsets and cultivating the observable actions, practices, and behaviors that ultimately shape and transform metamorphs. The language of metamorphosis,[31] with its emphasis on observable characteristics and activities, best reflects leadership as a verb—a "doing word."

Right from the outset, the Bible establishes the dual position of human beings as being part of the natural world but possessing the potential for advancement *and* degeneration. From Genesis to Revelation, the Bible provides an amazingly rich resource of wisdom on metamorphic leadership development for anyone willing to mine its depths, Christian or otherwise.

Developmental transformation is evident from the opening pages of creation to what it means to be like "a tree planted by streams of water" in Psalm 1:3 to the "time for everything" of Ecclesiastes 3 to the language of sowing and reaping in the Psalms (126:5), Proverbs (11:18, 22:8), and throughout New Testament books such as Galatians (6:7–8), 2 Corinthians (9:6), Luke (19:20–21), and Matthew (13:24).

Images of new birth are liberally sprinkled throughout the New Testament, and the language of discipleship is indelibly linked to learning, growth, and development in texts such as Matthew 28:19 and beyond. Metamorphic language is also evident in verses such as Philippians 2:6–7, Galatians 4:19, and specific accounts like the transfiguration in Mark 9:2–3 and Matthew 17:1–2 where Mark and Matthew employ the verb we noted earlier, "metamorphoo," meaning transfiguration, precisely because it depicts a complete change of form or appearance into a more beautiful or glorious state.

References to stages of maturity in passages like 1 Corinthians 3:1–3—where believers are weaned off milk while transitioning to meat—also highlight developmental themes. As does the language of little children, youth, and fathers found in 1 John 2. Even Jesus is said to have grown in wisdom and stature (Luke 2:52). And, as we shall see, the Bible is filled with stories of humans embracing the process of transformation (for better and for worse) and being changed from the inside out.

Indeed, the principles of growth, transformation, and observable development are so central to the biblical narrative that God's people are portrayed as being on a metamorphic development journey, paralleling their spiritual, social, and geopolitical journeys. And this rollercoaster of a journey is never truly "complete" this side of eternity.

For Christians, Jesus gives us the power of positive growth and change from the very beginning. If we participate with God in renewing our minds and transforming our practices, habits, and behaviors, we can become the powerful change agents God intends. The outcome of all this, of course, is leaders who are not easily "tossed back and forth by the waves" (Eph. 4:14), and who can "test and approve what God's will is" (Rom. 12:2).

When Metamorphs Go Wrong

We usually imagine the best and most wonderful outcome from metamorphosis. (It's probably all the talk of butterflies!) But, given humans' dual capacity for both advancement *and* degeneration, transformation can work both ways. Even as professing Christians, we can both embrace *and* resist change. This is starkly portrayed in Kafka's novella *The Metamorphosis*,[32] where a man (Gregor Samsa) wakes up one morning to find he has changed into what many modern translations describe as a "horrible vermin," very likely a giant dung beetle or cockroach! His transformation is so extreme and complete that he is unable to perform the "simple" tasks he'd been able to do before, like easily getting out of bed, communicating with his family, or eating anything other than partially decaying human food.[33]

Most people are averse to cockroaches, and I suspect there are good reasons for this, having never had a positive encounter with one in my life. The idea of waking up to discover you have transformed into something fearful or even repulsive is truly terrifying. Yet this kind of degeneration is a very real prospect for leaders and leadership.

The designers of the "Inner Development Goals" initiative[34]—an initiative aimed at promoting sustainable development for both people and planet—decided that what was needed to change the world had to come from within. It was becoming painfully clear that although people often know what must be done to bring about necessary change, they too often succumb to greed, selfishness, and indifference. In other words, the barriers to positive change stem from internal rather than external obstacles. Christians recognize in this the fundamental "fallenness" of human nature and the impossibility of turning the tide on such sinful self-interest without embracing God's intervention.

Thankfully, very few, if any, leaders actually plan to become "cockroaches" when they start out. Nonetheless, the disposition can creep up on us (forgive the pun). Leadership is not only in danger from degeneration but also from deformation.[35] The latter occurs whenever external pressures and temptations lead to the compromise of our personal or organizational integrity as leaders. We shall see some devastating examples of leadership degeneration and deformation in the subsequent parts of this book.

With this in view, humans share one other aspect of the metamorphic journey with caterpillars that is worth exploring briefly. We too can journey through life thinking we are one thing, unaware of our true transformative potential to become something entirely new and beautiful. But this is where the comparison ends. We are obviously not caterpillars (biologically or otherwise) who at least will naturally evolve into their fullest potential. Human beings, on the other hand, will sometimes resist the very possibility. Even when we do opt for transformation, we will quickly discover that, unlike a caterpillar, a once-in-a-lifetime transformation is woefully inadequate for our development needs.

This means that metamorphs must always be intentionally proactive about the divine expectation and imperative to morph toward becoming Christlike. However, in this, we cannot rely on discipline alone, whose demanding willpower "is like a muscle that tires."[36] Instead, we must free our seemingly limitless positive desires and proactively *long* for the perpetual inward remaking and continuous remodeling of our lives and leadership in ways that truly glorify and promote God's kingdom.

Thankfully, Christian conversion was never intended to be a onetime event but an invitation to a lifelong practice. Both the repentance (metanoia) associated with internal conversion and the transformation (metamorphosis) associated with external observable development are intended to be mutual, dynamic, and ongoing. This means they demand our engagement and cooperation virtually every moment of every single day.

Ultimately, both discipline and personal desire prove inadequate. Even when we "have the desire to do what is good, … [we] cannot [always] carry it out" (Rom 7:18). The change we need is only possible when we rely on something more dynamic and "out of this world" than our mere human desires (even those that are God-given), resources, and insight. Christ-oriented metamorphosis is possible only when God's Holy Spirit is invited, involved, and ultimately handed control of the entire process. This means we will need to proactively surrender control whenever we suspect we have taken it back again.

BEYOND ONE-DIMENSIONAL APPROACHES

Our ability to remain vigilant in our leadership development will be paramount because even Christian leaders are not immune to the temptations that accompany leadership. We too can degenerate or deform in the ways already outlined. We too can become preoccupied with the shallow measures of growth and one-dimensional approaches to success on display in the rest of the world. We too can become addicted to the acquisition of knowledge,[37] skills, facts, size, numbers, wealth, power, popularity, longevity, spiritual gifts, and so forth, and the misguided belief that we are actually changing something for the better. So, we too must become adept at drawing upon whatever resources we need in order to morph in ways that actually advance God's purposes and please God's heart.

We all know that expanding our knowledge and intellect, sharpening our skills, and acquiring all that our hearts desire do not necessarily lead to transformation or to being transformative. Like the story of Esau's bowl of stew in Genesis 25:29–34, leaders may have "unintentionally" sold their birthright too cheaply and settled for too little in pursuit of a singular dimension of leadership growth and development.

In contrast to these pursuits, our commitment to growing deeper with God[38] and in greater self-awareness leads to bigger hearts and minds that we eventually recognize as maturity, insight, and imagination. This dimension fuels our ability to transform necessary knowledge and intelligence into wisdom, grace, discernment, righteousness, and the ability to see life from someone else's point of view. Under pressure to "perform" and "succeed," many leaders have paid little attention to this dimension of their growth and have been all the poorer for it.

This dimension of development acknowledges that the road to growth is far from easy and inevitably involves painful moments of moral crisis and confrontation. It recognizes the vital necessity of actively involving others through diverse dialogue, collaboration across differences, commitment to life in community, and holding each other accountable with "feedback" and "feedforward," like Paul's confrontation of Peter in Galatians 2:11–14. This dimension actively embraces the power of failure, Rabbi Nahum Ward-Lev asserts:

> God supports falling forward, mistake-ridden risk-taking, and boundary crossing for the sake of growth in consciousness and relationship.... The God of the prophets continually calls a wayward people to return to right relationship that they might be healed of the consequences of their mistakes.[39]

Viewing failure as an intrinsic and expected part of this dimension of growth should come as a welcome relief to those of us who recognize within ourselves the same inclinations as the person in our earlier story who wanted to change the world.

Far too often, we expect leaders to enact a kind of positive change they have never personally experienced for themselves. They are taught to develop vision, mission, and strategic plans, make presentations, and be persuasive by following logic, listening to facts, crunching data, and writing algorithms as if there were no other way of operating. (By the way, other cultures do not begin with the premise that logic is the only way to think about the world.) They are encouraged to focus on using the "right" curriculum and being trained to market and mobilize, with little consideration for whether personal growth or transformation in themselves or the people they are leading is happening in the process. They are led to believe that it is what they accomplish rather than who they are becoming that amounts to true success. Often, it is too late before they recognize that what passes for success in many of our organizations, churches, and Christian ministries is virtually identical to the measures adopted by the "world" and ultimately a far cry from God's measure of faithfulness.[40] They are driven to achieve but with little notable progress toward either wisdom or maturity. Yet, as Richard Rohr reminds us, "A truly spiritual woman, a truly whole man, is a very powerful person. The fully revealed God of the Bible is not interested in keeping us as children (1 Cor. 13:11) or 'orphans' (John 14:18). God wants adult partners who can handle power and critique themselves (see Heb. 5:11–6:1)."[41]

Getting Comfortable Being (Mostly) Uncomfortable

In theory, Christians acknowledge this need for deep self-reflection and self-discovery work in order for leaders to align with God's purposes and achieve faithful, fruitful success. However, in practice, even Christians (myself included) can be highly resistant to embracing what may be deemed "unnecessary" discomfort. Hebrews 12:4–11 highlights the pain often associated with this necessary inner work. The passage concludes by suggesting that this discipline, though initially painful, eventually yields "a harvest of righteousness and peace for those who have been trained by it" (v. 11). This resonates with the "falling apart," breaking down, and reconstruction suggested by the metamorphic process and the pressure, heat, and time required to change metamorphic rock. Rick Warren's well-known phrase also echoes this sentiment: "There is no success without growth. There is no growth without change. There is no change without loss. And there is no loss without pain."[42]

Many of the non-Western leaders mentioned earlier also acknowledge this need. However, Western ideas of growth and change are often linear, upward, and optimistic in suggesting that things can only get better *and* bigger. They are based on the premise that correct knowledge and a better understanding of God will inevitably lead to right behavior. In contrast, in most non-Western cultures, leadership is learned through practice rather than primarily through accumulating knowledge (although this has its place). In these cultures, greater value is attached to experiencing God than understanding God. In past-oriented cultures like that of my birth (Ghanaian), change is viewed as circular and therefore not quite as optimistic as the Western idea of change. There is an expectation that whenever there is growth, it will be followed by loss, and that loss will be followed by growth. The ability to accept and adapt to the positive and negative in this cycle is the signal that growth is taking place. Development is not assessed by how long it takes, how much is learned, how many books are read, prayers offered, conversions clocked up, discipleship classes attended, Bible verses memorized, retreats taken, or conversations had, but by the evidence of actual inner transformation. Here, less interest is shown in how much a person knows *about* leadership and more in whether they actually know *how* to lead. Circular approaches to development are ultimately more realistic, lead to greater resilience, and are more likely to survive the pervasive uncertainty of our times. However, in the same way that a tree grows downward, upward, and outward simultaneously, growth is never simply limited to one dimension.

Leadership development is ultimately multidimensional and multilayered, regardless of culture and context. In my mind, it is like an onion, where delving into deeper developmental realms involves gradually removing layers of obstacles and resistance. Just like an onion, the journey that takes us deeper into ourselves and into God also invariably leads us to tears. Another way to envision this journey is as a spiral pathway. Instead of peeling away the layers until nothing remains (an improbable scenario considering the entrenched nature of some of our barriers), this describes a circular path that progressively delves deeper, narrows, and intensifies over time. However, unlike a spiral staircase that we climb upward, the path to growth is counterintuitively and relentlessly downward. Developmental progress is more like walking *down* a spiral escalator as it moves up.[43] The spiral nature of the pathway indicates that individuals often revisit the most stubborn and demanding parts of their leadership journey on multiple occasions, in different forms, usually under more challenging circumstances and at deepening levels of consciousness. It moves us up as we move on down, so there is no obvious end to the journey of growth, at least in this life. As a spiral, this circular development of growth followed by loss, and loss followed by growth has a trajectory. We are changed "from one degree of glory to another" (2 Cor. 3:18 ESV), so we should expect to meet new problems and make better mistakes. Tears are an acknowledgment that the losses involved are often accompanied by pain. (We shall meet this spiral escalator again briefly in chapter three.) Here, growth is less about progress and more about *shalom*,[44] with its appeal to the entirety of personal, interpersonal, and systemic aspects of growth. Lisa Sharon Harper defines the Old Testament Hebrew word *shalom* as well-being, wholeness, the perfection of God's creation, abundance, and peace.[45] Similarly, the New Testament Greek form of shalom, *eirene*, means restoration of relationship, wholeness, healing, and peace. We therefore "measure" our degree of transformation rather than the route it took to get us there.

Thankfully, the path to becoming mature leaders isn't solely paved by the pain of adversity, challenge, and failure. As cultural commentator David Brooks makes clear in his book *The Road to Character*, growth also springs from deep introspection and inquiry. It thrives when we absorb the best traits from our closest friends or seek to serve someone we love deeply or admire greatly. We grow and expand our emotional capacity when we experience great art or music. The causes we commit to also elevate our desires and help us channel our energies.[46] All these and more empower us to navigate the tricky spiral escalator of growth and development, which carries us up as we commit to the downward internal journey.

The Emergence of Metamorphs

What we lead may be "out there," but where we lead from is largely internal. Therefore, our spiritual, mental, emotional, and physical health affects our leadership for better or for worse. If we choose to ignore these aspects of ourselves, the integrity of our leadership will suffer as a result.[47] In his book *Bread for the Journey*, Henri Nouwen sheds helpful light on this:

> We like to make a distinction between our private and public lives and say, "Whatever I do in my private life is nobody else's business." But anyone trying to live a spiritual life will soon discover that the most personal is the most universal, the most hidden is the most public, and the most solitary is the most communal. What we live in the most intimate places of our beings is not just for us but for all people. That is why our inner lives are lives for others. That is why our solitude is a gift to our community, and that is why our most secret thoughts affect our common life.[48]

Nurturing each dimension of leadership is essential if we are to emerge as effective metamorphs. The external and internal, multilayered and multidimensional spirals of development are reminders that Christian leadership is primarily a call to transformation, not just information, education, or multiplication! Therefore, every believer and would-be leader is faced with the simple but inescapable challenge to "morph."

So, this book is about transforming leadership, but hopefully not the kind that adds endlessly to knowledge or merely produces greater understanding for its own sake. People are seldom transformed by facts or knowledge, and the limits of intellect and rationality are on display for all to see. The aim of this book is to encourage deeper reflection on the personal journey every leader, church, and organization must make as we navigate both our internal and external worlds in ways that provoke us toward leading better. This book is also an invitation to embrace your identity as a metamorph and to encourage yourself and the metamorphs around you to continue on a metamorphic leadership journey that personally transforms you, your churches, organizations, and the wider world beyond. Of course, the question we now face is: How do we get from where we are to where we really need to be? Thankfully, this is the theme of our next chapter. From one metamorph to another, as you embark on your very own spiral escalator, you'll discover, as I did, how storied stories and living parables have a profound part to play in your emerging metamorphic journey.

TRANSFORMING WISDOM

Living Parables, Leading through Story

> *The universe is made of stories, not of atoms.*
> MURIEL RUKEYSER
>
> *If you can tell a story well, you can move people to do something.*
> SOLEDAD O'BRIEN
>
> *The human mind is a story processor, not a logic processor.*
> JONATHAN HAIDT

Much of what we do to grow leaders in the West appeals largely to our heads rather than our hearts. Many leadership training courses focus on enhancing our cognitive capacity and feeding us information with little expectation of genuine transformation. They reward people for improving what they know rather than who they are becoming. In fact, the more a person, church, or organization knows, the more "advanced" we consider them to be. We have not only unquestioningly accepted this distorted vision of what leadership should look like, but we have also exported it everywhere within reach, all over the world. These courses rarely account for the evolving nature of leaders and leadership or the dangerous limitations of our cultural orientation and its broader implications. We train leaders to be experts on knowledge in the context of safety, stability, security, comfort, and convenience while overlooking the increasing insecurity and instability we and others actually face. All because, for us, knowledge is king.

Yet, the unique nature of the leadership challenges ahead and the swiftly evolving leadership landscape means we must resist our disproportionate reliance on the acquisition of knowledge as the primary transformative tool for leadership development. As we have seen, the gap between what we know and what we do is seldom one of understanding. And our semi-reverence for data, cognitive ability, theory, strategy, and well-articulated plans has so far delivered resoundingly mixed results! If the quest for knowledge, so prevalent in Western educational paradigms, was all that was required to generate great leadership, we'd have solved (rather than created) many of our toughest global challenges a long time ago.

LESS MESSING WITH OUR HEADS

Usually, it is not the lack of an adequate curriculum or information that holds leaders back from realizing their full potential or from leading well. Leadership specialist John Maxwell aptly notes that "understanding leadership and actually doing it are two different activities."[1] Marshall Goldsmith, a leading global executive coach, suggests the real challenge is "not understanding the practice of leadership; it is practicing our understanding of leadership."[2] A failure of leadership is rarely due to a lack of knowledge. Therefore, a far more fundamental approach to transforming leaders and leadership is required, if only because "our ability to know something intellectually is not the same as integrating or embodying that knowledge on an equally complex emotional and behavioral level."[3]

As important as it may seem to pursue better definitions, engage with the latest theories, follow the development of new schools of thought, and add to ever-increasing reservoirs of knowledge, these are simply no substitute for the ability to actually lead well *and* for the greater good. Indeed, our preoccupation with knowledge has led us to depend on our own abilities rather than God to get things done. More is being asked of leaders, and the stakes are significantly higher than ever. As a result, too many leaders simply find themselves out of their depth, or worse still, ill-equipped to lead consistently *or* for the common good. Unfortunately, there is always a price to pay whenever leaders fail, especially Christian leaders.

Clearly, we are no longer facing mere leadership training concerns (i.e., what good leadership looks, feels, and sounds like). Instead, we are facing far more daunting developmental challenges. We must now grapple with the monumental task of creating processes capable of not simply informing and educating but also enlarging hearts and expanding minds to see the world, our churches, organizations, and even ourselves in a whole new light.

While there are no simple solutions to improving leadership, foundational biblical cues can influence both the caliber and quality of future leaders and leadership. Given our need to adapt to a rapidly evolving leadership terrain and our responsibility to nurture emerging leaders—who could be anyone or indeed everyone—we must do everything we can to adopt or learn from these fundamental principles.[4]

More Heart than Head

The Bible emphasizes that the inner recesses of our private lives truly matter to God. According to 1 Samuel 16:7, "The LORD does not look at the things people look at. People look at the outward appearance, but the LORD looks at the heart."[5] Passages like Jeremiah 17:10 affirm this, "I the LORD *search the heart* and examine the mind" (emphasis added). Many Christian leaders act as if they don't truly believe God is watching them 24/7; we're functional atheists when it comes to our hearts. As a result, we often neglect this internal terrain. However, multiple biblical references underscore God's preoccupation with the heart and therefore our responsibility toward it.[6] When leaders pay insufficient attention to the obstacles littered throughout their inner world, they may neglect precisely what Jesus values most and hinder their own path toward genuine metamorphosis.

In the Bible, the heart is where our inner life begins. It's regarded as the core of our being, the source of our life and vitality, and the essence of our humanity. Among its attributes are the capacity for reasoning, contemplation, inspiration, and discernment. A person might be characterized by a clean, contrite, undivided,[7] or wise heart. Our heart defines and reveals our true nature to those who genuinely seek to understand us. Jesus expresses this in Luke 6:45: "Good [people] bring good things out of the good stored up in [their] heart, and evil [people] bring evil things out of the evil stored up in [their] heart. For the mouth speaks what the heart is full of."

The condition of the heart—the central core of a person—matters in leadership because this is where we nurture the internal scripts,[8] personal convictions,[9] and character commitments[10] that often guide our actions and words as leaders. Put another way, we can't improve our leadership efforts without considering what makes us do what we do and how we do it. In current leadership thought, it is Emotional Intelligence (EI) that focuses on this ability to manage our own internal world and understand the internal worlds of people around us.[11]

However, our heart is also influenced by the health of the environments in which we work and minister. These environments can liberate, confine, encourage, stifle, empower, or disempower us, and we may need help navigating or transcending them if we are to become better leaders.

Far from emerging in a vacuum, leadership is continually being influenced and molded by external and internal factors, both consciously and unconsciously, and the heart is impacted every single time this happens. This makes all metamorphosis an inside-out process requiring the full engagement of our hearts. Kouzes and Posner, two experts in leadership theory, highlight that "becoming a leader begins with an exploration of the inner territory as we search to find our authentic voice. Leaders must decide on what matters in life, before they can live a life that matters."[12]

More Wisdom than Knowledge

Any inability to understand our own mindsets, experiences, and mental processes, or the diverse perspectives and thinking of others, simply makes it harder for Christian leaders and believers to navigate our increasingly complex world. A lack of depth on our part will only be exacerbated by the constant shifts currently taking place across the leadership landscape. Many of these are already leaving some leaders feeling defeated, overwhelmed, and exhausted. But when combined with a lack of maturity, fear of embracing contradictions, defensive shallowness, and a scarcity of moral courage, these deficiencies soon lead to toxic leadership behaviors, vulnerability to the seduction of power, self-isolation, and a narrow focus on the technical aspects of leadership rather than its potential for transformation. Under the circumstances, we need more than mere insight; we need the kind of insight that displays wisdom.

In many non-Western traditions, leaders have always emphasized the importance of wisdom alongside knowledge.[13] As mentioned in the previous chapter, indigenous cultures—deeply connected to nature and attuned to their environments—often prioritize wisdom in their leadership paradigms. They highlight the interconnectedness of all aspects of life and emphasize qualities like awareness, empathy, collaboration, and collectivism (with its emphasis on the well-being of the group), as well as diverse paths to decision-making.

Even the Western scientific community is showing an interest in the nature of wisdom. Richard Rohr notes,

> In the past couple of decades, science has turned its attention to wisdom, an age-old character trait celebrated since ancient times yet almost entirely overlooked today. Wisdom, it turns out, can be defined, measured and cultivated. It is not the same as knowledge, intelligence or experience; in fact, it doesn't particularly correlate with those. (We all know smart people who aren't wise!) Rather, wisdom entails displaying emotional equanimity, viewing situations dispassionately, negotiating complex relationships, defusing conflict and giving good advice.[14]

This wisdom, only sometimes a function of age or experience, is primarily related to how we process and learn from both our personal experiences and the experiences of others. In their book *The Scientific Study of Personal Wisdom*, psychologists Michel Ferrari and Nic Weststrate outline the role of reflective practices in developing both personal and general wisdom and demonstrate how individuals can cultivate wisdom through deliberate effort.[15] They note that "without the ability to step back from one's own behaviour or one's own life priorities and without the ability to monitor feelings such as shame, anxiety, anger, pride, or greed, it is very difficult to increase self-understanding."[16]

Interestingly, attributes associated with wisdom—such as awareness, vulnerability, empathy, collaboration, and collectivism—are increasingly deemed critical "soft skills" for twenty-first-century leadership, and fostering wisdom is seen as a pathway to better decision-making, improved well-being, and more ethical societies. To paraphrase Einstein, "We cannot solve the problems we face using the same ways of leading we used when we created them."[17]

According to Proverbs 9:10, "The fear of the Lord is the beginning of wisdom, and knowledge of the Holy One is understanding." In the Bible, wisdom is viewed as a gift from God *and* a quality that can be pursued and developed through a reverence for God, prayer (James 1:5), a life of righteous practice (Prov. 2:6–7), studying Scripture (Ps. 119:98–100), godly advice (Prov. 12:15), observation and reflection (Prov. 6:6–8), and learning from experience (Rom. 5:3–4). Interestingly, these overlap with the activities already identified as vital to promoting and supporting metamorphic growth in the previous chapter.

The primary medium in the Bible for conveying, understanding, and applying wisdom is through stories. Biblical narratives, parables, and historical accounts are not just about transmitting historical knowledge or moral rules; they are primarily about embedding wisdom into the life and culture of the readers or listeners. To borrow from journalist Will Storr in *The Science of Storytelling*, "The gift of story is wisdom."[18] I would add that "the gift of wisdom is story," especially the transformed and transforming stories of metamorphs leading both from and for transformation.

When asked about the most revolutionary means of altering society, Ivan Illich—a prominent Austrian philosopher, Roman Catholic priest, and theologian—answered,

> Neither revolution nor reformation can ultimately change a society, rather you must tell a new powerful tale, one so persuasive that it sweeps away the old myths and becomes the preferred story, one so inclusive that it gathers all the bits of our past and our present into a coherent whole, one that even shines some light into the future so that we can take the next step.... If you want to change a society, then you have to tell an alternative story.[19]

It is notable that Jesus never sought to facilitate transformation by appealing to data, facts, theories, models, rationality, intellect, or even epic report writing! Instead, he directly engaged people's hearts through the power of storytelling. His ability to transform others through the simple tool of story suggests that those of us committed to the transformation of individuals, communities, and nations may be working with an impressive yet overly complex set of leadership development tools that simply lack the transformative power of story.

TRANSFORMED BY STORY

Following Jesus' example, much of my appeal will be made directly to the heart using interpretive stories.[20] The stories that follow in subsequent parts of this book are designed to bring about transformation. My hope is that they will go some way in revealing insights about ourselves, others, and our approaches to leadership and inspire leaders to embrace opportunities for metamorphosis.

Instead of relying on data and logic, biblical stories vividly depict the realities of God, humanity, sin, and salvation in the Bible. In *Leading by Story*, authors Vaughan S. Roberts and David Sim emphasize that storytelling is and always has been "a sacred activity in the Christian faith."[21] This makes the church, as an entity, essentially a storytelling organization. "It has a story to tell to those inside and outside, a story that it values and that it believes is well worth telling."[22]

Within Christian communities, storytelling is deployed, primarily through sermons and testimonies, to prompt us to reflect on our own narratives and consider who we are in relation to God and others. Missiologist Alan Hirsch highlights the significance of this: "In the logic of the Bible, stories, metaphors, and images don't have less truth than abstract propositions; they have more truth. That is why the Bible is mostly a book of stories and poetry. Its appeal is to more than the isolated rational mind."[23]

While we often associate storytelling with traditional verbal, written, and visual narrative forms, our entire lives are thoroughly immersed in a continuous flow of stories. Not only are they woven into music, sung through melodies, conveyed through poetic rhythms, reflected in artwork, communicated through drumbeats, and preached through sermons, but they are also expressed through dance and other forms of body language. In fact, important and meaningful information has always been passed down through the generations of virtually every culture through some kind of story. In West Africa, griots have been the traveling oral historians and storytellers for generations.[24] Even today, many cultures continue to use stories as their main medium for transmitting wisdom and the tribe's values in such a way that they end up representing the tribe itself.[25]

As a species, we not only tell stories, but we also craft our own narratives while enthusiastically absorbing tales told to us by others. Our brains are so hardwired to engage with stories that we proactively use them as a tool to better understand both ourselves and those around us.

This means we gravitate toward and increasingly adopt stories that specifically make sense of the way we see ourselves and those who live around us. Once again, Hirsch aptly captures this shift:

> People now identify themselves less by grand ideologies, national identities, or political allegiances, and more by grand stories: those of interest groups, new religious movements (New Age), sexual identity (gays, lesbians, transsexuals, etc.), sports activities, competing ideologies (neo-Marxist, neo-fascist, eco-rats, etc.), class, conspicuous consumption (metrosexuals, urban grunge, etc.), work types (computer geeks, hackers, designers, etc.), and so forth.[26]

In short, we not only narrate and immerse ourselves in stories, but we also embody a unique combination of different stories within who we are as individuals. The Bible also powerfully reflects the storied nature of reality, but our personal stories provide the patterns through which we understand our background, life experiences, faith commitments, and growth.

Ultimately, we need stories capable of reflecting our identity and nurturing its development. Facts and theories seldom help when we find ourselves "trapped" in narratives that limit our capacity to grow and change. Indeed, they are woefully inadequate for empowering leaders to become transformed or transformative. Instead, what is desperately needed are opportunities to rewrite our storylines and, if necessary, live a very different kind of story altogether.

At a time when people are eager to identify with powerful stories, a leader's ability to tell a better story, even about their own leadership journey, has never been more urgent. This echoes author Howard Gardner's advice that "the central task of leadership is to give people a better story to live. Not necessarily more convincing, not necessarily one that they enjoy more, but one that is a springboard to a better future."[27] By connecting with the powerful story of Jesus in particular and the gospel surrounding him, we can overcome any stagnation in our life or leadership journey. Vaughan S. Roberts and David Sims cite Hauerwas and Willimon in their appeal: "In Jesus we meet not a presentation of basic ideas about God, world, and humanity, but an invitation to join up, to become part of the movement, a people."[28] Only by engaging and reengaging with Jesus' story can we commit ourselves to an ongoing journey of personal growth and transformation. Stories can quite literally change everything.

Hearing from God through Story

I believe that virtually any biblical text, theme, statement, command, proposition, expression of poetry, praise, prayer, prophecy, parable, history, or mini-biography scattered throughout the length and breadth of the Bible can be storied and used to investigate episodes in our leadership formation.

Not only can leadership stories be illuminated through the great story of the Bible in emotional, sensory, and revelatory ways, but leaders can also write themselves into a story, either as one of the characters they encounter or as a completely new character of their own making. In other words, we can form a relationship with the narrative and become involved in creating or redirecting the story. Ferrari and Weststrate remind us that this is precisely the way wisdom grows:

> When it comes to developing wisdom individuals become wiser through simulating hypothetical situations that they could potentially encounter. Individuals can also project themselves into the narratives of literary and historical examples of wisdom, or of people they know personally and consider wise, so as to glean wisdom from the experience of these memorable people.[29]

However, the Bible isn't just any old storybook; we aren't shaped and transformed by interacting with mere words alone … God is also somehow active within the text, and if we wish, we can encounter him as we interact with it. In fact, only when we encounter God in the text do our hearts reveal our true desires, and our feelings and emotions rise to the surface. This is when the text becomes a mirror capable of reflecting our pain, fear, sin, and all that we are in a way that enables sometimes painful growth to occur. Some traditions refer to this process as lectio divina, and in *Who Stole My Bible?* author Jennifer Butler describes her own experience of this:

> The ancient contemplative practice of Lectio Divina—the belief that God speaks to us as we pray and ruminate on the ancient text—also inspires the way I read Scripture. Lectio is not study and analysis. It is more "hearty" than "heady," as one expert put it…. Rather than being merely a source of information about how to live, Scripture becomes, quite literally, a meeting place for a personal encounter with the Living God.[30]

Whenever we take the texts "to heart" in this way, we not only meet with God but also invite them to interpret us even as we seek to interpret them. This allows our ideologies, perceptions, and actions to be radically altered by the work of the Holy Spirit. Indeed, "the Spirit's work in Scripture is not unlike the Spirit's work in creation, namely, by groaning over the brokenness and brooding over the chaos, the Spirit calls forth new worlds."[31]

As you read through each chapter of this book, pause to consider the ways in which you would like "new worlds" to emerge within your story and the ways in which you would like to grow and change personally. But whatever else you do, be sure to invite the Holy Spirit along for the ride because this metamorphic transformation will not happen unless you do. Unsurprisingly, inner-life themes dominate the leadership-related narratives lining the biblical texts from Genesis through to Revelation, and these themes are focal points of the metamorphic process. Interpreted through the lens of leadership and with the Holy Spirit's help, the biblical stories introduced here will empower you to develop your personal and professional abilities and effectively release you to make your highest God-given contribution as a leader.

Participating in the Story

Although Paul's reference to "metamorphose" in 2 Corinthians 3:18 reminds us of the vital role of the Holy Spirit in shaping a Christlike heart within us, it would be foolish to think that God's Spirit is like some divine marinade, changing us whether we want to be changed or not! As I outlined in the previous chapter, our transformation occurs most effectively when we proactively rely on God rather than passively accept whatever happens to come our way. Revising and rewriting our stories is a fundamentally dynamic process, meaning we have a part to play in cultivating the predisposition that prepares us to receive God's Spirit and thus cooperate with God's work in our lives. Our active participation in the practices mentioned in the previous chapter guides us toward the godly transformation we so desire.

As we open ourselves to God's Spirit and engage deeply with the biblical story, we find our fundamental beliefs, assumptions, and emotions being reshaped in ways that lead us to make enduring shifts in our mindsets. However, it's metamorphosis we're after, so we must be wary and guard against any quick-fix or prized end-point mentality. Seasons of growth and periods of stagnation are a reminder that transformation is the work of a lifetime and is never truly complete this side of eternity.

In many ways, the stories and interpretive stories reflected in the three remaining parts of this book resemble the midrash of Jewish tradition.[32] They are a kind of interpretive story from which we can glean both insight and guidance. They also resemble the developmental models of coaching, mentoring, and spiritual development. These interpretive stories urge readers to align themselves with God's desire for their metamorphosis and also challenge leaders to grapple with the unique questions they raise. Their interpretive nature allows them to pointedly suggest where and how leaders might wish to engage or even disengage while simultaneously making it hard to control where the stories will likely lead them. Like the very best mentoring or coaching relationships, your personal interactions with these interpretive stories are unlikely to be the same as anyone else's. And, like every great mentor, interpretive stories intentionally share advice, insight, or anything else that fosters a desire for continuous growth and development in your heart.

Engaging with stories of any kind involves imagination, perspective-taking, and emotional engagement, which enables us to be "transported" to different realms.[33] Stories ask us to be involved in mystery, complexity, and ambiguity more than most other forms of communication. They are immersive and emotive, often leading to enlightening "aha" moments that inspire change and kick-start the transformational process itself. Multiple studies indicate that stories not only profoundly impact our emotions, thoughts, and actions, but they can also evoke tears, change our attitudes, opinions, and behaviors, and quite literally change the shape of our brains![34]

Given all this, it is not incidental that Jesus was quite literally the greatest storyteller of all time! Stories and interpretive narratives were the primary medium through which he conveyed his message and ignited transformation in others. Jesus explained that, through story, he sought to create optimum conditions for "those who had ears to hear" (Matt. 11:5). *The Message* version of Matthew 13:10–17 encapsulates his approach when Jesus responds to a pivotal question posed by his disciples: "Why do you tell stories?" (v. 10).

> He [Jesus] replied, "You've been given insight into God's kingdom. You know how it works. Not everybody has this gift, this insight; it hasn't been given to them. Whenever someone has a ready heart for this, the insights and

understandings flow freely. But if there is no readiness, any trace of receptivity soon disappears. That's why I tell stories: to create readiness, to nudge the people toward a welcome awakening. In their present state they can stare till doomsday and not see it, listen till they're blue in the face and not get it. I don't want Isaiah's forecast repeated all over again:

> Your ears are open, but you don't hear a thing.
> Your eyes are awake, but you don't see a thing.
> The people are stupid!
> They stick their fingers in their ears
> so they won't have to listen;
> They screw their eyes shut
> so they won't have to look,
> so they won't have to deal with me face-to-face
> and let me heal them.

But you have God-blessed eyes—eyes that see! And God-blessed ears—ears that hear! A lot of people, prophets and humble believers among them, would have given anything to see what you are seeing, to hear what you are hearing, but never had the chance."

Through story, Jesus challenged individuals to reassess their perspectives on themselves and the world around them. Crucially, Jesus employed parables that encouraged listeners to step into the shoes of others, inviting them to actively participate in the change. Historically, Jesus *told* parables people could project themselves into. However, personal experience suggests Jesus also invites us to experience new parables even today. At the beginning of this book, I recalled my experience of "living parables" during particularly intense and challenging seasons of personal growth. During these times I felt invited to engage in life-changing "curricula," specifically designed to get me from where I was in my change journey to where God wanted me to be. My experience of "living parables" is of biblical truth, reframed and recast with me in an observing role, leading role, or indeed every role. "Living parables" means that who I am in God's story is as important as the story God is telling. "Living parables" suggests God is invested in every metamorph's story of growth and development today, in real-time. Jesus' repeated refrain, "They that have eyes to see, let them see, and they that have ears, let them hear" applies to us in more ways than one. It underscores Jesus' desire for people to be attentive to their surroundings and engage with the realities right under their noses.[35] Jesus' storytelling also aims to ready each listener (and reader) to be transformed by new stories as well as older, timeless narratives. Jesus' stories are designed to awaken and prepare each of us for metamorphic transformation, often in the places we least expect.

Rather than introduce new knowledge to his hearers to educate or inform them, Jesus often simply subverts familiar everyday themes and concepts to transformative effect. Wisdom more than knowledge is being conveyed through his stories. I firmly believe that our desperate need for metamorphosis can be met by storying biblical stories in ways that inspire people to engage with Jesus' liberative intentions more fully. However, we must first bear in mind that our knowledge of Jesus has also been shaped for us by multiple storytellers, lest we find ourselves trapped by what Nigerian writer Chimamanda Ngozi Adichie describes as "the danger of the single story"[36]—how one perspective on anyone or anything risks a substantial misunderstanding. My hope is that some of what you read in this book will provide new perspectives on familiar stories.

VALUING DIVERSE STORYTELLERS

All of us, consciously and unconsciously, approach the biblical narrative from a particular social context and with a specific set of concerns. Traditional biblical studies have typically focused on examining the context of the biblical authors. However, there's been less emphasis on considering how the reader's unique perspective and worldview might influence their role as a storyteller.

British author Liz Shercliff highlights this aspect in preaching: "Despite the claims of some that we ought not to appear in our sermons, we already do. It is our body standing at the front of the church. It is our voice saying the words. It is our understanding we share."[37]

Our social location shapes our understanding and interpretation of the biblical text and inevitably influences what we observe or overlook, regardless of claims of impartiality, detachment, or objectivity. The acclaimed father of Black theology, African American theologian James Cone, eloquently articulates this in his influential book *God of the Oppressed*:

> Because Christian theology is human speech about God, it is always related to historical situations and thus all of its assertions are culturally limited....

> Although God, the subject of theology, is eternal, theology itself is, like those who articulate it, limited by history and time ... (Our image of God) is finite image, limited by the temporality and particularity of our existence. Theology is not universal language, it is interested language and thus is always a reflection of the goals and aspirations of a particular people in a definite social setting.[38]

Biblical scholars emphasize the distinct approaches of the four Gospels. Matthew, writing primarily for a Jewish audience, focuses on Jewish forms, Scriptures, and arguments. In contrast, Luke consistently references gentile sayings, poets, and philosophers for a gentile audience. Mark's style is rugged and straightforward, whereas John's Gospel engages an audience familiar with Greek and Jewish ideas, as well as the possible beginnings of Gnostic and mystical teachings about Jesus. There are few, if any, who would question the value of the distinctive approach the Gospels take or of their benefits to any and every audience they engage. They simply illustrate a dual-purpose vocabulary. In other words, they are four different books from four different authors, speaking from and appealing to four different audiences and simultaneously to every audience everywhere while being committed to expressing truths about the same person, Jesus Christ. Our own Spirit-inspired attempts at storytelling may not have the same authority, but they certainly reflect the same principles.

In this book, I will not pretend the neutrality or invisibility that so many Western storytellers do. Nor will I attempt to speak from everywhere and nowhere simultaneously. Western voices have generalized how these stories *should* be told for all of us. Hence, storytelling has been heavily influenced by Western values such as individuality, dualism, and linear thinking, as well as by colonialism and enlightenment thinking. This is, of course, a valid way of telling leadership stories, but it is only one among many. Instead, I will emulate the Gospel writers and other biblical storytellers by engaging with a dual voice. In other words, I will speak from who I am and what I represent, but I will do so for the benefit of everyone, everywhere.

A Little More about This Particular Storyteller

I approach the biblical text as a Black British woman. There is no ignoring who I am, even for those who'd like me to pretend otherwise. My identity, shaped both by where I was born and how I arrived in the UK is complex, as it is for many women of color.

I am aware that I see (and therefore am more likely to talk about) God's activity in just about everything I encounter. I do not save references about God for more overtly "religious" and "spiritual" occasions. This habit undoubtedly connects with my African heritage and likely started when I was a child. It also likely stems from the fact that many African languages do not have a separate term that translates directly to "religion." Consequently, God's involvement is never seen as a distinct category or limited to Sunday or other "worship" but is instead experienced as an inherent and ongoing part of reality. However, I'm aware that consistently referencing God is sometimes perceived as immature in certain Western church contexts, so at times, I have to bite my tongue to avoid being misunderstood. Ironically, a failure to acknowledge God in all things is equally viewed as "unspiritual" by many of African descent.

I have cultivated wisdom and skills from both my African and British cultural backgrounds. Yet, I've also had to develop leadership skills tailored to navigate a world that predominantly esteems whiteness. Deepa Purushothaman's reflection deeply resonates with me: "Until now, we have been told we weren't as good as those around us. We have had to assimilate to participate. We have had to survey the lay of the land and learn to anticipate. And we have had to learn what to do when we are gaslighted."[39]

I remember when one denominational leader suggested I should simply "stop standing out." Being the sole Black woman church leader in our denomination at the time, I pointed out that I had no choice in the matter and that his expectations presented the real problem!

No one can erase themselves from their endeavors. The storyteller, narrating the story about God from their perspective, inevitably brings forth certain themes, focuses, and insights while overlooking others (unless they have proactively taught themselves not to do this). This doesn't necessarily diminish what is being conveyed; it simply serves as a reminder of caution and humility for those engaging with the biblical text as hearers and storytellers, that theirs is unlikely to be the final word on any subject and that there is always more to learn.[40] Despite possessing remarkable insights, every person has unique and obvious "blind spots."[41]

One theologian soberly reminded us during a robust group discussion, "God is the only one here who doesn't need to do theology!" Simply put,

God isn't questioning the nature of his own existence, nature, or identity. We, however, are constantly grappling for a clearer comprehension of God, his narrative, and our place within his story. We only experience God within our own history and our own stories, so it is by consciously drawing upon God's activity in ourselves and others that we get a fuller understanding of God's story. Storytellers should therefore always identify who they are, where they are coming from, their particular limitations, and their specific interests. We should always be clear; we are engaging in the dual-purpose vocabulary that speaks both *from* a particular audience *to* every audience everywhere.

Ensuring the Whole Story Is What You're After

Our capacity to perceive differently isn't merely shaped by tradition or location. It's also shaped, as mentioned earlier, by our priorities and concerns. Our approach to reading and storying the Bible isn't solely tied to a specific culture, background, and history; it is also intertwined with our particular concerns. In other words, an evangelist might identify evangelistic themes, a missionary might see missionary themes, a pastor might recognize pastoral aspects, and a prophet might discern prophetic elements all within the same text.

I've shifted from incidentally or even accidentally considering leadership, diversity, justice, women, and mission while reading the Bible to intentionally focusing on these themes. I've realized these align with the primary concerns God has painstakingly equipped me to address. Liz Shercliff wisely states about preachers, "It isn't so much that God is going to give us something to say, it's that God has been forming us to say it."[42] For the prospective metamorph, being closed to a diversity of storytellers is a bit like an athlete expecting to achieve outstanding results based on a diet of apples. We all know that apples are good for you, but consuming apples 24/7 is decidedly unhealthy. Yet many of us expect to be transformed and transformative by hearing from only one type of storyteller, like Chimamanda's "single story." All the while, God has ensured that the story of Jesus (through the Gospels) and the entire Bible itself has been communicated through the voices of diverse storytellers—a reminder that the body of Christ has many parts, as in 1 Corinthians 12:12–27.

Alice Walker, an African American writer, beautifully encapsulates why we should interact with as many types of storytellers as possible regarding the biblical story. She writes: "I believe that the truth about any subject only comes when all sides of the story are put together and all their different meanings make one new one. Each writer writes the missing parts to the other writer's story. And the whole story is what I'm after."[43] I too am "after" the whole story.

There is, of course, a sinister side to all of this. As mentioned earlier, people can become entrenched in destructive storylines. Rachel Held Evans, in her book *A Year of Biblical Womanhood*, encapsulates this notion well:

> If you are looking for verses with which to support slavery, you will find them. If you are looking for verses with which to abolish slavery, you will find them. If you are looking for verses with which to oppress women, you will find them. If you are looking for verses with which to liberate or honor women, you will find them. If you are looking for reasons to wage war, you will find them. If you are looking for reasons to promote peace, you will find them. If you are looking for an outdated, irrelevant ancient text, you will find it. If you are looking for truth, believe me, you will find it. This is why there are times when the most instructive question to bring to the text is not what does it say? But what am I looking for? I suspect Jesus knew this when he said, "ask and it will be given to you, seek and you will find, knock and the door will be opened." If you want to do violence in this world, you will always find the weapons. If you want to heal, you will always find the balm.[44]

While individuals have the power to narrate stories of liberation, they are also capable of weaving narratives that are fueled by biases that reinforce unhealthy choices. Listening to other perspectives enables us to identify our biases and "blind spots" and get a fuller picture of God's story. It is also why we must ensure our compass is firmly set on becoming like Jesus as we are being transformed in response to the powerful stories of the Bible.

PREPARING FOR YOUR JOURNEY

You are fast approaching the end of the introduction of this book, and what you have read so far lays the groundwork for what will be built upon in the pages to come. Although each of the following chapters is like a self-contained short story, they will all make a great deal more sense after reading these first two chapters.

I've organized the rest of this book into three distinct parts that deliberately reflect the three key areas I believe Christian leaders need to experience the most: personal, community, and societal change. Although each chapter and section stand alone—with a mini-introduction to the theme, a middle, and an end—and stories can be read in whatever order you please, there is also a clear and structured progression, with each part of this book building on the previous one. The format is designed to provide an increasing sense of clarity and confidence as you apply the strategies reflected in the straplines of each chapter heading and throughout the chapter. These will guide you and promote your growth as a leader at each of the three individual, interpersonal, and systemic levels. And although I recognize there are many more stories also worthy of exploration in the pages of our Bible, there's a limit to what can be covered in any single volume, so for the remainder of this book I have focused on outlining just six metamorphic scenarios in three parts:

Part two of this book is dedicated to **transforming identity.** Here, you will focus on practices to help you become the kind of leader on the inside that God intends you to be. Although every chapter speaks to self-leadership, this chapter particularly focuses on this theme. You will learn about the critical practice of *nurturing curiosity from the inside out* from the story of Moses and chart a godly path to self-discovery. You will also journey with the Samaritan Woman from John chapter 4. She and Jesus' disciples will challenge you to identify and *defeat self-limiting mindsets* that may be obstructing your progress toward becoming the most effective and impactful metamorphic leader you can be.

Part three guides you through a process of systemically **transforming community** through your teams and organizational structures. You will draw inspiration from the story and friendship of Mary and Elizabeth. You will learn how to *leverage the power of friendship* and actively and practically develop crucial relationships in leadership while enhancing the influence and depth of your necessary friendships … and perhaps make a few more. And the story of the apostles appointing "the seven" will encourage you to *develop radical empathy to break systemic strongholds* as you confront and dismantle strongholds that interfere with developing healthy communities, particularly strongholds related to race.

Part four equips you for **transforming mission** through *discerning your "whys."* You will take a deep dive into Esther's story and explore the four pivotal questions that reveal your core purpose: Why me? Why this? Why here? Why now? These will not only help you focus as a leader, but they will also help align your leadership activities with the things that matter most in all God has called you to, so you can always lead on purpose. This section concludes with a focus on what it takes to *embed a strategic mission mindset* in an era that is both chaotic and heavily disrupted. You will learn from the example of the early 120 believers as they wait in the upper room and discover that sometimes the best response to chaos and uncertainty is to advance God's purposes through an intentional commitment to "multiply disrupted disruptors" whose mindset allows them to adapt and thrive in the midst of change.

Within each chapter of parts two, three, and four, you'll find an interpretive narrative based on a biblical character or biblical scenario. You will also find a case study based either on a single individual or a group of people I have had the honor of personally interacting or working with. To deepen your understanding and application, each chapter concludes with a section dedicated to silent coaching and reflection for individual readers or to be used for peer coaching, reflection, and discussion prompts for those journeying through the book together. Additionally, each chapter incorporates a time for prayer. Whether you're reading this book individually or as a group, you will find that you won't make much progress without engaging in prayer.

Getting a Bit More from This Book

As you go through the book, make sure to take note of the chapter headings as they provide an overview of the theme, and pay attention to the strapline as it suggests the strategy you are seeking to develop. However, as you journey through these interpretive stories, you might discern another strategy and predisposition that is more appropriate for your current season in life and leadership. The main goal is to move forward, regardless of how these stories enable you to do so. Forge a connection with the narrative and allow the Holy Spirit to *metamorphose* you into your most impactful self at this particular moment of your leadership. There is no right way to read each chapter. What is important is that you take whatever journey you need that best illuminates your path to transformation. If this includes dipping in and out of the chapter, feel free to do so.

In each of the biblical stories, reflect on whether what is being perceived is explicitly Christlike or not. We cannot develop as Christian leaders without imagining how Jesus would react in any of the roles within these stories. As mentioned earlier, our ultimate goal should be to stay centered on the person of Christ for our transformation and metamorphosis, lest we risk degeneration or deformation.

I have little doubt that the interpretive stories in this book will tell you a lot about me as a storyteller and as a leader. I've lived with these stories for many years, learned from them, and have told and retold them in various forms and contexts along the way. However, as you engage, interact, and grapple with these metamorphs and their interpretive tales, I pray they will reveal more about God and God's desire to transform, reshape, and empower you to lead in fresh and transformative ways wherever you happen to exercise your leadership in this season.

For leaders to positively impact anything or anyone, they must be prepared to combine an aspiration for Christlikeness with a commitment to become transformative leaders who lead both from and for transformation, namely metamorphs. Metamorphosis is a complex and lifelong process. In other words, God's work within us is never complete, so do all you can to avoid the danger zones of self-satisfaction and complacency. The stories within these pages are also cautionary tales that illustrate what's possible when we embrace our ongoing transformation in God, as well as what happens when we neglect it.

Changing the World Together

By reading this book, you've become part of a dynamic movement of leaders, each saying yes to God's invitation to intentionally lead with a transformative purpose. This commitment involves leading not only from a place of personal transformation but also with the aim of exerting a transformative influence and bringing transformation in others and the world around us.

Before concluding this chapter, it's important to recognize that our willingness to grow does not determine our inherent value to God. A leader's worth to God and God's love for any of us remains constant, regardless of whether we choose to change or not. However, these choices significantly shape our growth as believers, affect our credibility as witnesses, and may call into question whether we are even genuine followers of Jesus.[45]

There has never been a better time to press into all that it means to become a God-defined metamorph. Beyond mere reformation, our churches are in dire need of transformation, and we are living in a world that is equally desperate for transformative change. Indeed, Romans 8:19–21 captures this sentiment eloquently:

For the creation waits in eager expectation for the children of God to be revealed. For the creation was subjected to frustration, not by its own choice, but by the will of the one who subjected it, in hope that the creation itself will be liberated from its bondage to decay and brought into the freedom and glory of the children of God.

The "frustration" mentioned here mirrors our modern idea of disappointment with all of its unfulfilled desires and expectations. We are each being presented with a remarkable opportunity to not only be changed but to also become metamorphic agents of change in the world. That sound you can hear somewhere off in the background is me cheering you on as you commit yourself to simply go for it!

PART TWO

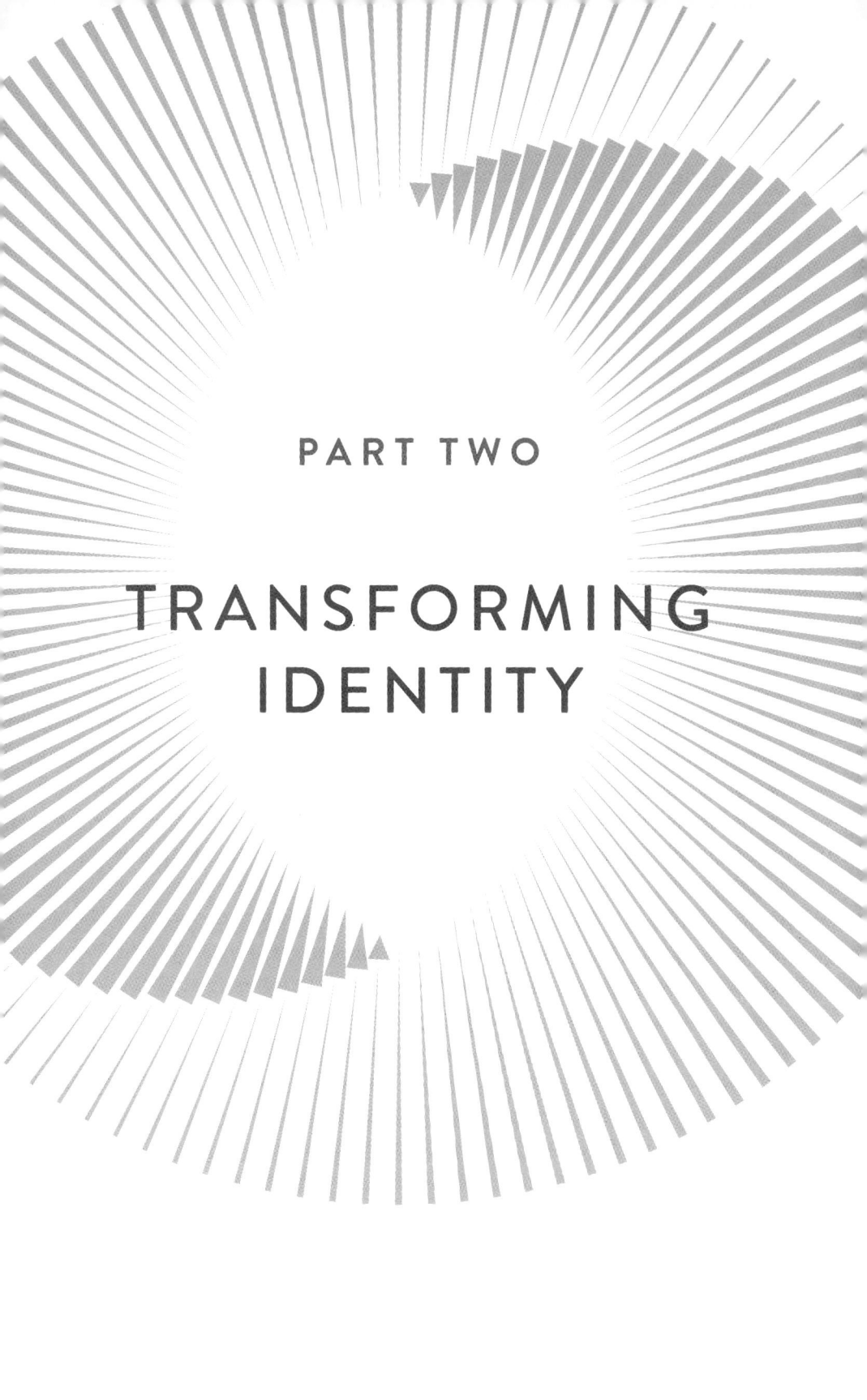

TRANSFORMING IDENTITY

3

MOSES
A PATH TO SELF-DISCOVERY

Nurturing Curiosity from the Inside Out

It takes courage ... to endure the sharp pains of self-discovery rather than choose to take the dull pain of unconsciousness that would last the rest of our lives.
MARIANNE WILLIAMSON

I am neither especially clever nor especially gifted. I am only very, very curious.
ALBERT EINSTEIN

Curiosity is an act of courageous vulnerability because every act of curiosity is admitting that we don't know something, risking a conclusion that makes us uncomfortable, and walking into a future that is uncertain. In other words, curiosity is an act of faith.
JARED BYAS

It's no secret that unhealthy Christian leaders foster unhealthy Christian communities. Leaders who neglect their own growth and development often struggle to facilitate the growth and development of the people they lead. Unfortunately, this awareness doesn't seem to deter leaders from behaving in ways that defeat what

God is trying to accomplish, in or even through them. Neither does it seem to prevent them from responding to new conditions, opportunities, and additional responsibilities with patterns of behavior rooted in deep-seated insecurities, old scripts, and unhealthy mindsets.

If left unchecked, these behaviors can sabotage their leadership and negatively impact their personal relationships, workplaces, churches, missions, ministries, and even their relationship with God. Although some behaviors are characteristic of men and others of women, others stem from socioeconomic, subcultural, generational, or even racialized realities. Regardless of their origins, individuals tend to take remarkably similar internal journeys to their respective behavioral destinations. But the type of leader they become ultimately depends on their readiness to foster a curiosity that allows them to navigate their unique developmental challenges successfully.

DID CURIOSITY REALLY KILL THE CAT?

The idea that an inquiring mind can prove destructive, or even fatal, is reflected in the proverbial saying, "Curiosity killed the cat." This is at least partially true. A pursuit of understanding and truth can indeed lead to adverse consequences, censure, sanctions, or even peril for those who probe deeper than others might wish. But the second part of this modern proverb is also revealing because it very reassuringly declares (rather smugly, I think), "But satisfaction brought it back." This suggests that the rewards of discovery can outweigh the costs by offering a reassuringly significant payback! The degree of satisfaction, however, seems directly related to the curiosity we're prepared to nurture and express in the first place.

All humans possess some passion for discovery when we start out in life. Children alone are thought to ask around forty thousand "explanatory" questions of their caregivers.[1] But as we mature, our curiosity and inclination to question seem to flourish or decline based on the responses we receive from those we look to for affirmation, such as our parents and friendship circles. Factors like ego, arrogance, fear of judgment, or a desire to avoid being canceled can also lead us to consciously or unconsciously suppress or even abandon our curiosity over time.

This is important because curiosity isn't just a key to personal development; it also promotes organizational growth and the forging of authentic connections with a wide range of people. Whether we're learning through new experiences or we're learning about our communities, the team we work with, or the world we live in, curiosity enables us to see familiar landscapes and people with fresh eyes. Curiosity challenges us to "see" what might have been previously overlooked or even disregarded.

If we're nurtured to be curious from a young age, it's likely we'll grow to embrace open-mindedness, be less resistant to uncertainty and change, and be willing to relinquish control in our exercise of leadership. Curious leaders seem to possess an innate drive to expand their knowledge and seek out fresh ideas, experiences, and opportunities. They also develop the habit of looking both backward and forward—because learning from the past helps them improve or innovate in the future. This type of leader excels in directing their curiosity *outward*, toward their environment, the people they interact with, the organizations they serve, or the situations they encounter. They understand that it's almost impossible to learn if you think you already know, a challenge some leaders still struggle to appreciate. These curious leaders crave knowledge.[2] But true transformative power emerges only when our curiosity is also directed *inward*, toward a leader's personal and often very private inner world.

At whatever stage in life they develop their abilities, transformative leaders prioritize inward curiosity and self-awareness; they acknowledge their limitations, failures, and mistakes and challenge their assumptions. They become curious about the one person they interact with in every waking and sleeping moment of their lives: themselves. They cultivate healthier leadership habits, such as asking the right people the right questions and genuinely listening to what those people say. As we explored in part one, these transformative leaders crave more than knowledge; they seek wisdom.

Unsurprisingly, leaders who lack curiosity are the exact opposite. They rarely ask questions, listen to others, or pause to consider their perspectives. For them, inward curiosity is limited to self-help, if it even includes that. Subsequently, they are at a disadvantage in the evolving leadership landscape as it shifts toward collaborative, "flatter" approaches that increasingly favor those who pursue and practice curiosity. Therefore, leaders who take time to cultivate curiosity will simply become better leaders over time.

Although the practice of curiosity can bring discomfort as well as satisfaction, it is nevertheless a critical practice for metamorphic leaders who long to lead both from and for transformation.

To understand the practice of curiosity, we will direct our own curiosity toward a specific figure from the Old Testament: Moses. The life of Moses is an important example because he is a would-be metamorph with a noteworthy commitment to God, whose narrative ironically begins with his resistance to God. His story is of particular interest because it is rich with the kind of internal scripts, personal convictions, and character commitments that are typical of both commendable and less admirable leadership practices.

Moses' narrative is impactful and inspiring but also deeply frustrating. It testifies to the power of curiosity but is also a cautionary tale regarding the consequences of neglecting to exercise curiosity during pivotal stages of our leadership development.

QUESTIONING TO EVADE

Exodus chapters 3 and 4 depict Moses' first encounter with God and illuminate his struggle with leadership. The story begins with Moses' curiosity to investigate a strange sight:

> Now Moses was tending the flock of Jethro his father-in-law, the priest of Midian, and he led the flock to the far side of the wilderness and came to Horeb, the mountain of God. There the angel of the LORD appeared to him in flames of fire from within a bush. Moses saw that though the bush was on fire it did not burn up. So Moses thought, "I will go over and see this strange sight—why the bush does not burn up." ... The LORD said, "I have indeed seen the misery of my people in Egypt. I have heard them crying out because of their slave drivers, and I am concerned about their suffering. So I have come down to rescue them from the hand of the Egyptians and to bring them up out of that land into a good and spacious land, a land flowing with milk and honey—the home of the Canaanites, Hittites, Amorites, Perizzites, Hivites and Jebusites.... So now, go. I am sending you to Pharaoh to bring my people the Israelites out of Egypt"
>
> EXODUS 3:1–3, 7–8, 10

This is one of the Bible's many "call narratives" that remind us that God's purposes are invariably worked out through imperfect and ordinary women and men, just like us. Whenever we sense a longing to do something for the church, community, neighborhood, or beyond, we may be recipients of a holy "nudge" and invitation to join in with God's plans. But, judging from

Moses' reaction to God's calling, he was anything but curious for further adventure.

As we delve into Exodus 3:10–17 and Exodus 4:1, 10–14, it becomes obvious that Moses is firmly set on the path of evasion. He tries to resist God's request for a "rescue" mission through three lines of questioning:

- Questioning authenticity (Exod. 3:13)
- Questioning credibility (Exod. 4:1)
- Questioning capability (Exod. 4:13)

Questioning designed to evade rarely emerges from a vacuum. Instead, like Moses, these inquiries typically arise when we are grappling with collective and personal history, issues of identity, and painful experiences. Moses' questioning reveals not only the impact of the many challenging circumstances he had faced throughout his relatively short lifetime, but they also reflect his limited grasp of God's activity in the history of his people and his own inadequate self-understanding at this stage of his leadership journey. Moses' story—and perhaps his reluctance to engage—reflects the larger, more complex story of God's people. The Children of Israel had endured four centuries of bondage before Moses' encounter at the burning bush, prompting questions about why God had not acted earlier. God's idea of the "right time" often contrasts starkly with our own, at least in my experience. Moses, of course, had already attempted a rescue mission of his own, resulting in him murdering an Egyptian, being rejected by his people, and fleeing a Pharoah trying to kill him. By contrast, God's timing of this intervention for his people—his kairos moment (the chosen time to act)—appears almost arbitrary, leaving us to ponder the uncomfortably long timeline of this narrative and thus the long, silent, and painful four-hundred-year pause in between. It is only much later in Numbers 11:12–13 that Moses actually lets slip what may have been troubling him all along, when he suggests that God has been a somewhat negligent mother: "Did *I* conceive all these people? Did *I* give them birth? Why do *you* tell me to carry them in my arms, as a nurse carries an infant, to the land *you* promised on oath to their forefathers?" (emphasis mine).

Far from neglect, God, it seems, prefers the "thirteenth hour" (that is, *after* all hell has broken loose) rather than the commonly lauded "eleventh hour" of many a sermon. However, what is never in question is God's compassionate, attentive, and loving commitment amid his people's tears and prayers.

We may not understand God's idea of a "timely" intervention or the means by which God chooses to act, but the resounding message here is that no grief or petition is wasted in God's economy. So, when God's time was right, he declares to Moses, "*I have come down to rescue my people*," but, in an ironic twist, promptly instructs Moses, "*I am sending you.*" Moses, though, struggling with his own sense of inadequacy and perceived abandonment by God, opts instead for a series of evasive "questioning" maneuvers.

Thus, Moses' line of questioning could scarcely be said to pass for genuine curiosity. On closer scrutiny, it is disingenuous at best and significantly problematic at worst. Yet God meets him precisely "where he's at" and responds to Moses with a set of counter questions that are, by contrast, sincere and earnest. It's important to note that God is not asking for information or education, despite Moses' attempts to provide both. God already knows the painful truth about Moses. Instead, God's questions appear aimed at enlightening Moses about himself.

The entire encounter is tragic and laughable and plays out like an African morality tale or a scene from a Shakespearean comedy. Instead of cornering God, Moses' futile attempt to dodge God's call on his life ends with him cornering himself. Rather than obscuring the truth, each question only serves to uncover and clarify Moses' inner thoughts and feelings. And if we permit them, these questions will do the same for us too.

Often, the "questions" we present to God under similar circumstances are merely excuses that feel like genuine reasons at the time. Moses' efforts to avoid responsibility might have backfired, but they also led to the very challenge and reassurance he so desperately needed.

Questioning Authenticity

"Moses said to God, 'Suppose I go to the Israelites and say to them, "The God of your fathers has sent me to you," and they ask me, "What is his name?" Then what shall I tell them?'" (Exod. 3:13). In other words, Moses seems to be asking God an authenticity question. *Are you really who I think you are? Are you (God) the genuine article?*

Authenticity questions can surface at any juncture of our Christian journey and leadership. They arise when we project failed relationships, disappointments, and past struggles onto God. We often wrestle with authenticity questions when things go wrong or when we make mistakes with far-ranging consequences. However, we also, somewhat predictably, ask authenticity questions even after witnessing miracle upon miracle and breakthrough after breakthrough. In this instance, Moses had his very own perpetually combusting bush right under his nose, yet he was still asking an authenticity question.

Are you really who I think you are?

In the Western world, this question often emerges in existential terms: "Can God truly exist if ... ?" However, the certainty of God's existence is rarely challenged in the East and the Southern Hemisphere. Instead, the query tends to revolve around God's nature: "What kind of God is this?"[3] Despite our different starting points, both lines of inquiry eventually converge on a similar theme: "Are you the Almighty God?" "Are you trustworthy?" "Are you truly in control?" "Are you going to let me down?" "Are you going to mislead me?" "Are you going to make me look bad or stupid if I go along with you?" *Are you really who I think you are?*

One might argue that Moses' inquiry was a sincere attempt to learn more about the entity he was now engaging, especially considering God's seeming absence in the preceding four hundred years. However, the direction of the discussion suggests otherwise. Far from seeking a genuine solution, Moses seemed to be crafting what he perceived to be a valid reason (or excuse) to evade the very task being asked of him. Yet, God responds to Moses' attempt at sabotage with grace and mercy and in the most spectacular way possible. God answers by unveiling his true nature: "God said to Moses, 'I AM WHO I AM. This is what you are to say to the Israelites: 'I AM has sent me to you'" (Exod. 3:14). God also said to Moses, "Say to the Israelites, 'The Lord, the God of your fathers—the God of Abraham, the God of Isaac and the God of Jacob—has sent me to you'" (Exod. 3:15).

While Moses is looking for the name of the god he can argue with, God reveals his identity by declaring, "I AM." In this one statement, God reveals to Moses his sovereignty, omnipotence, and presence from beginning to end. The God who is beyond comprehension, called "I AM" or "YHWH," has been and will be with Moses in every breath.[4]

When we find ourselves wrestling with authenticity questions, we may also need a fresh revelation of who God is. I sometimes need this sort of reassurance and revelation after a mere forty minutes, let alone four hundred years of apparently unanswered prayer!

However, while God was unveiling his true nature, Moses, rather than attentively absorbing the revelation, seemed otherwise preoccupied with crafting his next excuse—which suggests he wasn't really listening at all. We don't know if God's self-identification as the God of Moses' ancestors Abraham, Isaac, and Jacob was particularly comforting or a source of additional consternation, but we do know what Moses did next.

Questioning Credibility

"Moses answered, 'What if they do not believe me or listen to me and say, "The LORD did not appear to you"?'" (Exod. 4:1). In other words, *What if they don't believe that I'm who you think I am?* Essentially, Moses was voicing doubts about his own credibility, and he had good reason, given his earlier failed rescue attempt.

Moses was asking, *What if I can't prove myself? What if they laugh in my face? What if I just don't have the credentials to be a deliverer? God, are you sure you came to the right address? Am I really who you think I am? And even if I am, what if no one else believes me? It's all very well and good speaking to me out of a burning bush, but at the end of the day, I'm the one who's got to convince everyone else that what you say is true. They are the people who will judge me, and say, "Who do you think you are?"*

If any of this resonates with you, read on, and take encouragement from what happens next. God appears to answer this credibility question by revealing Moses' own capabilities to Moses himself: "Then the LORD said to him, 'What is that in your hand?'" (Exod. 4:2).

When we doubt our credibility, God often goes to great lengths to redirect our attention to our inherent abilities and resources. He points us to what we ourselves are holding and prompts us to recognize the gifts and talents he has given us, as well as the gift he is making of us.

In Moses' case, God highlighted the staff in his hand, demonstrating just what he was capable of if he allowed what he held to be empowered and energized by God. As Moses named his staff, it turned into a serpent, which in view of its superior God-given authority would swallow the staffs-come-serpents Pharaoh sought to counter with (Exod. 7:10–13).

When we are wrestling with credibility questions, we often need a fresh revelation of who we are and of what God can do through us. But this is only when we are prepared to surrender all we have to become the "instrument"

God holds in his hand. Moses' staff would, after all, ultimately be known as the "staff of God" (Exod. 4:20).

However, as the story unfolds, it becomes apparent that even this objection does not lie at the root of Moses' real concern, and his deeper apprehension is finally revealed in Exodus 4:13.

Questioning Capability

"But Moses said, 'Pardon your servant, Lord. Please send someone else'" (Exod. 4:13). The question here is inferred rather than explicitly stated, reflecting Moses' final evasion tactic. *Surely there must be someone who would do a better job of this than me?*

Capability questions surface when we step outside our comfort zones, enter unfamiliar territory, and face daunting challenges. Capability issues arise whenever we are stretched beyond all we have become accustomed to.

The capability question wonders, *Am I really up to it?*

The problem with this question is that although it sounds incredibly spiritual, humble, and even self-effacing, it often originates from a blend of fear and pride. It implies, *Lord, I know myself better than you do.* Or *Lord, I can't. I shouldn't; perhaps I won't.* No wonder we read in the very next verse, "Then the LORD's anger burned against Moses" (Exod. 4:14). However, it's important to note that God's burning anger serves a purpose beyond the expression of mere frustration. Rather than impatiently incinerating Moses on the spot (as my anger might have led me to do), God offers Moses another option to deal with his overwhelming anxiety and insecurity. In anger, God presents Aaron as a potential solution, not to release Moses from his own unique responsibility but possibly as a reminder of the community support that has always been available to him.

Could it be that God's anger stemmed from Moses' assumption that he had to go it alone? Is it possible that the God who exists in community and who creates community for us becomes exasperated when we forget this? As someone accustomed to both collectivist and individualist cultural outlooks, I find it surprising that Moses was not thinking more collectively about God's call on his life, even in Exodus chapter 2, when, in his first attempt to aid the Israelites, he acts on his own without consultation or collaboration, as if he is alone and without aid himself. He was, of course, never alone, even when it may have felt like it. Although born in a collectivist culture, Moses seems to have become accustomed to an individualistic approach to problem-solving. We see evidence of this again in Moses' later interaction with Jethro.[5]

When we are wrestling with capability questions, perhaps we should revisit "burning anger" from God's point of view to discover what we might also be missing. We too may need God to shed more light than heat on the anxieties and concerns we often unnecessarily carry on our own. Aaron, Moses' actual brother, was exactly the kind of support Moses needed to make progress in his calling. God orchestrated Aaron's involvement, just as God knows what and who we need for our leadership journey. Aaron's presence also reminds us that no divine calling is a solitary heroic venture. You would think we'd readily grasp this, given the entire Trinity is engaged in our salvation. Even God seemingly avoids the kind of rugged individualism we often take for granted in the Western world.

God used Moses' questions not to excuse him from his calling but to reveal the root of his self-doubt. Moses needed a revelation of who God is as the "I AM" of his ancestors. He needed exposure to the gifts he held and the gift he could become in God's hand. He also needed insight into the kind of support that was available all along to propel him forward in his calling.

Ultimately, God's calling of Moses serves as a reminder that embracing curiosity and facing internal challenges are essential steps toward transformative leadership.

QUESTIONING TO TRANSFORM

Moses' initial questioning was designed to evade God's calling, and it revealed his internal fears and doubts. Numbers 12:3 affirms that "Moses was very meek, more than all people who were on the face of the earth" (ESV). Although some translations use the word "humble," "meek" seems to fit better with Moses' initial struggles with self-doubt and fear. Despite his "meekness," he eventually earned recognition as one of history's greatest leaders across three major religious traditions.[6] However, he didn't emerge from the womb with these credentials; instead, they were gradually etched into his character throughout the course of his life and leadership.

Like all those called to lead, Moses encountered challenges that threatened to sabotage his leadership at virtually every turn. If our aim is to serve Jesus and become the kind of leader God entrusts to further his purposes, we're bound to face many of the same leadership obstacles Moses faced.

These challenges don't always follow a straightforward, linear sequence. Instead, they tend to overlap, creating the spiral pathway I highlighted in chapter one of this book. This is another reminder of the *multilayered* as well as the multidimensional nature of metamorphic leadership development and of the inevitable tears that come from peeling back our "leadership onion."[7]

While it's impossible to cover every aspect of Moses' leadership journey in a single chapter, we will focus on the following three wisdom-seeking questions that can be employed when we face leadership challenges. This should help us identify transformative themes capable of facilitating our leadership progress:

- What do you know about yourself that no one else knows?
- What do others know about you that you may not know?
- What do you and others not know about you that God alone knows?

In many ways, facing each challenge with these questions is an opportunity to cultivate a kind of inside-out curiosity that can profoundly transform our approach to our personal leadership development.

By reading Moses' narrative from Exodus to Deuteronomy (ideally in one sitting), we uncover where and how these hurdles manifest in his life. And by exploring the following questions—originally directed at Moses' inner world—we can begin excavating our own inner territory to transform our own lives and leadership too.

What Do You Know About Yourself That No One Else Knows?

Moses serves as a poignant reminder that our capacity to lead others often hinges on our ability to lead ourselves. We cannot lead others where we ourselves are not willing to go. Some of us may resonate with Moses at this crucial stage of his leadership development: "Here I am, Lord. Send *anyone* else!"

Moses came face to face with what he knew about himself (or at least suspected) that possibly no one else knew; and, like an inexperienced driver behind the wheel, he almost stalled before he'd even begun. His deep-seated insecurities nearly hindered him from embracing the path of true leadership altogether.

Moses' narrative underscores the fundamental truth that leaders do not emerge from a vacuum, much like metamorphosing butterflies. We all come from somewhere, and we all come with baggage. Moses had a history, background, and culture. But he also had experience, trauma, and struggle. Inevitably, all these yearned for the metamorphic transformative power of the Holy Spirit. Just like us, there are things Moses knew about himself that possibly no one else knew, which posed a genuine threat to his ability to lead others well. And just like us, most of these issues were rooted in his identity and sense of who he was.

Identity shapes our individuality and sets me apart as "me" and you as "you," yet how we feel about our identity can inadvertently obstruct even God's best intentions for us. Identity encompasses our "objective" inherited traits like culture, ethnicity, sex, and race. These largely remain beyond our control but greatly influence our sense of belonging within particular social groups. For example, Moses would always belong to a generation of Hebrew males subjected to ruthless genocide.

However, alongside our inherited traits, our identity also involves acquired characteristics and the things that set us apart, such as our distinctive beliefs, qualities, personality traits, appearance, behaviors, and expressions.[8] Although many Hebrew men were likely slaves in Moses' era, some may have been rescued and assimilated into Egyptian culture just as he had. Moses himself had been raised in the distinctive setting of a palace. He therefore enjoyed education, authority, and the influence that likely accompanied this upbringing, which would have set him apart from others.

Moses' combined inherited and acquired characteristics would have shaped his perceived identity and sense of belonging, just as it does for us today. It's been said that "identities tell *us* who we are, and they announce to *others* who we are."[9] Unfortunately, who we believe we are and where we feel we belong can become quite confused along life's journey, just as it did for Moses.

Moses' perceived identity was clearly a source of contention. He was a Hebrew boy raised by an Egyptian family—but not just any Egyptian family. Moses was raised as the son of Pharaoh's daughter, the same Pharaoh who sanctioned the genocide of male Hebrews his age. In other words, he lived among people who despised what he was, who he came from, and what he stood for—people who considered themselves superior to his people of origin.

According to Exodus 2:11, Moses strongly identified with the Hebrew people and evidently harbored animosity toward at least some Egyptians—so much so that one day he witnessed an Egyptian mistreating a Hebrew slave and subsequently killed the Egyptian. We know this was premeditated because

Exodus 2:12 informs us that before he acted, he "looked this way and that." But having taken the law into his own hands, Moses then encountered rejection from his own people the very next day when he intervened in a scuffle between two Hebrews. Instead of acknowledging him as a fellow Hebrew or a potential "savior" figure, they challenged him as a murderer: "The man said, 'Who made you ruler and judge over us? Are you thinking of killing me as you killed the Egyptian?'" (Exod. 2:14).

Notably, when Pharaoh learns of the incident, he also views Moses as a potential threat, branding him a common murderer or a possible danger to other Egyptians. "When Pharaoh heard of this [the murder], he tried to kill Moses" (Exod. 2:15). Not exactly the kind of adopted grandfather any of us would wish for.

This moment starkly reveals the lack of familial affection between the two men. Pharaoh doesn't call Moses in for a chat about the "unfortunate incident" or offer him royal leniency. There's no hint of anything other than contempt toward Moses, and Pharaoh swiftly seizes the tragedy and the opportunity to rid himself of yet another "Hebrew boy."

Moses finds himself caught in a cycle of rejection. He is taken from a rejected and enslaved people, those who raise him eventually reject him, and he is also rejected by the Hebrews to whom he wished to belong. We meet him, apparently struggling with his own hurt and resentment, unable to find his place, and, like so many of us, trapped in the mold life had shaped for him.

For followers of Jesus, our core identity is rooted in Christ. Neither inherited nor acquired, fixed nor felt characteristics determine our belonging to him. We are whoever God says we are ... no more and no less. Our identity lies entirely within God's domain, which makes it unshakable and unaffected by our status, conduct, or unique characteristics, no matter how strange, displaced, or rejected we may sometimes feel. However, our inability to maintain a conscious awareness of what it is to be "in Christ" means we are often confused about our identity in him, fail to live in alignment with this identity, or behave in ways that contradict it altogether, and subsequently create unnecessary obstacles for ourselves.

There are things we know about ourselves that, if we're not careful, will hinder us from responding fully to our calling in any and every season of our leadership or ministry. The specific issues differ from person to person and are influenced by our history, experiences, gender, ethnicity, challenges, weaknesses, and temptations. However, we ignore these issues at our own peril. When we meet Moses in this story, he's a shepherd caring for his father-in-law's sheep. Perhaps he believed this was all he was capable of. Perhaps this was all he aspired to. It wasn't glamorous or sophisticated, yet God interrupted him, got his attention (aka burning bush), and urged him to reconsider his calling and leadership. Inevitably, in the contest of questions Moses initiated with God, Moses was destined to lose.

It's fair to assume Moses was good at leading sheep, but he was now being tasked to lead people and, in time, would be called upon to lead an emerging nation. Unfortunately, Moses remained firmly entrenched in the quagmire of his past. Despite being away from Egypt for four decades, he hadn't healed his wounds or resolved his inner struggles. He had started a new life, married, had a child, and adopted a new identity in a different land, but he still hadn't resolved the stuff he knew about himself.

It matters little what accolades we possess, titles we hold, material possessions we've acquired, or the societal status we've achieved. Even if we're married, or we've raised families or gained recognition, unless we confront the hidden aspects within ourselves, we risk stagnation in leadership. Longevity as a Christian doesn't guarantee our readiness for anything.

If we hope to lead from or for transformation, help anybody or anything, divine interruptions designed to confront what lies hidden within us and what we know about ourselves are inevitable. The secret desires, sins, overwhelming needs, fears, and barely contained anger are potential stumbling blocks that could incapacitate us if left unaddressed.

The most effective leaders possess a deep understanding of people, but the true litmus test of this understanding lies in how well we get to understand ourselves. To fully embrace God's purpose in each phase of our lives, we must foster a curiosity that directs us to confront what we already know or at least suspect about ourselves, address what we find, and grow in our leadership. By heading back to lead his people, Moses was also finally able to accept his own ethnicity. The journey of self-discovery spans a lifetime, but the crucial step forward is the one that gets us started on that path today.

This journey of self-discovery starts with asking yourself, "What do I know about myself that no one else knows?" What hidden aspects of yourself do you grapple with that others might not be aware of? What feelings, thoughts, or desires have you kept concealed—longings, resentments, pride, or even insecurities? We don't usually become who we are in one defining moment; instead, our metamorphosis tends to happen in stages. As you begin to address the issues you know about yourself but keep others blind to, you'll likely encounter the next challenge of the leadership journey: issues about yourself you're blind to that others can clearly see. This represents yet another layer of the leadership onion and is, unfortunately, a whole new reason for tears (sorry!).

What Do Others Know About You That You May Not Know?

We have to be more than a little curious to address the things we know about ourselves that others may not know. However, confronting our leadership blind spots demands another level of curiosity altogether.

As we continue to summarize Moses' narrative, a new avenue of inquiry arises—one that prompts us to consider the insights we might glean from those within our spheres of influence and our relationships. Unless we're curious enough to explore the perspectives others may have of us, our pursuit of self-understanding and leadership wisdom will remain severely limited. Not only will we constantly struggle with willful blindness, but we will also find ourselves prone to the habitual denial of truths that deserve our attention.

Consider the journey Moses undertook—from rejection, abandonment, resentment, murder, escape, and despair … to the acceptance of a new people and family. From facing reluctance, anger, and fear … to encountering acts of God such as the staff turning into a snake, the plagues of blood, frogs, gnats, flies, hail, locusts, and darkness. From the death of Egypt's firstborn, the Passover, the exodus, consecration, and the crossing of the Red Sea … to the song and dance, water from a rock, manna, and quail. Through it all, Moses transformed from a man who doubted his own ability to speak convincingly—as expressed in Exodus 6:12, "If the Israelites will not listen to me, why would Pharaoh listen to me, since I speak with faltering lips?"—to one who stood with unwavering confidence, reassuring his people with the words, "Do not be afraid. Stand firm and you will see the deliverance the Lord will bring you today" (Exod. 14:13). This journey was marked by moments of doubt, triumph, and divine intervention, illustrating Moses' growth as a leader and ultimate faith in God's deliverance.

At this juncture in Moses' story, he has received a revelation of God, a clearer understanding of his own capabilities, and the available support needed to plug the gaps in his perceived gifts and shortcomings. Having achieved transformative feats he might never have imagined possible, he faces his second major hurdle, which prompts him to engage in an even deeper level of curiosity. When we are making progress in our leadership, we will *always* reach a place where others will know things about us that we may not know about ourselves. These will encompass both positive and negative aspects of our leadership.

In Exodus 18:13–23 Jethro, Moses' father-in-law, sees something that Moses cannot see. After celebrating all the things God has done through Moses to rescue the Israelites, Jethro witnesses Moses presiding as the lone judge for all of Israel from morning until evening.

If you are making significant progress as a leader, you *will* eventually hear an echo of Jethro's inquiry, "What is this you are doing?" (v. 14), from someone you hold dear and respect. If you are extremely fortunate and someone is genuinely invested in your growth as a leader, you will also hear something like Jethro's challenge, "What you are doing is not good" (v. 17).

It's interesting that in Moses' lifetime, he goes from believing he is incapable of serving his people to believing that he alone is capable of serving his people!

Unlike Western culture, the Afro-Asiatic cultures of the Bible did not consider criticism and correction as signs of failure or disaster or even as personal attacks. Instead, they were more likely viewed as evidence of growth and maturation.

The Bible itself is clear that correction is a natural part of Christian progress. Proverbs 3:12 advises, "But don't, dear friend, resent GOD's discipline; don't sulk under his loving correction. It's the child he loves that GOD corrects; a father's delight is behind all this" (MSG). Similarly, Hebrews 12:6 reiterates, "It is the child he [God] loves that he disciplines; the child he embraces, he also corrects" (MSG).

If we seldom hear the question, "What is this you are doing?" it may suggest we're doing little worthy of comment. Alternatively, it could also suggest that the people around us are not sufficiently invested in our leadership to offer honest feedback. However, it's also possible that our demeanor, reactions, and attitudes deter people in our circles from sharing candid truths with us. If we are too fearful, proud, or arrogant to take correction or direction, we will short-circuit our development as leaders.

If our actions are toxic and harmful to others, it's crucial that we learn to embrace the question, "What is this you are doing?" A friend of mine likens toxic leaders to people who carry around leaky barrels of gunpowder. These leaders inadvertently leave a trail of potential hazards as they go about their business. All they need is for some "bright spark" to come along and ignite it all.

Moses had no idea he was a liability to himself as well as to the very people he was seeking to serve. It simply hadn't occurred to him that he might be exhausting everyone, including himself. He genuinely thought he was helping. What seemed like self-sacrifice was, in fact, inadvertently sacrificing others to his need to feel "useful." The remarkable thing is when this was brought to his attention, "Moses listened to his father-in-law and did everything he said" (Exod. 18:24). To fully inhabit our calling, we will sometimes require correction and redirection and how we respond will be just as critical as recognizing our need for it in the first place.

I've often pondered why God designed humans with physical blind spots when (presumably) alternative options were available to him. On top of this, we also blink fifteen to twenty times a minute, leaving us fully blind for 10 percent of every waking day.[10] These biological limitations mirror the personal blind spots that constantly evade our attention. These are only accessible to us through the perceptions and insights of others—family, friends, mentors, peers, team, and community members—who often see what we do not. Although we may not realize we are moody, vindictive, petulant, bullish, or manipulative, someone else definitely does and may be longing to enlighten us!

> **ROBERT: IN NEED OF A METAMORPHIC JOURNEY**
>
> When I met with Robert, it was clear he was remarkably gifted, but it was also clear he had a frustrating tendency to make himself indispensable. Having conducted a brief 360 call with those who interacted with him on a regular basis, there was an underlying and recurring theme: Robert would design systems and processes that he alone could properly manage or interpret. In fact, he operated in a way that kept him in constant demand and therefore the go-to person for information in or about the organization. Instead of the dynamic catalyst he had been when he'd started in the role, he had become the predictable bottleneck. His selective sharing and withholding of critical pieces of information, depending on whom he was dealing with, were a source of comfort and assurance to

> him but drove everyone else to near distraction. His tendency to be generous with his direct reports while withholding from peers only exacerbated the problem. Robert compounded this further by stubbornly refusing help from anyone he deemed "incapable" or "unworthy." Instead, he clung to his need to be needed, oblivious of the impact it was having on others around him and met any direct challenges to his mini fiefdom with his now infamous "meltdown" and withdrawal tactics. His behavior proved so frustrating that despite Robert's brilliance at everything he did, his colleagues had begun to exclude him from key meetings, initiatives, and activities.
>
> In our first meeting, three things became immediately apparent. First, Robert's sessions with me had been foisted on him in a last-ditch attempt to help him break poor habits and make progress on the issues. Second, he was afraid, defensive, and clearly in no mood to cooperate with someone he feared had been instructed to render him "controllable." It was unlikely our sessions would go well—those who have such things forced upon them in this way seldom engage enthusiastically. Third, Robert's days were already numbered if he continued to resist the help he so evidently needed. The question was who would jump first: Robert, his boss, or his peers ...

As we reflect on Moses at this stage of his leadership journey, our own growth as leaders might similarly accelerate if we simply opened ourselves to the observations of others. Like Moses in Exodus 18:17, Robert was in danger of destroying himself and those he thought he was "helping." He could only be a metamorph if he opened himself to the transformative power of deeper curiosity.

Like Moses, we need more than the peer support of an "Aaron." We also need those who will show us our insecurities, shortcomings, idiosyncrasies, and weaknesses impacting people around us destructively. Thankfully, Jethro could see directly into Moses' blind spots and was willing to communicate what no one had noticed or perhaps dared to convey. To overcome this leadership hurdle, Moses would have to heed Jethro's insights and wisdom, which urged him to expand his leadership capacity by empowering the gifts and capabilities of other similarly talented prospective metamorphs who were just as dependable. Indeed, Moses would never have realized others were also capable of making astute decisions if he hadn't made room for their input.

Moses needed a comprehensive 360-degree system that encompassed his peers, mentors, and mentees, yet he couldn't see this for himself. It took the insight, intervention, and counsel of Jethro to reveal the God-given resources already available to him (yet again). This model of support remains crucial in today's landscape, where the best leaders learn to collaborate, share the load, and involve others in leadership, just as Moses was advised to do. Ultimately, Moses led best by redistributing the responsibility entrusted to him by God and by recognizing what had rightly been entrusted to others.

Having a reflective 360-degree group of people around us allows us to receive feedback on our more and less favorable leadership traits and behaviors. We often lack the ability to see ourselves as others do. So God places us in communities of those who are ahead of us (e.g., mentors, coaches, counselors—relationships that exist for accountability, wisdom, and growth), those who are beside us (e.g., partners, friends, colleagues—fellow leaders and peers facing similar challenges), and those who are behind us (e.g., mentees, coachees, employees—those with whom you share your insights and accumulated wisdom). If empowered to speak into our lives, these people can help us grow into reasonably well-rounded and teachable human beings.[11]

Without an openness to questions, challenges, and feedback from our community, we may never grow beyond a certain level of leadership maturity and therefore wisdom. Perhaps our biology and inherent blind spots are partly designed to remind us of this reality. Only the most dangerous leaders fail to invite questions, challenges, or insights from those committed to their well-being. (Let's face it—who would accept these from anyone else?) However, it's possible to be surrounded by loving friends, great colleagues, insightful mentors, and people who report to us who have never been explicitly empowered to tell us what they're really thinking. If this resonates with you, empower them now. Personally, I'm blessed to have mentors, peers, friends, and mentees unafraid to tell me the truth about myself, though as I often jest, I sometimes wish they weren't quite so ready and willing!

Moses' story stands out not just because he learns to delegate responsibilities but also because of his openness to learn and act upon the advice of someone who wasn't leading a multitude through a wilderness at the time! While insights from peers in similar roles are valuable, the mark of an exceptional leader lies in their readiness to embrace wisdom from unexpected sources such as their would-be "Jethros." The latter might differ from us in multiple ways, but they possess divine wisdom crucial to our ongoing journey! Their readiness to share invaluable insights that benefit us and those around us should always be welcomed with open arms!

What *Moses knew about himself that others did not know* almost prevented him from getting started on God's purposes for his life. But *what others knew about Moses that he was unaware of* almost prevented him from making further progress in his leadership journey.

In this phase of his leadership, Moses faced what he'd kept hidden from others, and others had revealed what had been hidden to Moses. However, to mature his leadership and equip him to further guide the people into God's Promised Land—a pivotal goal set by God—there was a third hurdle Moses would have to overcome. And it meant yet another layer of that leadership onion to peel away and weep his way through.

What Do You and Others Not Know About You That God Alone Knows?

Things that lie within our knowledge of ourselves but may be hidden from others require deliberate personal curiosity and courage to uncover. By inviting and empowering those around us to share their insights, we can receive invaluable perspectives that we may be wholly oblivious to and that can aid our growth as leaders.

However, there are aspects of who we are that are so shrouded in shadow from both ourselves and those closest to us that we only catch glimpses of them in moments of anger, pain, jealousy, or self-doubt. Unearthing these aspects demands the deepest level of curiosity, while neglecting them could do untold damage to our very best leadership efforts. Leadership is always a "we," not just a "me" endeavor. Ignoring these hidden aspects of ourselves can have a devastating impact on the entire leadership ecosystem, affecting not just the leader but also everyone influenced by them. We are ultimately responsible for the health of our leadership and cannot afford to abdicate the final responsibility to anyone else.

This third line of inquiry presents the most formidable obstacle to our development as leaders because these concealed aspects seem impenetrable to us and are often unnoticed, overlooked, or simply inaccessible to those closest to us. Fortunately, this realm belongs to God, whose view of our innermost landscape is awash with light. However, if we truly want to know what God alone knows, we must turn to him for that revelation.

Numbers 20:2–12 marks a pivotal moment in Moses' leadership journey and illustrates precisely what is at stake. During these closing stages of Moses' story, God makes this severe pronouncement: "Because you did not trust in me enough to honor me as holy in the sight of the Israelites, you will not bring this community into the land I give them" (Num. 20:12). Initially, God's reaction seems an extreme response to what appears to be a minor mistake on Moses' part. Instead of speaking to the rock as instructed, Moses strikes it with a staff. This is reminiscent of a previous incident in Exodus 17, where he is specifically instructed to strike the rock. Based on Numbers 20:2–11 alone, one might perceive God as a harsh and capricious taskmaster.

However, a deeper examination of Moses' life and leadership reveals a recurring pattern that we catch a glimpse of in this seemingly isolated event. A habitual behavior becomes evident, not just in Moses but also in Aaron, who shares in the devastating consequence. Although Moses had an exceptional relationship with God, there was one thing that competed with it: his relationship with God's people. This major flaw remained unaddressed and unresolved for so long that it became almost imperceptible to everyone, including Moses himself.

Moses' relationship with the people posed a constant threat to his leadership. They occupied a significant place in his thoughts, at times overshadowing his relationship with God entirely. At crucial moments throughout his leadership journey, his anger and frustration with them even surpassed his faith in God. In one incident, Moses descended a mountain carrying two stones handcrafted by God, only to witness the people worshiping a golden calf, facilitated by a colluding Aaron, now heavily implicated. Moses was so angered by what he saw that he smashed the stones entrusted to him (Exod. 32). Yet in many ways, Moses' reaction was understandable. The people weren't just worshiping other gods; they were worshiping the antithesis of everything God had revealed himself to be thus far. However, in his anger, Moses smashed the very commandments God instructed him to bring to the people. This mirrors instances where Christian leaders feel tempted to destroy what God has entrusted to them because of their frustration with those they lead. Leaders have been known to forsake their calling, their work, their church, and sometimes even their faith because of the hurtful words, behavior, and indifference of fellow believers. Thankfully, at least in Moses' case, the tablets were later replaced. Not everything we destroy can be.

This, of course, was not the only time Moses' anger got the better of him. In Exodus 16, Moses instructs the people to gather as much manna as they need but to not save any for the next day. When the people ignore his instructions, and the manna begins to rot and stink, Moses becomes angry with the people (Exod. 16:20). In Numbers 11, when the people complain that all they have to eat is manna, Moses complains to God, "Why have you brought this trouble on your servant? What have I done to displease you that you put the burden of all these people on me? … Why do you tell me to carry them in my arms, as a nurse carries an infant, to the land you promised on oath to their ancestors?" (Num. 11:11–12). Having developed an over-inflated sense of self-importance, Moses begins to see himself as the rescuer and carrier of Israel's burdens, which causes him to grumble at God and resent the people.

The true source of Moses' anger toward the people is revealed in Numbers 20:10 when Moses says, "Must *we* bring you water out of this rock?" (emphasis added). In his anger, Moses takes credit for what is clearly a work of God. Moses isn't just angry because the people are dishonoring God as their rescuer; Moses feels the people are dishonoring *him* as their rescuer. Unlike God's anger, which is meant to expose the sin of the Israelites, Moses' anger exposes his own sin. And by placing himself as the savior of the people, Moses dishonors God, and God declares Moses will not enter the Promised Land with his people. Every Christian leader must reckon with the possibility that they may one day love their followers more than they love God and fear their rejection more than they fear God's.

Moses' leadership journey goes from believing he couldn't lead the people, to believing he didn't need others to help him lead, to believing that he didn't need God to lead the people. Ultimately, his over-developed sense of self-importance as a leader manifests as both pride and entitlement.

Every leadership journey experiences similar pivotal moments that reveal something in us that God knows but has been hidden from others and even ourselves. If you had asked Moses anywhere along his leadership journey if he believed that he didn't need God, he probably would have said, "Absolutely not!" But slowly, those hidden thoughts became hidden beliefs, expressed through little outbursts, until they were revealed in a tragic public act.

Aaron, who is also included in the verdict, was of little help to Moses at this critical point in his leadership journey. Instead of challenging Moses as he should, Aaron—who colluded with the people in the event with the golden calf, then with Miriam against Moses in Numbers 12:1–2—makes Moses complicit here in the worst possible way. As helpful as the people around us can be, they can also fall prey to shortsightedness and self-interest.

So many stories of leadership failure involve scenarios where a leader and their closest associates overestimate the leader's importance to "God's work" and literally "turn a blind eye" to their excesses, be they sexual, spiritual, emotional, physical, or financial. The leader becomes centered, to the detriment of everything and everyone else. Worse still, the over-inflated sense of importance attached to them makes God seemingly superfluous. Deception of this magnitude masks wrongdoing in ways they now find hard to recognize or acknowledge and is only further compounded when leadership ecosystems resist naming their own complicity even once the sin has been finally exposed, failing to recognize both its gravity and devastating impact on God's honor and God's people. In this instance, Aaron appears to have enabled Moses to live above "the rules" and to engage in behaviors that would otherwise be condemned in others. There's nothing more disturbing than a room full of leaders who do not seem to understand they have been complicit in overlooking and disregarding warning signs, closing ranks, defending offenders, suppressing evidence, and shielding perpetrators over victims, while prioritizing their rapport with whomever they deem to protect their interests.

Gender justice specialist and author Natalie Collins points to Judith Herman's book *Truth and Repair* where she challenges the notion of neutrality in phrases like "objective bystander" when facing the impact of such collusion. Collins writes, "Herman suggests that 'bystander' is too benign a description for such ancillary figures. Instead, she borrows the term 'implicated subjects' from the scholar Michael Rothberg, who has argued that almost all of us contribute to or benefit from structural injustice, and so almost none of us is innocent of implication."[12]

Like Moses and Aaron, it is usually only a matter of time before the little outbursts no longer perceived as wrongdoing, even by those closest to us, end up being publicly revealed alongside damning stories about the "implicated subjects."

Status and privilege have a way of working to inoculate us from the demands of both metanoia (repentance) and metamorphosis (transformation). So the following guidance from Natalie Collins is a critical means to protect both leaders and those around them as we seek to honor God's holiness and navigate our way through the most crucial aspects of leadership:

> If we are all Implicated Subjects, we must regularly ask ourselves, is power misuse taking place in my life/workplace/church/family at the moment? Where might I need to be vigilant to my own tendencies toward turning a blind eye to the things that grieve God's heart? Have I surrounded myself with people who will tell me when I am wrong?[13]

There's the inclination to deny or hide our brokenness to safeguard ourselves, our interests, or existing relationships. But God searches our hearts and wants our brokenness to come to light so it can be addressed before it's too late. Jeremiah 17:9–10 says, "The heart is deceitful above all things and beyond cure.... 'I the LORD search the heart and examine the mind, to reward each person according to their conduct, according to what their deeds deserve.'"

This third line of inquiry aims to reduce the extent to which we become involved in these concealed practices veiled in shadow that God perceives but that we and those around us apparently do not. We may ignore or mask our brokenness in layers of deception or just passively accept stuff that both we and those around us seem indifferent to. Those things that God knows about us, yet we and others around us seem oblivious to or ignore, are often revealed in what we excuse or seek to justify.

We may not see these clearly until we find ourselves neglecting to honor God as Holy before the entire community, like Moses and Aaron before Israel in their final act. They do this at a critical juncture in the development of Israel's understanding of who God is and who they are to God. What we model as leaders matters, especially when we fail to act in ways that safeguard God's honor and protect those who may be vulnerable to mistreatment.

To every onlooker, Moses was a man of God, unequivocally the meekest man on earth, and a revered prophet who had stood in God's presence. His time in God's presence had so imbued him with holiness that he radiated with a brightness too overwhelming for others, prompting Moses to, quite literally, have to cover it up![14]

Moses is rightly celebrated as a remarkable leader. Leading two million people through any wilderness would be considered a success story by many of today's standards. He's lauded for his faith in Hebrews 11, and in Deuteronomy 34, we are reminded that "no prophet has risen in Israel like Moses, whom the LORD knew face to face.... For no one has ever shown the mighty power or performed the awesome deeds that Moses did in the sight of all Israel" (Deut. 34:10, 12). Yet, for all his great deeds, Moses was barred from entering the Promised Land. Throughout the years, his unaddressed anger and unresolved relationship with the people seemed to erode his commitment to God, leading to moments of carelessness and complacency. Ultimately, he is disqualified from leading these same people into the Promised Land.

There will always be things that *no one else but God knows about us.*

Self-awareness, self-reflection, and friendship will get us started on God's purposes for our lives. Tools like Myers-Briggs, StrengthsFinders, and the Enneagram offer valuable insights into our personality traits and strengths and can aid our self-awareness.[15] Feedback from trusted colleagues, supervisors, mentors, and those affected by our leadership also contribute significantly to our growth, provided we give permission and cultivate open and transformative relationships.

Yet, these have their limits, leaving us to learn some things about ourselves only through a *God-inspired revelation or insight.* These come to us only when we take time to retreat and pray about what we do and how and why we do it. It is during these moments that we can understand our motivation behind our actions—whether it's ego-driven, God-honoring, or a result of our own need to be needed. Taking time to reflect on who God is to us, and who we are to God and those we serve can reveal whether we are truly concerned with God's will or with other people's opinions of us. These insights can propel us beyond the initiation of our God-given assignments, driving us toward progress and, hopefully, ultimate *completion.*

This kind of curiosity enables us to discern what is barely visible or audible to us and those around us. And it is this curiosity that allows us to read between the lines, hear what is often left unsaid, and transform our relationships with Jesus, others, and leadership itself.

Moses received assurances, divine tools, and a whole burning bush. Yet despite this, he let his anger with the people overshadow his call. His pride obscured God's holiness and led to his exclusion from the Promised Land. The Bible is not a fairy tale! Not every story in its pages has a happy ending. When we resist the call to morph, it hinders us from achieving our full potential, regardless of our many gifts.

It's crucial to note, as mentioned in chapter two of this book, that although our worth to God remains unchanged, our readiness and suitability for a God-given task may be in question. God challenges us, much like Moses, to face three pivotal questions in life and leadership. If we nurture curiosity throughout our leadership journey, even amid the potential tears that might accompany our many discoveries along the way, we'll be ready to metamorphose in the ways God intends.

FOR PERSONAL REFLECTION OR GROUP DISCUSSION

Questioning to Evade

1. Which of the three questions below do you most often use to evade what God may be asking of you and why?
   - Authenticity: *Are you (God) really who I think you are?* (Exod. 3:13)
   - Credibility: *What if they don't believe I'm who you think I am?* (Exod. 4:1)
   - Capability: *Am I really up to it?* (Exod. 4:13)
2. How do these evasion tactics or doubts affect your life and leadership, including your decision-making, relationships, and personal growth?
3. What can you do to practically address your evasion tactics or doubts?
4. Do you have a 360-development group? If yes, who are they? If no, identify potential members using the outline below:
   - Who are those ahead of you (e.g., mentors, coaches, pastors, therapists, counselors, and supervisors—relationships that exist primarily for accountability, wisdom, and growth)?
   - Who are those beside you (e.g., partners, friends, colleagues, or collaborators—fellow leaders and peers facing similar challenges)?
   - Who are those behind you (e.g., mentees, coachees, supervisees— those with whom you share your insights and accumulated wisdom and who remind you of your need for consistency and integrity in your own leadership)?

Questioning to Transform

1. Which of the three transformative questions below do you need to wrestle with most and why?
   - *What do you know about yourself that no one else knows?*
   - *What do others know about you that you may not know?*
   - *What do you and others not know about you that God alone knows?*
2. On a scale of 1–10 (where 1 = not at all and 10 = brilliantly), how well do you cope with criticism, correction, change, and exhaustion; and how do you know this?

3. Who would you invite to tell you when things are going wrong? Who are the people who can tell you when you are misusing your power, grieving God's heart, failing to honor God as holy, or in danger of destroying what has been entrusted to you by God? Why would you select those people?
4. What approach should these people (from your response above) take to illicit the best response from you? (Don't forget to let them know your thoughts on this.)
5. What additional steps, such as engaging in regular self-reflection, can you take to strengthen your curiosity?

TIME FOR PRAYER

Take a moment for personal or group prayer. If part of a discussion group, lift up each member, asking for guidance, strength, and clarity as they navigate through their challenges and seek growth in their personal and leadership journey toward *greater curiosity*.

4

THE WOMAN AT THE WELL
THE ART OF BECOMING

Defeating Self-Limiting Mindsets

One of the most useful questions an adult can ask a child is—What do you want to be when you grow up? As if growing up is finite. As if at some point you become something and that's the end.
MICHELLE OBAMA

Our very lives succeed or fail gradually, then suddenly.
SUSAN SCOTT

It takes courage to grow up and become who you really are.
E. E. CUMMINGS

People who experience mysterious physical discomfort during their childhood and early adulthood often attribute it to "growing pains." Though considered harmless, these pains can manifest as severe cramps and persistent aches that may linger on for months or even years. Yet, despite the very real discomfort, there is no clear or definitive evidence that physical growth actually causes pain.

Nevertheless, the term "growing pains" remains popular in both medical circles and among the general public today. Perhaps this is because it offers a shorthand for unrelated but intense physical discomforts, such as those I experienced when my wisdom teeth were determined to make their way into the world throughout my twenties and early thirties. It also speaks to distressing experiences that go beyond mere biological pains, such as the disappointments and frustrations of unwelcome, often hard-to-ignore "choices" our hormones seem to make in collusion with our DNA.

Whether we love or hate these changes, we all must make decisions about "painful" aspects of our lives over which we have little or no control. Sometimes, hormones seem to have the upper hand in dictating our actions under the influence of our DNA and other biological factors.[1] At other times, we wrestle with circumstances, difficulties, structural or systemic issues, and cultural pressures thrust upon us without our permission. There are also those moments when we're left pondering the best course of action in response to the ill-considered words or actions of malicious or even well-intentioned people.

Wherever these challenges come from, they force us to carefully consider our choices. As with our ever-changing bodies, we aren't faced with the question of *whether* to grow (it's usually too late for that!) but rather about *how* we choose to grow and what we aim to *become*.

BECOMING: A NEVER-ENDING JOURNEY OF GROWING UP

Growth is not only intrinsic to life; it is also a force of nature that we have little power to resist. Cells in the average human body continue to grow by reproducing every single day of our lives.[2] As we age, this process slows, becomes less accurate, more destructive, and ultimately less efficient and reliable. However, our cells continue on their course regardless, leaving us with little to no control over the inevitable process of physical aging, despite our human efforts to the contrary. By contrast, we have almost absolute control over our attitudes, disposition, responses, and behaviors, giving us significant power over who we actually want to become. Ultimately, it appears that although "who we are is God's gift to us, who we become is our gift to God."[3]

Our lives continue to evolve physically, emotionally, spiritually, or mentally, whether we want them to or not. But unlike the growth that inevitably leads to our physical and mental decline, the process of becoming who we are requires close nurturing and careful monitoring if we wish to grow into something better. This is particularly important because we make developmental choices that affect "how" we grow, both intentionally and unintentionally, year by year, month by month, week by week, day by day, and even moment by moment. Regrettably, our choices are not always in our best interests or those of the people we claim to care about the most.

However, despite our human inclination to sometimes self-destruct developmentally, we also possess an almost limitless capacity for positive transformation. Whether we have been leading for years or are relatively new to the experience, we are never as fixed in our ways as we might think. Nor are we entirely at the mercy of the circumstances or conditions we constantly face.

Though aging is inevitable, thanks to neuroplasticity our brains possess an almost infinite capacity for rewiring. This allows us to form new mental pathways relatively quickly in response to fresh information. While plasticity is most robust during childhood and adolescence, our adult brains also retain a significant capacity for change. So, contrary to popular opinion, we really are "never too old to grow up," and it's even possible to "teach an old dog new tricks." The crucial question is whether the old dog really wants to learn new tricks in the first place!

With God's help we often can and do change the way we believe, think, and behave. The Christian principle of repentance, or metanoia—changing one's mind—relies on this premise for its success. Thus, we are perpetual candidates for transformation and always prospective metamorphs, given new chances to determine who we are becoming in life and in leadership.

The term metanoia also suggests that what we become requires our proactive engagement—our "yes"—and is therefore determined by our choices and our willingness to make them. Viktor Frankl, the Austrian neurologist, psychologist, and Holocaust survivor, is often credited with a poignant statement that underscores this: "Between stimulus and response there is a space. In that space is our power to choose our response. In our response lies our growth and our freedom."[4] In other words, we are always at liberty to determine who we become, despite, and sometimes precisely because of, the circumstances we encounter along the way.

None of us remains static—there's always more growing up to do, and although we're no longer what we once were, we have not yet reached our full potential either. Thankfully, with God's help, we possess the capacity to become more than we ever thought or dreamed possible.

BECOMING: MORE THAN THE SAMARITAN WOMAN AT THE WELL

The account of the Samaritan woman in chapter 4 of John's Gospel powerfully illustrates that we can indeed choose how we grow. Her story vividly reminds us that metamorphosis—the ongoing transformation of heart, mind, life, prospects, possibilities, and ultimately leadership—can happen to each of us, either gradually or suddenly, given the right conditions. John's narrative also demonstrates that metamorphosis can also apply to entire communities and people groups.

The Samaritan woman's story begins when Jesus, mindful of the Pharisees' growing scrutiny of his ministry, is compelled to depart from Judea and head back to Galilee with his disciples. As events unfold, we notice Jesus intentionally breaks from the typical Jewish custom of avoiding the Samaritan territories between Judea and Galilee. Rather than following the longer, conventional route favored by Jewish travelers that circumvented Samaria via the Transjordan,[5] Jesus chose a more direct path through Samaria. The phrasing in John 4:4 makes it clear that Jesus "had to" take this route, implying that this was somehow part of a divine imperative. In other words, God was well and truly up to something.

To fully grasp the profound significance of these events, we must briefly explore the historical relationship between these ancient Jews and Samaritans, the reasons for the social and geographical apartheid that existed between these communities, and why the Jews treated Samaritans with such contempt in the first place.

Stepping Back

After Solomon's death in 930 BCE, the kingdom of Israel fractured into two distinct entities: Israel (consisting of ten tribes in the north) and Judah (comprising Judah and Benjamin in the south) (see 1 Kings 12). Initially, Samaria was simply the name given to the new capital of the northern kingdom by King Omri in 1 Kings 16:24, but it eventually became shorthand for the entire northern region itself. The events surrounding the splintering of the kingdom of Israel were the source of the tension and division so evident between Israel and Samaria during Jesus' time.[6]

What began as a political division soon erupted into religious and cultural tensions. Over time, these ancient Jews perceived themselves as an inherently superior and chosen race destined for heaven. They also came to regard the Samaritans as an inferior, mongrel race, "the children of political rebels, racial half-breeds whose religion was tainted by various unacceptable elements."[7] This perception stemmed from the intermarriage between Samaritans and Assyrians, as well as the Samaritans' belief that they could worship at Mount Gerizim instead of the Jerusalem temple. Despite their shared ancestry, with both groups claiming Abraham as their father, claiming Moses as their liberator, worshiping the God of Jacob, and belonging to the children of Israel, the Jews harbored a deep hatred toward the Samaritans.

By the time of Jesus, the animosity between Jews and Samaritans was so intense that John chapter 4 could just as easily have been titled, "Jesus Engages with a Racially Inferior Heretic at the Well!" Moreover, the Jewish antipathy toward Samaritans was so pervasive that, by the first century BCE, calling a Jew a Samaritan was considered one of the worst insults a person could utter. Shockingly, this is precisely how Jesus' critics labeled him in John 8:48, saying, "Aren't we right in saying that you are a Samaritan and demon-possessed?" The choice of words was deliberately intended to humiliate Jesus both publicly and personally in the worst way imaginable.

It is this background that makes the "had to" language of John 4:4 so very intriguing and the unfolding story of the interaction between Jesus and the Samaritan at the well so incredible. Weary from walking all morning through Samaritan territory, Jesus and his disciples reach Sychar, where Jacob's Well is located. At this point, the disciples head into town to buy food while Jesus stays at the well to rest. What follows is unique to John's Gospel and is one of the most extraordinary dialogues of the entire New Testament. Although many Bibles title it "Jesus Talks with a Samaritan Woman," so much more than mere "talk" takes place in this historic moment.

Back to Her Future

If we fast-forward through her life's journey, we discover that the woman at the well holds the distinction of being the first person to whom Jesus discloses his identity as the Messiah, as well as being the first recorded evangelist in the New

Testament. Acts 8:4–40 reveals that by the time Philip arrives in Samaria, many Samaritans have already embraced Jesus, and this remarkable woman is often acknowledged as the catalyst for this growth in Samaritan Christianity.

In post-biblical literature, she's referred to as Photini or Photina, meaning "enlightened," "radiant," or "shining" (a name she is believed to have taken at her baptism). Within Russian Orthodoxy, she's recognized as Svetlana. Throughout Greek sermons spanning the fourth to the fourteenth centuries, she earns titles like "apostle" and "evangelist." These sermons frequently draw parallels between the Samaritan Woman and the male apostles, often suggesting she surpasses them all.[8]

Some stories recount her extensive travels alongside her five daughters or possibly sisters (Anatole, Photo, Photis, Paraskeve, Kyriake) and her two sons (Photeinos and Joseph). Her influence is said to have extended from Africa to Rome, where she transformed many lives and communities.

One such story describes how, following her arrest and torture by Nero, she is placed into the custody of Nero's daughter, Domnina. Shortly after, Domnina and around a hundred of her servants embrace Christianity and receive baptism. This unexpected turn of events must have been immensely frustrating for Nero, who had clearly intended Domnina to persuade Photina to renounce her faith. Eventually, Photina and her entire family are said to pay the ultimate price and are martyred by Nero.[9]

On the Greek Calendar, St. Photina is remembered on February 26, although various Orthodox communities commemorate her on slightly differing dates. Within the Greek Orthodox tradition, she occupies a place of honor among their apostles. Indeed, one of her titles is "Great Martyr St. Photini, Equal to the Apostles."

Her story is a treasure trove of invaluable insights into the metamorphic journey of *becoming*. In both John's gospel and beyond, she emerges as an exceptional leader, further empowered by Jesus to make a significant contribution to the expansion of Christianity throughout the ancient world. Yet her biblical narrative begins without fanfare, without prestige, and without reference, even to her name.

INVITING TO CONTRIBUTE: KEYS TO TRANSFORMING OTHERS (AND OURSELVES)

How did this seemingly solitary woman of John chapter 4 transform into the Great Martyr St. Photini, and how does she become someone of such clear repute, significance, influence, and impact? I suggest it begins with Jesus' simple request, "Will you give me a drink?" (v. 7).

Essentially, Jesus invites her contribution amid a culture in which Jews did not typically ask anything of Samaritans, especially Samaritan women; and Samaritans, in turn, would not ask anything of Jews. Jesus' request for help stands in stark contrast to Zerubbabel's rejection of Samaritan aid to rebuild the temple many centuries earlier in Ezra 4:2. So, whatever else may be going on at this point in John's Gospel, there is already something of great prophetic significance in what Jesus asks of the Samaritan woman rather than what he offers her (initially, at least). This single act of inviting the woman to contribute seems to unlock the proverbial floodgates: Her metamorphic journey of *becoming* is accelerated, setting her on a path from a "solitary woman" with no name into "Great Martyr St. Photini, Equal to the Apostles."

In the journey of life and leadership, there are always defining moments that can awaken our leadership potential in unforeseen and extraordinary ways. Becoming convinced of the value of our personal contribution is one of them, and it is not incidental that this theme particularly resonates with women leaders and others from underrepresented groups.

Extensive research indicates that becoming a leader involves much more than developing a skill set, adjusting our styles to fit the specific needs of a particular role, or simply occupying a leadership position. Instead, becoming a leader involves a far more fundamental shift of identity than the mere giving of a title suggests.[10]

Something specific must happen to support our motivation to lead and give us a sense of ourselves as leaders. This *something* is sometimes referred to as "leader identity." It is considered a critical component for aspiring leaders, especially for women and underrepresented groups.

Leader identity recognizes that we do not become leaders in a social vacuum. Leadership develops not only when we take purposeful action but also when those around us validate or resist it. Their verbal and non-verbal reactions convey whether they perceive us as leaders. Something as simple as being noticed, paid attention to, or being seen and championed can significantly contribute to our perception of ourselves as leaders and influence our willingness to take further leader-like actions. Leader identity evolves each time actions viewed as *leadership* receive affirmation from significant individuals. It is an iterative process. To put it simply, "Such affirmation gives the person the fortitude to step outside a comfort zone and experiment with unfamiliar behaviours and new ways of exercising leadership. An absence of affirmation, however, diminishes self-confidence and discourages him or her from seeking developmental opportunities or experimenting."[11]

Yet even today, leader identity is more likely to be assumed in men, often irrespective of any real supporting evidence. Women, however, have a long history of being persistently denied the recognition and validation so often accorded to their male counterparts, even when they undertake the same actions or display similar leadership qualities. This is often painfully obvious within churches and other contexts, where male leadership has become normalized over time.

But in John 4:7, Jesus said to the woman at the well, "Will you give me a drink?"

It is, of course, her response that sheds light on the groundbreaking nature of Jesus' request: "'You are a Jew and I am a Samaritan woman. How can you ask me for a drink?' (For Jews do not associate with Samaritans)" (John 4:9). Given the historical background outlined earlier, the circumstances of this particular interaction, and Jesus' evident passion for engaging with those in the margins, we should not be entirely surprised that the Holy Spirit chooses to introduce the Samaritan woman to the biblical story in this way and at this time. Far from being presented in the posture of a petitioner seeking Jewish help (which a Samaritan might not readily accept anyway), she is initially presented as an outsider capable of contributing to the well-being of a fatigued, depleted, and very Jewish Jesus!

We often focus on what Jesus offers the woman: the promise of living water. Yet, as important as this is, it's crucial not to overlook Jesus' apparent determination to disrupt the prevailing power dynamics and gender relations that existed between the Jewish and Samaritan communities at what was to be a critical moment in their shared history.

The conversation doesn't begin with Jesus showcasing his ability to offer life-altering water or perform miracles. Instead, it begins with Jesus' request for the woman's help and, by implication, his recognition of her value to God and her agency and ability to act. Some speculate that Jesus was pretending to be tired and thirsty to create a teachable moment, but this view overlooks Jesus' human experiences and the likely physical impact of his long journey to the well. I have little doubt that Jesus was genuinely exhausted and dehydrated by the time he sat down. And Jesus was willing to use his current condition to orchestrate a powerful transformative event for a person disregarded by everyone else.

The interaction between Jesus and the woman at the well sets her free to step into her calling in a way that wouldn't have been possible if Jesus had simply arrived with a bucket of living water and declared the superiority of his offering from the outset. This encounter is far from accidental; Jesus intentionally shapes the conversation to pique her natural curiosity. His engagement seems specifically aimed at eliciting a response, and despite societal norms and cultural expectations, she responds. Initially cautious, she gradually becomes more comfortable interacting, engaging, and questioning Jesus. It all starts with a simple request for a drink, followed by the mention of living water—an intriguing proposition that naturally attracts her. Then, unexpectedly, Jesus shares personal insights about her life, which could have stopped the conversation in its tracks but instead seems to add even more proverbial fuel to the conversational fire! There's an undeniable quality about Jesus that seems to draw her out further, compelling her to embrace any growing pains while contributing more and more to this improbable unfolding scenario. In fact, the more Jesus talks, listens, and responds, the more she appears to contribute.

Indeed, before we know it, this becomes Jesus' longest recorded conversation in the New Testament and marks the first time he reveals his identity as the Messiah (to a Samaritan woman, of all people). As a result of the interaction, she rushes off to make her most significant contribution of all, at least within the biblical narrative, to her townsfolk—the very people she may have been trying to avoid in the first place! The rest, as they say, is church history (or at least hagiography).[12] However, I'm now getting ahead of myself.

Growth through Affirmation

It's unlikely the woman at the well would have been accustomed to interacting with strangers, particularly Jewish men, in such a candid manner. Her disclosure, "I have no husband" (v. 17), is a pivotal moment in the biblical account and often produces a collective intake of breath, but perhaps for all the wrong reasons. Many interpret her admission of having had five husbands and currently not being married as a confession of grave moral misconduct. To many Western ears, she has betrayed herself as being casual or even flippant in her attitude toward marriage and relationships. Yet, other aspects of her story, particularly the surprising response of her townspeople, challenge assumptions about her alleged moral failings or social ostracism and cast doubt on the presumption that she was a prostitute.

People from the Global South or East might more readily grasp that her situation is unlikely to be explained by appeals to her imagined sexual promiscuity. Considering the cultural context in Israel during the New Testament era, it's improbable that five men would willingly marry a woman without fame or fortune and with a reputation for adultery. Moreover, in a culture where women typically couldn't initiate divorce, it's unlikely she was a serial divorcee by choice. Additionally, given the high value placed on having children, especially sons, it's hard to imagine five men marrying a woman known to be infertile, as some commentators suggest.[13]

Instead, her five marriages and current circumstances might have been the consequence of far more mundane yet tragic circumstances, reminiscent of the Old Testament story of Ruth. Given the harsh reality of rural life, perhaps a series of unfortunate events led to the deaths of several of her husbands. Or, a levirate arrangement might have been enforced with one or two husbands, while divorce could have played a role too. As far as her current circumstances were concerned, not being married to the man she now lived with might not signify grave sin; rather, it could just as easily be due to her lack of a dowry, resulting in her settling for a status similar to that of a concubine. Perhaps the man she was currently with was old and required care, and his children didn't wish to share their inheritance with her, leaving her without a dowry document. Similar scenarios arise in some cultures even today. Scripture doesn't clarify why she'd had five husbands, but exploring first-century realities and cultures that live more closely to these realities today helps us imagine how her circumstances might have unfolded.

In the ancient world, being a serial widow or divorcee was exceedingly rare, even for men. So, any sharp intake of breath at this point in her narrative should be reserved for the fact that no one outside her community, including Jesus, could have deduced her unlikely and highly convoluted set of circumstances, whatever they were. The only way of knowing would have been through divine revelation. Jesus' extraordinary ability to uncover what was perhaps the most complex, elusive, and painful issue in her life leads her to acknowledge the divine source of his insight. Instead of reacting with offense or resentment, she becomes even more captivated and liberated by the revelation, thereby crossing another potential pain barrier. Satisfied that he is indeed a prophet, she unexpectedly, from our point of view, shifts the conversation to theology, a subject a woman had no place engaging with at the time.

And yes, Jesus corrects her misconceptions, but notably, he also addresses the misperceptions within his own Jewish tradition: "Believe me, a time is coming when you will worship the Father neither on this mountain nor in Jerusalem.... God is spirit, and his worshipers must worship in the Spirit and in truth" (John 4:21, 24). He corrects her without belittling her theological inquiry or making her feel inadequate.

What's intriguing is how unthreatening the Samaritan woman finds Jesus, despite the social and cultural norms that required deference to this rabbi, someone she should have considered her superior in every way. The woman at the well is a woman in a man's world, where men did not engage women in conversation in public and where women certainly didn't answer back, engage in debate, or challenge the dominant group's claim as the ultimate standard for measuring spirituality, theology, and philosophy. Yet, there was something about Jesus and the value he placed on their interaction that empowered her to challenge, question, and boldly express her opinions. She not only conversed with Jesus but also posed pointed questions. This, of course, is a masterclass in empowering leadership from Jesus!

Painful experience often leads underrepresented individuals to assume their voices won't be heard or taken seriously when they attempt to contribute their thoughts and ideas in leadership discussions. Nevertheless, like the woman at the well, many persevere anyway, even if they fail at the first, second, or third hurdle.

This story illustrates the extent to which Jesus is prepared to go, quite literally, to enable this woman's contribution—and, by extension, ours as well. He not only understands what it takes to identify underrepresented leaders, but he also knows how best to affirm and empower them to grow beyond their pain barriers.

I occasionally find myself engaged in conversations with senior leaders, predominantly men, who express a genuine interest in involving and supporting women and people of color in their leadership circles. However, they frequently lament what they perceive to be a lack of confidence and competence among these groups. My response to such comments is much the same every time because developing underrepresented groups—be it women, people of color, or others—really isn't rocket science. It requires the same kind of commitment and investment that is needed to nurture all those already overrepresented leaders (because there really is nothing new under the sun)!

The challenge in identifying underrepresented leaders typically doesn't stem from their lack of confidence or competence. What can be perceived as a lack of self-confidence is perhaps a natural response to being overlooked and undermined time and time again. Instead, the challenge often lies with existing leaders who fail to build meaningful relationships beyond surface-level connections, which are crucial for nurturing any leader, let alone those from underrepresented communities. A disproportionate amount of informal time and effort often goes into reinforcing the leadership identities of the "usual suspects." Meanwhile, there is usually a lack of consideration for the specific training and development needs of underrepresented groups. Additionally, there is often a scarcity of opportunities, platforms, challenging assignments, or the kind of consistent practice that is often taken for granted by overrepresented leaders. To make matters worse, underrepresented leaders are sometimes expected to exercise their leadership as if they were culturally identical to the overrepresented leaders. No wonder confidence and competence are perceived as issues. Pretending to be someone else is quite literally exhausting.

The transformation of butterflies and insects in nature highlights the need for environments that optimize conditions for metamorphosis. As leaders, our *becoming* is more closely aligned with God's purpose when we and those around us actually acknowledge the value of each other's contributions. Growth happens and limiting beliefs are weakened when we regularly reinforce this kind of affirmation. A supportive environment fuels our empowerment to contribute positively to God's mission and to the needs of our world. As the history of so many Christian grassroots movements reveals, if we fail to affirm leadership in others, God usually takes the matter into his own hands and finds another way.[14]

Growth through Vulnerability

Following Jesus' example and inviting the contributions of others invariably helps us to become more like Jesus. This process often results in a spiritual and emotional gush of "living water" that reveals just how close the Holy Spirit has always been throughout the process. God is never a mere bystander in metamorphosis; he's always an active participant, even more so than we are.

The more we embrace the dynamic process of transformation, the more we find ourselves experiencing him.

In 2022, I found myself navigating uncharted waters. As I mentioned in the preface, I spent several months recuperating from two significant surgeries. It was my first experience of hospitalization and confronting such severe health issues. After being discharged from the local hospital, my world shrank to the confines of my room and my bed. By the end of the year, I was exhausted and physically weaker than ever before, and trust me, I've had my moments! I needed assistance for not just getting up and down the stairs but also with getting in and out of bed. My housemate, though incredibly supportive, drew the line at changing my clinical dressings, fearing she might do more harm than good. We've been best friends for years, and although I trust her implicitly, the thought of her removing dressings that felt almost glued in place improved my prayer life more than my faith. So, when she expressed her reluctance, I silently breathed a sigh of relief.

However, there were pandemic-related restrictions at the local hospital and a lack of nearby support, so we had to pray as never before for an alternative solution to my health needs. Eventually, we reached out to our neighbors, none of whom were Christians, and discovered two highly skilled nurses living directly across the street from us. They not only handled my dressings, but they also expedited my transition through the health system—a reminder that in such instances, you just don't know what you don't know. Soon, other neighbors began to call in on us, offering their assistance and support. In a season where so many were already feeling vulnerable and challenged, we realized that far from being burdensome, our neighbors relished the opportunity to contribute to our well-being.

I am eternally grateful to God for those neighbors and the lessons I learned about the limits of self-reliant leadership. Their support was an amazing blessing during what felt like the least "useful" and "productive" phase in my life. Ironically, I was a greater blessing to them by "asking for a drink"—lying "flat on my back" in a state of helplessness—than I had ever been during my more deliberate efforts at trying to be an actual blessing.

As leaders, we often lean toward self-sufficiency. We avoid making requests for help or depending on others because it sometimes feels like the easier option. Leadership can become more about showcasing our strengths than acknowledging our needs and more about being depended upon than showing dependence on others. Unfortunately, some of us prefer it this way and find comfort in being needed rather than being in need ourselves. This sometimes suits us far more than we're willing to admit.

If Christian leadership is primarily perceived as a platform to demonstrate Jesus' power to make us seemingly invulnerable to life's challenges, then our success metrics will seldom align with kingdom values. Our idea of leadership will revolve around having the right answers and feigning reliance on God when what we're actually practicing is self-reliance. When we adopt this approach, collaboration becomes little more than lip service. We dominate others by presenting all the ideas, allocating all the resources, and providing all the solutions, often in an attempt to "save the day" but not necessarily in a way that Jesus would approve of. This approach to leadership and ministry can, unfortunately, resemble a colonial campaign or imperialistic enterprise rather than servant-hearted leadership.

Jesus' idea of *becoming* is less about showcasing our amazing leadership abilities and more about enabling others to realize their own leadership potential. By asking for help, as Jesus did, we cross a necessary growing-pain threshold during which the abilities and agency of those asked are highlighted and valued.

In the Western world, there's a slow but emerging shift away from viewing "vulnerable" individuals and communities as merely helpless recipients in need of our rescue. We are becoming increasingly proactive in partnering with people in the restoration of dignity and self-determination. International Aid and Development fields have long practiced Asset-Based Community Development (ABCD),[15] which focuses on identifying and utilizing a community's existing strengths and assets rather than concentrating primarily on its needs and deficiencies. Even now, Western Christians are increasingly reflecting on whether our approach to aid might sometimes cause more harm than good. The necessary shift involves more asking and less dictating, more listening and less telling, and much more invitation and less imposition in leadership. Furthermore, those traditionally seen as "beneficiaries" are less likely to accept a "savior" mentality, especially "white saviorism," and now expect to be treated as equal partners in any attempts at problem-solving.

Even with these developments, we have yet to fully explore leadership paradigms based on vulnerability and inviting the help of others. Perhaps the real challenge lies in inviting contributions in ways that are neither demeaning, tokenistic, nor exploitative. For the Samaritan woman, her contribution began not with Jesus' offer to do something for a poor marginalized "nobody" but with his request and tacit acknowledgment of her ability to do something for him!

The story of the Samaritan woman captures a moment in the life of someone who, by the standards of many, was unlikely to achieve much of significance. In many circles, she would have been dismissed as having little to contribute and certainly not viewed as appropriate leadership material. Yet her encounter with Jesus changed everything for her, just as our encounters with Jesus have the potential to change everything for us too.

ENCOUNTER: KEYS TO BEING TRANSFORMED AND TRANSFORMATIVE

The Samaritan woman's encounter with Jesus was undoubtedly the most foundational and formative moment of her life. Not only does it have metamorphosis written all over it, but without this meeting, everything we know about her would not have been possible. Its significance cannot be overstated. It quite literally changed everything.

As she ventured out for what appeared to be a routine part of her day (never underestimate the potential of the mundane), she experienced an unexpected and life-altering metamorphosis. In her culture (and in many cultures today), women usually collected water during the cooler hours of the morning and evening. They often congregated together at the well to exchange news and gossip as they collected their life-sustaining load. However, her decision to go out at noon, under the harsh sun, might have been an attempt to avoid her neighbors and the usual social scene at the well, as some suggest. But we should note that the text itself does not explicitly state her reasons for going about her task in this way.

Some interpreters imply she was intentionally seeking encounters of a very different kind. These views portray her as a marginalized figure within her community, a woman of dubious morals, a sexual predator venturing out at an unusual hour, deliberately avoiding her own townsfolk while seeking other prospects or "customers." In addition, a perceived curse associated with repeated adversity led to the ostracism of women in some communities and is still the case today. This may well have been the fate of our lone Samaritan woman. However, neither interpretation fully explains the warm reception she later receives from her townspeople when she shares news about Jesus. So, we must consider other, more plausible explanations for her solitary journey to the well.

Although it might seem to be more convenient for her to fetch water earlier in the day, not all ancient societies adhered strictly to this practice. In some cultures, women washed and dried clothes in the mid-afternoon sun so they could prepare food later and socialize with neighbors. (The same is true of contemporary societies with similar customs.)

Interestingly, John's narrative is only concerned with the reason for Jesus' fatigue and thirst as he sat by the well; it makes no attempt to speculate or explain why the woman arrived there at that same time. Regardless of her motive for being there, and given the Jewish aversion to Samaria, it's unlikely she would have expected to meet a Jewish man on a trip she must have made on multiple occasions. Yet, this particular visit transformed her life and subsequently changed the lives of countless others because of her.

Commentators on this story often emphasize Jesus' decision to travel to the well but sometimes overlook the significance of the Samaritan woman's journey toward Jesus, set against the backdrop of the tense Jewish-Samaritan relations. Even at a distance, it would have been clear that a Jewish man sat between her and the water she'd presumably journeyed some way to collect. She faced a choice: return home without water or brace herself for potential hostility and abuse.

Whenever we make journeys toward God, we often craft the conditions for an encounter. These journeys might include practices like prayer, fasting, Bible study, retreats, and any effort we make to connect with or listen to God and to those around us. But we must make these journeys intentionally because, like the woman at the well, we may have reservations about embarking on the journey in the first place or turning back once we get there. Trepidation, cynicism, reluctance, or other forms of resistance are growing pains always seeking to deter us. We have our own expectations of how the encounter will unfold. However, whenever we advance toward these potential encounters, we invariably find that Jesus is already there, ready to meet and enable us to become people who can significantly impact the lives of a multitude of others.

For us to metamorphose and *become* who God created us to be, we must attune ourselves, first and foremost, to God's actual voice, not our expectations of what we think he will say. And we also need to listen to the voices of both our allies and our adversaries. We are metamorphosing and *becoming* whenever we heed the voices of global and local communities, particularly the poor, dispossessed, persecuted, and marginalized—essentially, the groups Jesus spent so much of his time among.

Allow God to Transform Your Vision

As we practice these disciplines, we realize that encountering God not only transforms us spiritually and emotionally, but it also grants us a new perspective and enables us to see what we couldn't see before. Up until this point in her narrative, the prevailing sentiments of her day limited the Samaritan woman's entire identity and life possibilities. We too can find ourselves confined by external and internal narratives, mindsets, attitudes, and behaviors that can distort or even thwart God's intentions for us, in us, and through us.

In John 4:27, when the disciples return and see Jesus conversing with a woman, the text notes their reaction: "His disciples … were surprised to find him talking with a woman. But no one asked, 'What do you want?' or 'Why are you talking with her?'" It seems their surprise was not initially due to Jesus speaking with a Samaritan—they had just been in a Samaritan village themselves to purchase food—rather, their astonishment stemmed primarily from the fact that Jesus was engaging in a conversation with a woman, and the interaction was far from one-sided. In other words, Jesus was giving her voice.

Their astonishment is a stark indicator of the deep-seated and harmful prejudices prevalent in their era. The teachings of certain rabbis reflected the prevailing Jewish views on women at that time. Men were instructed: "One should not talk with a woman on the street, not even with his own wife, and certainly not with somebody else's wife, because of the gossip of men…. It is forbidden to give a woman any greeting."[16]

The prevailing attitudes toward Samaritan women were even more severe, summed up by another rabbinical statement: "The daughters of the Samaritans are [deemed unclean as] menstruants from their cradle."[17] To understand the gravity of this, it's important to note that in the Old Testament, the community isolated menstruating women outside the camp (Lev. 15). Samaritan women were regarded as being in a perpetual state of menstrual impurity (*niddah* in Hebrew) from birth. For the disciples, Jesus was in conversation with the worst possible kind of Samaritan: a woman.

The woman at the well would have been acutely aware of how she might be perceived by Jesus during their conversation. In essence, although purchasing food or drink was one thing, engaging in social exchange—which could involve sharing food, drink, and utensils—was an entirely different matter altogether. The NIV footnote of John 4:9 not only highlights this tension, but it also makes it even more explicit: "Jews will not use the same dishes that Samaritans use."[18]

As a woman at the well, she would have faced the sexism of both Jewish and Samaritan men; and, as a Samaritan, she would have faced the ethnocentrism of Jewish women too. Here was a Samaritan who happened to be a woman and a woman who happened to be a Samaritan: a double jeopardy in her society. And as a "single," unmarried woman who had been married five times and was now living with a man who wasn't her husband, her social standing was likely at the very bottom of the social hierarchy. So, perhaps her situation might be better described as a triple jeopardy.

In what must have been a potentially loaded conversation, this extraordinary woman was able to grasp the visionary perspective of Jesus. This encounter starkly contrasts with the disciples' reactions, revealing how very different they were from Jesus at this point in their transformative journey. Jesus was raised in the same society as them, breathing the same air and being exposed to the same views on women and Samaritans. Yet, he was neither compelled nor constrained by these societal prejudices.

We can almost picture the disciples, seeing Jesus engaged in conversation with the woman as they approached the well, whispering in shock and disbelief while they were still far enough away to not be overheard: "Who's she?" "I don't know who she is!" "Why's he talking to her?" "I don't know; you ask him!" "I'm not asking; you brought it up!" "Yeah, but you were thinking it!" Although they may have been sufficiently surprised to discuss Jesus' interaction with the Samaritan woman among themselves, it seems they lacked the courage to question Jesus about it directly.

Evidently, Jesus' vision of this woman was based on divine insight and informed by his Father in heaven rather than by the prevailing sentiments of his day. He had God's perspective and saw something quite different from his disciples as he engaged with this woman at the well. And the longer she spoke with Jesus, the more she began to share this perspective too. Fortunately, her future did not depend on the disciples' vision of her. Indeed, had it been left to them, there might have been no story to tell!

The disciples serve as a powerful reminder that mere association with Jesus does not automatically lead to transformation. Similarly, there is nothing inherently transformative about engaging in spiritual disciplines like reading the Bible, praying, or fasting. As mentioned earlier, although aging is inevitable, *becoming* takes intentional transformation. I've met enough theologians to fill a football stadium, and if mere Bible reading was sufficient for metamorphic transformation, our world would be a very different place indeed. I also know numerous "Holy Spirit-filled" believers from all over the world, so if prayer and fasting were all that was needed to assure a profound change, the world would have already seen a monumental shift with no need for further mission. Unlike aging, *becoming* requires intentional transformation, often through a multitude of growing pains we often choose to avoid. Despite most of us knowing otherwise, we often behave as if mere association with Jesus is enough to ensure transformation.

There's a significant difference between merely "hanging out" with Jesus and having a true encounter with him. The risk with the former is it gives a false sense of closeness that can mask whether any real change is actually taking place or not. In contrast, a genuine encounter with Jesus is transformative, propels us on the journey of *becoming*, and leads us to a profound metamorphosis.

It's all too common to be a disciple who spends each day with Jesus, admiring him, "absorbing" his teachings, engaging in meaningful dialogues, and even exalting him. Yet, like Jesus' earliest followers, it's possible to do all this and still return to him to discover that we are more culturally captive than we imagined, and significant transformation is still required.

In Jesus' presence, the unnamed woman at the well began to perceive things she hadn't necessarily been able to see before. It was something beyond the presenting "facts" and beyond her current reality. She not only saw Jesus for who he was—the promised Messiah—she also saw another world in which she was not simply a woman, divorcee, or despised Samaritan. In Jesus' world, she was a potential catalyst for change and transformation.

Despite spending three significant years immersed in his company, the disciples took quite a lot longer to fully adopt Jesus' perspective toward women, Samaritans, and outsiders.[19] Even then, Peter, at least, seemed in need of a repeat prescription! It wasn't until he received a divine vision in Acts 10 that he understood gentiles to be included in the invitation to salvation. In contrast to the disciples, the Samaritan woman caught Jesus' vision in just a brief encounter, probably because she recognized who Jesus truly was: "Could this be the Messiah?" (John 4:29).

Transformation isn't a passive process that can be absorbed through mere proximity; it demands an active, open posture that willingly says yes to God, accepts the inevitability of growing pains, and takes responsibility for the renewing of our own mind. Rather than a byproduct of self-discovery or self-help methods, transformation is a dynamic process—a result of encountering Jesus, his perspective, and recognizing him for who he truly is. It was recognition of *who* Jesus was and *how* he was that was so pivotal to the Samaritan woman's transformation. Genuine encounters with Jesus allow us to see him clearly and to see the world as he sees it. By seeing him and seeing like him, we begin to understand our true selves. This realization is never accidental or automatic; it is always a deliberate act. Whether it's Peter's admission of his sinfulness in Luke 5:8 ("Go away from me Lord for I am a sinful man") or the Samaritan woman's revelation ("Could this be the Messiah?"), *becoming* is never accidental, incidental, or inevitable. It is always, always intentional.

Like the disciples in this narrative, our past experiences and preconceptions can leave us short-sighted, immobile, or even paralyzed as leaders. These perspectives can obscure the truth about Jesus, ourselves, and others. They can hinder our progress and inhibit our growth, causing one person to take years to become what might take another person mere moments.

Our self-imposed limitations come from our beliefs about ourselves, our perceptions of others, and what others think of us. Interestingly, both the disciples and the woman at the well reveal how privilege or disadvantage can distort our self-image and prevent us from seeing others or ourselves as they and we really are. Both can leave us prone to overestimating or underestimating our true value to God and each other. Both can severely impede our ability to develop into metamorphic leaders. Had the Samaritan woman been subject to the disciples' vision of who she was, her story would probably have unfolded quite differently. Unfortunately, this scenario is an everyday reality for many remarkable women worldwide who are similarly overlooked by those who, like the early disciples, interact with Jesus but seem unable to see or know better despite their interactions. Surely, it's time for us to break free from these constraining narratives and embrace the power of transformative encounters with Jesus.

PRECIOUS: A METAMORPH IN THE MAKING

Precious sat beside me during a dinner at a two-day conference where my best friend, Cham, and I were keynote speakers. I tend to believe that God orchestrates seating arrangements for divine appointments, so I anticipated some meaningful connections.

We soon got talking, and I invited Precious to share what God had put on her heart. It quickly became clear that God was orchestrating something significant in and through Precious's life and that major doors of opportunity were about to open. Her story and her deep desire to transform lives in her home country captivated both Cham and me. How could God resist such passion? We certainly couldn't!

As we talked, the atmosphere changed; we sensed the presence of God's Spirit, realizing we were seated beside an exceptional person. Curiously, Precious herself seemed unaware of her own extraordinary potential. So, we knew what we had to do: We both felt called to mentor her right there and then, believing that offering her the chance to see herself through our eyes and comprehend what Jesus revealed about her as a world changer was the greatest gift we could provide.

Within weeks, she began glimpsing this vision for herself. She soon gathered support from significant figures and organizations—the queen, the national bank, the health service, and eventually even the prime minister rallied behind her cause. It was evident that grace and favor accompanied her everywhere she went. With a clearer vision of herself aligned with how God saw her, the possibilities for her were boundless. All we had to do was buckle up and enjoy the ride!

Scholars frequently highlight Jesus' defiance of social taboos in conversing with the Samaritan woman, yet often fail to equally acknowledge her own boldness in challenging these conventions. She was undoubtedly aware of the societal rule against men speaking with women in public—even their own wives—yet she chose to engage with Jesus anyway and on her own terms.

In a society that pressured her to conform, she was quite simply and refreshingly herself. It requires vision and courage to break free from personal, spiritual, and societal constraints. No wonder it is often said, "Courage is the first virtue because it makes all of the other virtues possible."[20]

Courage involves the willingness to change, embrace the pain of growing, see through our biases, and believe we can become who God originally created us to be. This transformation gives us the audacity to be our true selves, lead in our own unique way, validate our own experiences, and trust our God-given interpretations and insights. This isn't to say we shouldn't learn from those who have gone before us; disregarding the wisdom of others gained from experience would be both foolish and arrogant. However, since individuality and individualism are not the same thing,[21] our greatest achievement lies in becoming the best version of our Christlike selves as possible. When Precious, from the story above, discovered all this, she became a force to be reckoned with and has not looked back.

The Samaritan woman also did something unprecedented: She committed to following the one she had begun to believe was the Messiah and took up the challenge of sharing her newfound conviction with others. In an almost comical turn of events, she leaves her water jar behind at the well—presumably with Jesus still thirsty—seemingly forgetting the initial purpose of her visit. Her actions mark a significant shift, not just in her story, but also in what it means for each of us to follow Jesus and share his message.

Allow God to Transform Others through You

After her life-changing encounter with Jesus, the Samaritan woman sought out the very people she had possibly been previously trying to avoid (even if just for some time alone). Filled with joy and a newfound purpose, she urgently invited her neighbors to meet Jesus, saying, "Come, see a man who told me everything I ever did. Could this be the Messiah?" (John 4:29). Transformed by Jesus, her focus shifted to how she could extend this same blessing to others.

This story beautifully demonstrates how *becoming* is a journey of encountering Jesus *while* encouraging others to encounter him too. It is a story about the power of metamorphic connection to transform both ourselves and those around us.

Jesus engaged with an unlikely figure: a Samaritan woman, possibly divorced more than once, perhaps a widow, and likely living in a less-than-ideal arrangement. Yet, she raced toward her townspeople with a message of hope and transformation. She turned what could have been a barrier into a bridge when she entered a town where animosity toward Jews was the norm and somehow managed to persuade them to listen to the Jewish rabbi seated at the well, suggesting he might be the actual Messiah. She inspired connection across a historic divide of hatred and distrust, forging a bond that seemed humanly impossible.

The quick and enthusiastic response of the townspeople is remarkable, especially considering the societal constraints on women's voices at the time. In a culture where women's testimonies were often disregarded, and women of questionable reputation (if that is indeed what she was) faced severe consequences, her ability to be heard and followed is miraculous. The fact that the townspeople listened to her testimony at all suggests she was not the outcast many assume. In short, many miracles were taking place simultaneously. Clearly, their subsequent belief in Jesus as the Messiah was not sparked by the preaching of the male disciples, nor by any sudden transformation in her lifestyle, as some seek to suggest. (It was far too soon for that.) It was based purely on the testimony of the woman herself, a woman who would eventually transform Samaria and become "Great Martyr St. Photini, Equal to the Apostles."

If we define leadership as a willingness to partner with God in transformation, coupled with the ability to guide others toward a transformation they might not initially embrace, then Photini exhibited remarkable leadership. Her actions mirror the kind of leadership Jesus exemplifies and encourages us to follow. Her story is a testament to the fact that although transformation begins *in* us, it is not simply *about* us or even primarily *for* us, our families, or our churches. If it is to be the kind of metamorphic transformation the Bible speaks about, the benefits must extend beyond our immediate circles.

This is the story of a woman introduced with no name, yet before we even get into her story, she compels us to recognize the extraordinary truth that a renowned name or an amazing, credentialed background is never a prerequisite for greatness in God's eyes. She embodies the idea that metamorphosis is central to God's interaction with us and that the process of transformative *becoming* is not solely our endeavor but primarily resides in God's domain. Ultimately, God is the initiator and facilitator of this transformation, and if we are wise, we will choose to actively partner with him in pursuit of our own journey of *becoming*.

FOR PERSONAL REFLECTION OR GROUP DISCUSSION

Areas of Your Leadership Where You Are Experiencing Growing Pains

1. How do you respond to these painful changes (positively or negatively)?
2. Why do you think you respond in the way you do during times of change?
3. What steps can you take to help yourself make positive choices in times of change?

Inviting and Empowering the Contributions of Others in Your Leadership

1. Who have you invited and empowered to contribute to your leadership this week?
2. Identify who you struggle to invite to contribute to your leadership and why?
3. What will you put in place to deliberately include others in your leadership development?

Inviting and Experiencing Transformation in Your Jesus Encounters

1. How will you proactively let go of your preconceived expectations of God?
2. What "vision" of yourself or others do you hold that undermines God's intentions for you or them?
3. What changes of mind (metanoia) are needed for this transformation to occur?

TIME FOR PRAYER

Take a moment for personal or group prayer. If part of a discussion group, lift up each member, asking for guidance, strength, and clarity as they navigate through their challenges and seek growth in their personal and leadership journey of *becoming*.

PART THREE

TRANSFORMING COMMUNITY

5

MARY AND ELIZABETH
TOGETHER IS BETTER

Leveraging the Power of Friendship

If you want to go quickly, go alone. If you want to go far, go together.
(POSSIBLE) AFRICAN PROVERB

I am because we are, and since we are, therefore I am.
JOHN S. MBITI

You can't make old friends.
DOLLY PARTON AND KENNY ROGERS

My best friend, Cham, and I are literally a study in contrasts. We differ from one another in so many ways. Yet, paradoxically, we are also predictably similar in almost every way that counts. We share an unwavering dedication to Jesus, a zeal for our common vision and mission, and a love for doing life together in community (most of the time!). We also share a limitless appetite for spicy, flavorful food and will try almost anything in pursuit of our fondness for seasoning (though, in all honesty, we appreciate all good food).

Cham is a second-generation culturally Punjabi Sikh Christian woman, born and raised in Birmingham, UK. By contrast, I am a first-generation (just about) West African woman, born in Ghana and raised across Ghana, Nigeria, North London, Brighton, and now Birmingham, UK. This means Cham and I differ from one another both ethnically and culturally. But our distinctions extend beyond our geographical roots and upbringing. We also differ from one another in many of our likes and dislikes, our gifts and skill sets, as well as in our respective temperaments. Cham tends to see the glass half-empty, while I am definitely (and sometimes irritatingly, according to Cham) a glass half-full type of person. Having said that, we have also been known to switch perspectives on occasion. Thankfully, our collective outlooks mean our glass is mostly full for much of the time!

As I write this, Cham and I have been friends for nearly twenty-five years. As you can imagine, over the years, we have learned an incredible amount about each other, life, the universe, and, of course, God.

I am profoundly grateful for my friendship with Cham because, with God's help, she has played a crucial role in my becoming a better follower of Jesus, a better human being, and hopefully, a better friend.

THE CHALLENGES OF FRIENDSHIP

Although friendship is critical to our metamorphic transformation, Jesus' own experiences of friendship—from John, the "disciple Jesus loved,"[1] to Judas, the friend who betrayed him—illustrate the many ways these relationships can be fraught with life's greatest challenges as well as life's richest rewards.

In the Gospel of John, Jesus exemplifies true friendship through his life and death and forms deep bonds with all those who follow him. In John 15:12–14, Jesus commands his disciples to be friends, saying, "My command is this: Love each other as I have loved you. Greater love has no one than this: to lay down one's life for one's friends. You are my friends if you do what I command." His resurrection further empowers his disciples to go into the world with a mandate to both befriend and make befrienders of others. American historian Diana Butler Bass captures this beautifully: "Christianity did not begin with a confession. It began with an invitation into friendship, into creating a new community, into forming relationships based on love and service."[2] Perhaps unsurprisingly, the early Christians were renowned for their exceptional sense of community, powerful relationships, and their ability to transform their world through the simple yet profound practice of friendship.

Reflecting on the metamorphic nature of friendship, author Dana Robert observes that "friendship makes us human" and asserts that "friendships form individuals, create neighborhoods and churches, and knit together the fabric of society."[3] Genuine friendship surpasses mere social ties and goes beyond superficial connections. Although friendships may not last forever, as some proverbs seem to suggest, their impact can remain and influence us for a very long time indeed. Ultimately, true friendship is prophetic and spiritual in nature because it reflects the character of God, brings us closer to Jesus, and offers the profound possibility of an actual friendship with God.

Physicist Neil deGrasse Tyson highlights the reality of our connection to each other biologically, to the earth chemically, and to the universe atomically.[4] In other words, relationship with one another is already an inescapable fact. Yet, to have a "meaningful" friendship, a relationship must stem from a conscious decision and the investment of time, effort, and above all, courage.

Family relationships are typically defined by blood ties and the proverbial "blood is thicker than water" obligations that often underpin expectations and heighten family tensions. By contrast, friends tend to be the people we choose to associate with, based on mutual interests and values. Nevertheless, friendships also come with their own commitments and are subject to their own, often equally complex, set of expectations. If the full expression of our "blood is thicker than water" proverb is, "The blood of the covenant is thicker than the water of the womb,"[5] as some suggest, it would imply that the relationships we choose for ourselves, like friendships, are paradoxically *more* significant than the ones we are born into. And, like all relationships, they can also be costly.

Navigating the complexities of genuine friendship can be challenging when physical, mental, spiritual, and emotional closeness are often misinterpreted as having sexual undertones. This complicates the understanding of intimate, honest, and vulnerable friendship. On the other hand, the fact that I can become a "friend" of my local arts charity, public library, or animal shelter by simply making a donation only adds to the confusion! Social media further muddies the waters by suggesting that "friends" can be made by browsing through carefully curated snapshots and engaging in digital exchanges that are frankly more likely to leave us feeling anxious and lonely than genuinely connected.⁶ Many seem content with these superficial, transactional exchanges, which is incredibly disheartening for those who genuinely care only to discover that others weren't particularly interested in the first place!

This prevailing dynamic propels real interpersonal relationships into superficial territory. So, it's no surprise that despite our inherent connectedness, loneliness is a fast-growing social "epidemic" in the Western world. Without appropriate action, pervasive loneliness will be normal in our societies, including the US, within a matter of years. The UK's appointment of a "Minister for Loneliness" is a testament to this growing concern.⁷ However, the solution to our social dilemma surely lies in fostering a deeper understanding of what it means to build and experience true friendships, coupled with the courage and necessary skill to initiate and cultivate this type of relationship in the first place.

Having commanded his disciples to be friends, Jesus goes on to provide profound insight into the nature of friendship by contrasting the demands of friendship with those of servitude. He says, "I no longer call you servants, because a servant *does not know* his master's business. Instead, I have called you friends, for everything that I learned from my Father *I have made known to you*" (John 15:15 emphasis mine). To put it another way, unlike servants who primarily engage in allotted tasks and the fulfillment of duties, friends gain a deeper understanding of each other's unique interests and true intentions. Friends are welcomed into a circle of trust and are privy to intimate insights and details of the heart that are not usually disclosed to servants. Friendship also requires a level of vulnerability and openness not typically cultivated in a servant-master relationship. Friends often experience and understand each other's feelings as if they were their own. Whereas servants focus on their master's requirements, friends invest in mutually sustaining their relationship. And although servants can be friendly, and friends will inevitably serve one another, these relationships operate on different levels of sharing and caring and are not directly comparable in terms of their quality and depth.

It's not surprising we should hear such words from Jesus, because we find no greater embodiment of this kind of friendship than in Jesus himself. This is more than can be said for Jesus' friends, who, shortly after hearing his profound declaration of friendship, sadly fail to live up to the ideal themselves. At least one of them betrays Jesus in pursuit of personal gain, and then, following the crushing disappointment of Jesus' arrest and crucifixion, virtually everyone else goes on to desert him wholesale.

Jesus is not the only victim of problematic friendships, of course. Millions of people all over the world experience pain-filled and broken relationships. They are among the many reasons why the pursuit of genuine friendship is so incredibly challenging, and openness and vulnerability are such risky endeavors in the first place.

There are myriad reasons why friendships disintegrate. Friends sometimes fall out if they develop increasingly divergent views on the so-called contentious subjects of religion, politics, sex, and money (apparently to be avoided at all costs in polite conversation!). Friendships sometimes fracture when churches split or someone deconstructs their faith. Other friendships implode as the result of betrayal, unresolved disagreements, or outright arguments. In some cases, friends drift apart when they realize they no longer share common interests or that their needs have evolved. However, not all friendships conclude on a sour note—some simply fade away, become redundant, or gradually shift in a whole new direction.

Whatever the cause of broken, painful friendships, they often hurt us far more than we care to admit and leave us hesitant to deepen existing relationships or even embark on new ones. This can be especially true of some church leaders who, despite the potential benefits of supportive friendships, are cautious about trusting others or forming deep connections. Past hurts and experiences of betrayal or rejection can, understandably, cause them to withdraw or maintain their distance in an effort to protect themselves from further hurt.

THE POWER OF FRIENDSHIP

If we long for metamorphic change in our lives, our communities, and the wider world, we cannot shy away from the pursuit of true friendships—not just because Jesus sets a high standard for us but also because friendships are crucial for attaining metamorphic transformation! Jesus' interactions alone suggest that God both intends and ordains critical friendships in order to effect meaningful metamorphic change. I personally believe that God presents us with opportunities for friendships in every phase of life and that part of our task is to recognize and engage with these opportunities whenever and wherever they show up.

Leadership itself is also a fundamentally relational dynamic, and it demands a level of relational engagement that utilizes many of the skills essential for fostering great friendships. Leadership and organizational experts Margaret J. Wheatley and Deborah Frieze emphasize the relational nature of leadership networks, stating,

> In spite of current ads and slogans, the world doesn't change one person at a time. It changes as networks of relationships form among people who discover they share a common cause and vision of what's possible. This is good news for those of us intent on changing the world and creating a positive future. Rather than worry about critical mass, our work is to foster critical connections.[8]

True friendships, however, transcend common interests and are about more than co-laboring together in community. Friendships allow us to genuinely share in each other's burdens. St. Augustine insightfully noted that in friendship, "rough things become smooth, heavy burdens are lightened, and difficulties vanquished."[9] C. S. Lewis, in one of his most quoted passages from *The Four Loves*, describes friendship as the profound connection that occurs when we say, "What! You too? I thought I was the only one."[10]

True friendships are life-giving as well as transformative. In the twelfth century, Aelred of Rievaulx, in his seminal work *On Spiritual Friendship*, declared, "The best medicine for life is a friend."[11] This sentiment is echoed throughout the classic literature on friendship by thinkers like Aristotle, Montaigne, Emerson, and, more recently, C. S. Lewis. They all recognize that true friendship offers much more than mere companionship. In fact, friendship is difficult to define, but it is also rarer and more precious than companionship can ever be. Montaigne was definitely onto something, although perhaps overstating it when he suggested there may be only one true friendship in every three hundred years![12] Proverbs 18:24 reflects on this rarity and depth: "A man of many companions may come to ruin, but there is a friend who sticks closer than a brother" (ESV). Proverbs 17:17 notes that "a friend loves at all times, and a brother is born for a time of adversity." Not all Jesus' friends abandoned him, of course. Some continued in friendship even beyond the bonds of death. In her book *Our Unforming*, Cindy S. Lee paints a poignant picture of these faithful friends:

> The Gospels tell us that a group of women stay with Jesus. Women with no voice and no power choose to do what others don't: they accompany Jesus to the cross. They are present as he dies; they are still there when he is buried. Perhaps these women also feel the same disappointment and doubt and ask the same questions as the other disciples, but more important than their mental questioning is their love for a friend.[13]

By supporting our friends through their challenges and acknowledging our impact on them, whether positive or negative, we do more than share their burdens; we actively participate in their transformation for better or for worse.

I believe that the single most powerful factor in determining the sustainability of someone's ministry in leadership or pastoral roles is the presence of a "full-disclosure friend," with whom we share complete transparency and have no secrets. In the absence of such profound friendships, those in church ministry and leadership are often more vulnerable to serious challenges like depression, moral failings, or overwhelming urges to abandon their ministry all together. Ironically, churches with small groups often intend to foster such intimacy and accountability, yet the groups often fail to achieve the transformative depth of true friendship because they turn friendship into an event that primarily values attendance and service. Event-based communities aim at creating better productions and numerical growth and can seldom cultivate the authenticity, degree of disclosure, accountability, and vulnerability required for deep relationships. Friendships cannot be made to order, so these groups inevitably default to easier, conceptual Bible studies instead, leaving people lonely when even in the midst of a crowd. The unique strength of true friendships lies in the risks taken in sharing ideas and hearts. These help sustain a calling and bring to life the vision and mission of God in us, our church, or organization. In other words, whatever needs to happen does not always happen without the relationships capable of releasing us and others around us into all we can be in Christ. I know this firsthand because I have personally experienced how friendship can and does keep us on course and helps facilitate the desired metamorphosis in our journey as followers of Jesus.

However, although friendship is powerful, it has its limits. Dana Robert aptly states, "Friendship has limitations. It does not solve all the world's problems. It does not cure cancer or HIV/AIDS. It does not eliminate structural injustice. It does not involve perfect people who practice perfect mutuality. Friendship is not an adequate social policy or political ideology."[14] But while friendship alone won't solve the world's problems, we cannot get started on any of these problems without actually engaging in meaningful friendship in the first place. Ultimately, it is friendship that changes the people who go on to change everything else. In the aftermath of the genocidal violence in Rwanda in 1994, where one group of Rwandan Christians murdered those they considered "ethnically" different, theologian Emmanuel Katongole wrote, "We engage in mission to establish friendships that lead to the formation of a new people in the world."[15] Friendship is an integral part of our calling to follow Jesus and an overtly Christian practice. Therefore, although friendship should never be reduced to a mere strategy or program, we should proactively and purposely pursue friendship as a transformational key. Friendship ultimately offers us opportunities to bear witness to Christ and to engage our friends as coconspirators in subversive acts of faith that defy racial, cultural, and political powers to testify to the kingdom of God!

Unfortunately, friendships charged with such revolutionary potential are not easy to come by for some of the reasons previously outlined. The power of friendship to bridge divides—including generational, ethnic, and cultural barriers—is often underestimated and underutilized, precisely because the transformative potential of unconventional relationships has not been fully recognized.

One of the most profound and pertinent examples of an extraordinary friendship is found in the New Testament story of Mary (the mother of Jesus) and Elizabeth (the mother of Jesus' cousin John the Baptist). This narrative is far more than the familiar biblical account often associated with Christmas; it also captures the life-giving force and transformative power of friendship.

EMBRACING THE RISKS AND REAPING THE REWARDS

Luke chapter 1 introduces us to a young woman named Mary. We learn she is approached by God's messenger angel, Gabriel, with what turns out to be a life-altering message. (Please note that it is Mary—not her brother, father, uncle, or even her husband-to-be—who is chosen for this pivotal role in God's grand plan. God selects her without seeking any permission from or giving prior knowledge to any male figure in her life, making it patently clear that, in God's eyes, her body and choices are primarily her own and not theirs.)

God entrusts Mary with a responsibility and opportunity unlike any other—not for national glory, immense wisdom, fame, wealth, or any of the things usually associated with success and power. Instead, she is entrusted with something infinitely more valuable: the care of God's ultimate gift to humanity—the Son of God, Emmanuel, no less than God with us. However, she is not presented with the "finished article" of an obviously all-powerful savior. Instead, she is entrusted with the baby Jesus, who starts out (as we all do at the beginning of life)—vulnerable, wholly dependent, and in need of Mary's nurturing, love, and protection. This is a profound reminder that the most significant responsibilities and possibilities often start in the most humble and dependent forms.

Elizabeth, on the other hand, is entrusted to bear the forerunner, John, who would prepare the way for the Messiah that the younger Mary would carry, give birth to, and nurture into adulthood. Unlike Mary's intended, Elizabeth's husband, Zechariah, is given advance notice of his wife's miraculous pregnancy. Yet, Zechariah's encounter with the angel leads to an unexpected outcome: In stark contrast with the faith that Mary exhibits, Zechariah becomes temporarily mute because he struggles to accept God's Word at face value (Luke 1:20). In many ways, Zechariah's response is unsurprising; neither he nor Elizabeth had reason to expect or perhaps even hope for a child at their late stage in life. Luke chapter 1 explains that although "both of them [Elizabeth and Zechariah] were righteous in the sight of God, observing all the Lord's commands and decrees blamelessly … they were childless because Elizabeth was not able to conceive, and they were both very old" (vv. 6–7). Elizabeth and Zechariah's story is a poignant reminder that life's trials, disappointments, and tests of faith affect everyone—righteous or not, leaders or not. We need the support of friends in such circumstances. Zechariah's response also reminds leaders to cultivate a readiness and receptiveness to God's unforeseen acts, irrespective of when they eventually materialize. Friendships help us with this too.

Sometimes, God's calling seems delayed, as it was for Elizabeth (and Zechariah), making us feel as if we've missed our moment and are somewhat past it. Yet, the truth is, *we're never too old to give birth to something new*. Conversely, sometimes God's calling finds us early in life, like Mary, and we wonder, a bit like Moses in chapter three of this book, whether we're really up to it. But the truth is, *we're never too young to be called upon or chosen by God!* Either way, whenever we receive God's calling, we're going to need friends, and we're going to need to be the kind of friend who can support others to nurture and realize God's intentions for them.

God's vision for Mary is as decidedly Mary-shaped as it is God-sized! This is exactly how our vision and mission should be. Like Mary, we should never be able to enact a vision that God entrusts to us without his help and the help of those he places around us at pivotal moments in life. Our metamorphic transformation requires us to recognize our dependence on both God and others. Despite some obvious risks in making such a journey, Mary chooses to proactively seek friendship. In doing so, her story converges with Elizabeth's in ways that reveal precious insights about the mysteries of God, the essence of friendship, and qualities we should aspire to if we are to forge meaningful and impactful friendships along the way.

Although Gabriel told Mary about Elizabeth's pregnancy, Elizabeth had no prior knowledge, as far as we know, of Mary's situation until Mary had literally walked through Elizabeth's front door. In this narrative, it is Mary who undertakes the journey to Elizabeth and who ensures that they both have the support they need when they need it most.

As already intimated, the pursuit of friendship is often hindered by a fear of intimacy and the discomfort of allowing others to get close to us. It takes courage to embrace this vulnerability and take the first step on the journey toward true friendship, especially when there's a risk it might all go wrong and end up in pain. Not all journeys to friendship are as physically demanding as Mary's or as emotionally intense as Elizabeth's. Some are geographical, others are emotional, psychological, spiritual, or a combination of all of these. Our relationships sometimes require us to open our doors to others, and at other times, we'll find that doors have been opened for us, allowing us to become exactly the right encouragement and breakthrough that someone needs to take their next step or to try their new thing.

In Elizabeth, Mary found a confidante who would understand and believe her extraordinary story. In turn, Elizabeth found in Mary someone who needed no explanation. This is often the hallmark of great friendship because friends are people you don't have to explain yourself to. They already "get it," and they "get you." You don't have to spell everything out because they already know where you're coming from or at least are willing to learn. Friends like this take you seriously and don't look at you sideways with incredulity when everyone else does. In fact, they declare you innocent until proven guilty, and when you are as "guilty as sin," they are the ones who insist you confront your "stuff" and get it sorted.

Sometimes a really good friend can read your expressions. They will know what the "look" means, what the sigh communicates, and what the silence is really all about. Good friends read between the lines and sometimes know what you're about to say even before you say it.

Such friendships usually take years to develop, but there are times when shared experiences—a birth, death, marriage, illness, or moments of joy—act like an emotional and spiritual adhesive, binding people together in a short time, even across differences. Sometimes a common vision, shared challenges, troubles, and struggles connect even the least likely people in the most unexpected ways, transforming mere acquaintances into true friends.

At this juncture in their lives, Elizabeth and Mary needed each other for understanding and support. Both women have a powerful, divinely orchestrated God-given bonding experience when they meet, simply by virtue of their shared experience. Despite the possibility that Elizabeth knew nothing of Mary's situation, Luke 1:41–45 states,

> When Elizabeth heard Mary's greeting, the baby leaped in her womb, and Elizabeth was filled with the Holy Spirit. In a loud voice she exclaimed: "Blessed are you among women, and blessed is the child you will bear! But why am I so favored, that the mother of my Lord should come to me? As soon as the sound of your greeting reached my ears, the baby in my womb leaped for joy. Blessed is she who has believed that the Lord would fulfill his promises to her!"

I have no doubt that my friends would prefer greetings from me that are just as potent and spiritually empowering as this one. Quite honestly, I would seriously love it too!

UNLIKELY FRIENDS

Mary and Elizabeth's friendship exemplifies the potential of a powerful metamorphic cross-generational connection. According to scholars, Mary is around fourteen years of age when we meet her in this biblical story, and the Bible itself points to Elizabeth's "old age" (Luke 1:7), indicating she was already likely a senior citizen and post-menopausal with her childbearing years firmly behind her.

However, this unusual pairing is not an isolated instance in the biblical narratives. Instead, we find many examples of unique and groundbreaking friendships throughout Scripture, which God uses to unveil his metamorphic kingdom and to progress his purposes. Some of these noteworthy pairings include:

Moses and Joshua. Joshua, significantly younger than Moses, was not only his mentee but also his eventual successor as the leader of the children of Israel. But their friendship wasn't all one-sided; Joshua also supported Moses' leadership and stayed close in his victories *and* in the midst of his struggles. This pair were unlikely friends, not so much because of their age or because a mentor/mentee relationship existed between them, but because of the likely differences in their personalities and respective dispositions. Moses was much more likely to be a sensitive, reflective, prophetic-intercessor type, while Joshua was more likely to be the practical warrior and a man of strategy and action.

David and Jonathan. This pair is another example of extraordinary friendship. Jonathan remained fiercely loyal to David, even as King Saul (Jonathan's father), attempted to kill David. David and Jonathan's friendship was so strong that Jonathan not only risked his father's wrath to protect it but also his own claim to the throne to honor their bond. Their deep connection stands as a testament to the profound impact genuine friendship can have and how it can transcend both personal ambitions and familial expectations.

Esther and Mordecai. Their relationship was initially one-sided, and although they were cousins, Esther was more like a daughter to Mordecai. Their relationship evolved until, by the end of their story, it was almost entirely equal and mutual. By this time, Esther had become Queen of Persia and elevated Mordecai to become one of the king's most trusted royal advisors.

Paul and Barnabas. This is easily one of the New Testament's most tumultuous relationships and is another example of a friendship that started out fairly one-sided with Barnabas advocating for Paul. Despite its rocky phases, their relationship matured into mutual respect and support, with Paul eventually emerging as the more prominent figure. It is unlikely that Paul would have become the man he was without Barnabas's advocacy and investment. It was this friendship that allowed Paul to throw off the regrets and mistakes of his past and embrace what was to be his future calling. Their friendship exemplifies the love that Paul writes about in 1 Corinthians 13 (which may well have been written with Barnabas in mind) and is mirrored in the way Paul advocates for, encourages, and prays for his own fellow coworkers.

Contemporary social norms often leave men, in particular, struggling to cultivate the level of emotional and psychological closeness necessary for their personal growth and well-being. So, notwithstanding Mordecai and Esther, these examples demonstrate the potential for meaningful and genuine friendships, especially among men. By contrast, stories of women like Mary and Elizabeth, or better still, Ruth and Naomi, suggest that women may be hardwired for friendship despite the strains that tragedy, loss, and relocation might inflict. A landmark UCLA study suggests that besides the typical "fight, fright, or flight" response to stress that all people have, women can also adopt an alternative "tend and befriend" response.[16] In difficult times, women seem to deliberately seek out other women, as we see in Mary and Elizabeth's story. The resulting friendships appear to reduce women's stress levels, and the authors of the study propose that they also account for their longer life spans.[17]

There are, of course, other unlikely pairings that could be mentioned, but I highlight these because, like Mary and Elizabeth, they specifically demonstrate the power of friendship across the boundaries of difference.

More Different than Alike

Leadership can be powerfully enriched when we forge friendships across difference with people who neither look like us nor share our social or cultural background. Cham and I have discovered this for ourselves over the years and have learned a great deal from each other through our differences. Friendships across boundaries work to broaden our vision and reveal insights we would still be ignorant of were it not for them. They inevitably introduce us to things we could never have discovered by ourselves, especially if we remain within a small circle of like-minded people and inevitably narrow perspectives. However, these relationships are most fruitful when they are rooted in mutual respect, devoid of condescension, and committed to treating each other as equals.

Not long ago, I was speaking to a good friend who resides in the suburbs of another city. He knew that, at the time, I was living in an area of Birmingham, UK that was almost 80 percent Muslim, including a small, radicalized minority. He spoke about the prevailing fears in his community about Islam and Muslims in general. I shared that it had never occurred to me to walk around my community in fear and that despite being a committed Christian and far from shy about it, I always felt incredibly safe.

I recounted stories from my Muslim friends about their experiences during times of national tension around Islam. I shared how they had spoken of women being harassed and spat on in supermarkets, hijabs being forcefully removed by strangers in public, and young men being arbitrarily stopped and searched by hostile police. I also mentioned the killing of a South Asian man in a racially motivated attack in our area, a tragedy that had barely made the news and left the community extremely angry with some ready-to-reciprocate hostilities. His response was telling: "We never hear about that stuff." And had it not been for our friendship, he still would not have heard about "that stuff."

I'm fortunate because I do hear about that stuff, and it helps me appreciate why people do what they do and feel the way they feel. I've made a point of pursuing friendships across all kinds of difference, including theological and political ones, even when I strongly disagree with conclusions reached and views expressed. I believe it makes me a better leader and more able to appreciate what others sometimes find hard to understand. It also allows me to say things that people are willing to listen to, even though they may be very different from me and from each other. There are things my friends will tell me that I would never hear on a television debate or spoken of in public.

My penchant for befriending a diverse array of people stems from the realization that friends can be challenged in ways that perfect strangers or even casual "colleagues" cannot. This doesn't mean I befriend everyone or even make friends with just anyone. I do neither. Some people simply aren't open to friendship with people like me, and I've had to learn to avoid situations that can lead to my abuse, even if others initially seem well-intentioned. Despite this, I've made friends with some of the most unlikely people imaginable, as well as with those I've really needed to learn from.

My earliest mentors were significantly older than me, yet they treated me as a friend. We were more than mere colleagues, mentor, mentee, or even just pals … we were friends. They opened up their hearts to me and told me things … I mean, really told me things. They shared their deepest thoughts and experiences in ways that helped me grow and mature. I also learned invaluable lessons from them about being a good friend that have helped to make me the person I am today. I am profoundly grateful for all they invested in me and for how much they believed in me, even when I didn't believe in myself!

I also remember, with no small degree of embarrassment, some of the things I shared with them in the early days of my discipleship and leadership journey when I wasn't thinking straight, and worse still, when I was! I'm grateful for the way they simply "heard me out" with patience, respect, and without judgment, offering challenge or encouragement wherever needed. Although I'm sure they must have learned something from me on those occasions, I strongly suspect the learning was an overwhelmingly one-sided affair. (If any one of you mentors are reading this today, I thank you …)

Proverbs 27:6 insightfully states, "Wounds from a friend can be trusted, but an enemy multiplies kisses." To put it another way, true friends are not afraid to share difficult news with one another. Polite acquaintances who say what we want to hear or share only what they're willing to divulge simply will not do. We are already quite capable of telling ourselves what we want to hear. What we need are friends prepared to open our eyes to what's "out of the box" and who will candidly present us with the harsh realities in ways that only close companions can. Friends not only share in our joys but also in our pains, and they share in our strengths as well as our weaknesses. Diverse friends, in particular, help us to change the way we see the world. They also help us change the world we see so that together, we can make the world a more God-inspired place.

At this point in her life, Mary needed an Elizabeth far more than her peers and the men and women she'd grown up with. Likewise, although much later in years and finding herself in a most unexpected condition, Elizabeth needed a Mary, perhaps ironically even more than her own contemporaries.

Maybe you are facing boundary-crossing opportunities and feel the call to develop new friendships across difference. Go for it! Smile and introduce yourself to new people, show a genuine interest in them, and ask how they and their family are doing. Look for simple ways to share life together, especially over meals. In most cultures, true friendship doesn't begin until you've at least eaten together. However, beware of reducing hospitality to merely "entertaining" and "throwing dinner parties." Instead, actively build community, practice mutuality, learn to receive as well as give. Avoid transactional and agenda-laden interactions. If you are persistent and patient and people feel at home with you, genuine friendship can and will be forged. These budding relationships will introduce you to new experiences, challenge you in unexpected ways, and prepare you for the emergence of new transformative possibilities.

More Alike than Different

Friendship across difference doesn't mean we have no more in common than our humanity. In this biblical account, while the specifics of their relationship remain unclear, Mary and Elizabeth are referred to as "kinswomen," indicating that, despite their differences, they were related to each other in some way. And they suddenly found themselves sharing far more relationally and emotionally than ever before.

Not only did they suddenly have some rather serious family matters to discuss, but they'd also both experienced life-altering events that resonated deeply with the other. These included supernatural encounters, divine interventions, visitations from angels, unexpected pregnancies, being misunderstood, and societal judgments—Elizabeth for her childlessness in a culture that prized motherhood, especially of sons, and Mary for becoming pregnant in a culture that demanded everyone be respectfully married first.

Both were probably also having to deal with, at least a little, unwelcome public scrutiny and curiosity! Elizabeth's experience is hinted at in Luke 1:24, where it's mentioned that she kept herself "in seclusion" for five months of her pregnancy, a period when she was hidden from public view. This was unusual, as cultures that practice seclusion usually encourage it to happen immediately *after* the birth rather than during the pregnancy (unless there is fear of miscarriage, which could have been the case here). Elizabeth's pregnancy shifted her social standing significantly, meaning that her news would have been considered big news! She herself acknowledges how the community's perception of her changed: "'The Lord has done this for me,' she said. 'In these days he has shown his favor and taken away my disgrace among the people'" (Luke 1:25).

And then, six months into Elizabeth's pregnancy, an angel appears to Mary, and announces not only the forthcoming events in Mary's own life but also what was already happening with Elizabeth. Given their similar circumstances, it is hardly surprising that "Mary got ready and hurried to a town in the hill country of Judea, where she entered Zechariah's home" (Luke 1:39–40).

As Christians, we often talk about the incredible benefits that come with being part of the faith and of belonging to a larger Christian "family." I remember being very excited by this news as a young believer until I realized that the Christian "family" can be quite dysfunctional too! However, our bonds should not simply remind us of who we have to "put up with," like it or not, for eternity! They should also remind us of what we have in common, spiritually speaking. Our familial connections affirm that we share enough spiritual DNA to prove both our divine "paternity" *and* "maternity." They remind us that we have indeed originated from the *same* "womb."[18]

However, common lineage doesn't mean there is only one way of being a family member, especially with a family as large and diverse as ours. Similarly, our friendships shouldn't turn us into identical twins with uniform tastes and opinions. Yet, this is what some Christians expect of their fellow believers. Each of us is uniquely crafted by God, with different talents, backgrounds, and perspectives. It's in embracing these differences that we truly understand the depth of our unity.

There may have been many reasons why Mary was eager to visit Elizabeth, but one thing is clear: Up until this point in the New Testament, no one, male nor female, had been entrusted with a responsibility as significant as bearing i) the savior of the world or ii) the one who would prepare the way for the savior. Then, remarkably, two people receive this precise divine news within six months of each other.

As already intimated, Mary and Elizabeth were undoubtedly different in many ways—in age, in life circumstances, and even in their roles in the grand story of redemption. Yet, their common bond as bearers of extraordinary news united them in a profound way. They found solace and encouragement in each other's company, recognizing that although their paths were unique, they shared a divine purpose that connected them at the deepest level.

In our Christian journey, we too encounter people who seem vastly different from us—in culture, backgrounds, and even the way they express their faith. Yet, in our diversity lies our unity, and in this unity lies our true metamorphic potential. Just as each member of a biological family contributes to its richness, the diverse members of the Christian family also add to its vibrancy, depth, and ability to bring about impactful metamorphic change. Our unity does not come from conformity but from our shared commitment to following Christ and living out his teachings in our own uniquely metamorphic ways.

GIVING HONOR WHEREVER IT'S DUE

The most notable thing about Mary and Elizabeth's interaction is how Elizabeth, and all she carries and is entrusted with, still honors and celebrates Mary and all that she carries and is entrusted with. In their culture, it would have been customary for Mary to show deference to Elizabeth due to her age. However, under the Holy Spirit's influence, Elizabeth reverses these expectations. Not only does Elizabeth's baby leap at the sound of Mary's voice and Elizabeth herself is filled with the Holy Spirit in Mary's presence, but Elizabeth also openly proclaims God's favor upon Mary (rather than herself). She exclaims in Luke 1:42–45:

> "Blessed are you among women, and blessed is the child you will bear! But why am I so favored, that the mother of my Lord should come to me? As soon as the sound of your greeting reached my ears, the baby in my womb leaped for joy. Blessed is she who has believed that the Lord would fulfill his promises to her!"

Protestants tend to be a little dismissive of Mary, and in some cultural contexts, elders can be dismissive of the youth; but there is no denying the high regard the elder Elizabeth, and even the unborn John, gives to the young Mary. This dual recognition of Mary's blessedness, by both Elizabeth and her child, speaks volumes about the extraordinary nature of her calling and the respect she is due.

In other words, Elizabeth was physically, spiritually, psychologically, and emotionally carrying what Mary needed at that precise moment. Mary wasn't just carrying her own hopes and dreams but also the future promise of Jesus, embodying the hopes, dreams, and potential of all humanity. Because of societal expectations, it's doubtful that Mary had yet shared this immense burden with Joseph or anyone else, and she still faced the daunting task of having to explain to her husband-to-be how she was now at least three months pregnant after a "visit" to her "cousin's" house. Mary needed all the encouragement and support she could get, both because of all that had already taken place *and* because of all that was still to come.

Although this is Mary and Elizabeth's story, aspects of their husbands' narratives are also included. They reveal how everyone in the story needed a revelation from God in order to understand and accept what was happening. However, the nature of each revelation is notably different and highlights the contrast between the characters who respond with belief and affirmation despite societal expectations, and those who do not. Zechariah fails to believe *despite* his angelic visitation, and Joseph needs to hear directly from the angel's mouth *before* agreeing to share Mary's burden. In contrast, Elizabeth, filled with the Holy Spirit, not only accepts Mary as the pregnant virgin she claims to be (despite Elizabeth's lack of personal experience), but she also recognizes the significance of Mary (as "the mother of my Lord") and that of her unborn child within God's purposes. The timeliness and significance of their emerging friendship is heightened still further. Mary found in Elizabeth the person who shared her burden, affirmed her calling, recognized her significance, and celebrated along with her.

The interaction between Mary and Elizabeth highlights the importance of recognizing and honoring each other's divine callings. Elizabeth's reversal of societal norms and her acknowledgment of Mary's blessedness, under the Holy Spirit's influence, underscores the extraordinary nature of Mary's role and God's great love of reversals. Their encounter serves as a reminder of the importance of supporting one another in our spiritual journeys and of giving honor wherever it's due.

No Competition, No Contest

In this crucial moment, Mary needed support, not competition or disparagement. She did not need someone more interested in diminishing her role out of envy or insecurity. She needed none of the comments and remarks that leaders sometimes make in the name of "support." Nor did she need condescension regarding her youth or capability: "You're a bit young for all this, aren't you?"

What Mary needed is what we all need when we're struggling to honor God's call for our lives, organizations, and churches: a supportive, affirming friend—someone who recognizes the value of what we carry and encourages us to persevere. We need someone who inspires us to go on ... especially when we feel like doing neither.

Being a good friend involves letting what God has placed in us—our talents, possibilities, aspirations, and all that we carry—validate and celebrate what our friends are carrying. As a friend, you will need to stay attentive to what God has placed in others so you can offer confirmation when needed, affirmation wherever possible, and support continually, even when you feel you need it more than they do. Help them see their significance within God's plan and keep encouraging and challenging them to aim higher.

This journey of friendship isn't just about being nice for the sake of it or telling people what they want to hear. What Elizabeth offered Mary was the unfiltered truth, which just so happened to be wonderfully affirming and precisely what Mary needed at the time because she would soon face harsh criticism, accusation, innuendo, and disbelief from a variety of sources.

Elizabeth's choice to speak "in a loud voice" (v. 42) could signify her excitement ... or maybe she was making a public declaration and affirmation. When God places a call on our lives, there will always be skeptics who question that calling. There will always be those who doubt what you are "carrying." And there will always be individuals prepared to oppose and resist you as you seek to walk in obedience with God. There may even be moments of doubt when you wonder whether you were visited by an angel at all or even heard from God in the first place. It's at times like these that we need to seek out a friend who will tell us and everyone else how it really is and who will affirm us loudly, if necessary, without holding anything back.

Celebrate and Endorse

Friendships may last a lifetime or a season. For Mary and Elizabeth, their time together was brief—Mary stayed with Elizabeth for three months until possibly just after Elizabeth gave birth, and thereafter, there's no record of any further interaction between them. The reality is that some friendships are indeed seasonal. This doesn't mean they are necessarily fair-weather friends, but instead they are forged by shared vision, location, and a calling that lasts for only a "moment."

Regardless of the duration of their relationship, the impact Mary and Elizabeth had on each other remains with us even today. Mary's response to Elizabeth's Spirit-filled affirmation is immortalized in what is known as The Magnificat, or Mary's song, in Luke 1:46–55. This song reflects Mary's profound realization of her role and blessing:

> "My soul glorifies the Lord
>   and my spirit rejoices in God my Savior,
> for he has been mindful
>   of the humble state of his servant.
> From now on all generations will call me blessed,
>   for the Mighty One has done great things for me—holy is his name.
> His mercy extends to those who fear him,
>   from generation to generation.

He has performed mighty deeds with his arm;
> he has scattered those who are proud in their inmost thoughts.

He has brought down rulers from their thrones
> but has lifted up the humble.

He has filled the hungry with good things
> but has sent the rich away empty.

He has helped his servant Israel,
> remembering to be merciful to Abraham and his descendants forever,
> just as he promised our ancestors."

We all need friends who leave us inspired to declare great things about ourselves and God's calling upon us. And we should aim to be such friends to others. A simple interaction, like Mary's with Elizabeth, can be enough to provide supernatural clarity and confidence about our purpose and impact. As a young woman, Mary probably didn't expect to be taken seriously or to make the kind of contribution that would change anyone's life, and yet Elizabeth's impact enabled her to declare the truth of God's metamorphic purposes for her own life. So, Mary, devoid of all false humility, confidently acknowledges the significance of what God was doing "to her," "through her," and "for her," declaring, "From now on all generations will call me blessed." And she wasn't wrong!

GAIL: RELATIONALLY METAMORPHIC

I met Gail over breakfast at a conference celebrating Black professionals. Her demeanor commanded both respect and attention, and she looked every bit the powerful Black professional she was! Our paths had already crossed a few times during the event, so we fell into easy conversation. When I asked her where she was located, it turned out we were both based in the same city, so as she described the building, I had a pretty good idea of where she worked.

"Funny thing is, I was originally employed as the cleaner in the same building," she laughed.

"So, what do you do now?" I asked.

"I'm the Head of Service, responsible for exploited and vulnerable children for the entire Trust!"

As it turns out, Gail and her story are well-known in the sector.

"When I was fourteen," she said, "I was permanently excluded from school ... and I left with no qualifications. I also had criminal offences on my record, making my journey after school even more challenging."

Her life took a turn when she became pregnant at sixteen and a mother at seventeen. Following a violent attack and robbery at her home, police relocated her for safety reasons. These challenges marked a significant turning point for Gail, and she sought to transform her life.

Now, many years later, Gail tells her story to motivate and inspire and reflects on the people who came alongside her at critical points in her journey and helped her on her way. These people recognized her potential and the gifts she carried, and they presented her with opportunities despite her challenging past. One personal tutor remains a significant figure in her life. Gail's work progresses not just from her expertise but also from the relationships she forms with clients and their families. Her approach to changing the world around her is rooted in friendship.

Gail's message is inspiring but simple: "You are not on your own. When you experience challenges, find your support network and pull on them for help, guidance, and support. Make sure you have a committee of people around you that can be open and honest with you, challenge you, celebrate, support, and, most importantly, guide you along your next steps." Gail's journey and her current role as a mentor and friend highlight the transformative power of relationships and the importance of a supportive community.

CREATING IMPACT AGAINST ALL ODDS

Perhaps the most powerful thing we learn from this passage about Mary and Elizabeth's friendship is that it enables us to do what we're called to do against all the odds! This is a theme powerfully echoed in Mary's song, The Magnificat, which not only highlights the impact of God's work in her life but also underscores the significance of her friendship with Elizabeth. Mary's song is a reminder of how God often chooses the most unlikely individuals from the most marginalized groups to make world-changing metamorphic contributions. This is one of those moments God proves to be utterly predictable, for, throughout the biblical narrative, we can always count on God's activity to happen through the least expected people.

God's choice of Israel, a nation described as the least among nations, is a prime example of this. One scholar points out, "If God had chosen as the 'holy nation' the Egyptian slave masters instead of the Israelite slaves, then a completely different kind of God would have been revealed. Thus, Israel's election cannot be separated from its servitude and liberation."[19]

Our central religious text, the Holy Scripture, is predominantly the work of an oppressed and occupied minority, and the Exodus event reveals God as a champion for a weak and defenseless people. The Ten Commandments, a cornerstone of Israel's law, begin with a profound acknowledgment of their social and political history of oppression and liberation, as God declares in Exodus 20:2–3, "I am the LORD your God, *who brought you out of Egypt, out of the land of slavery*. You shall have no other gods before me."

At various points in their history, the children of Israel were slaves, exiles, or a small fledgling nation amongst the giants that surrounded them. Even during prosperous times, like Solomon's reign, greater superpowers overshadowed them, and by the time we meet them in the New Testament, they are a colonized minority.

The reality is that the peoples described and addressed in the Bible texts were oppressed and marginalized at virtually every stage of their social and political development. And the very story of Scripture is about a displaced, colonized, and oppressed community.

In contrast, many Western Christians have grown up in nations that were once colonial powers. This background significantly influences our perception and interpretation of the biblical narrative and means we often view and interpret the story from the perspective of colonizers rather than the colonized. We also have an unhealthy tendency to teach others to do the same.

We are so used to winning and having determinative power on our side that our faith takes on a different texture than that of an oppressed people. Power becomes the ability to control our own destiny and the destiny of others rather than the power to live faithfully before God or to advocate for the marginalized. We also tend to prioritize self-preservation, which may be why sacrifice, persecution, and martyrdom are often alien and challenging concepts for us, to be avoided at all costs. Our colonial commitment to self-preservation, often at the expense of others, explains why we behave as if

God's main task in our universe is to keep us safe, secure, and wealthy, even when two-thirds of the world clearly are not. Consequently, when God doesn't deliver on these expectations, it explains why we become distressed and even "faithless."

The shock and dismay expressed by some church leaders following one of the deadliest terrorist attacks on UK soil—the Manchester bombings of May 22, 2017—were revealing.[20] Some confessed they nearly lost their faith, while others pondered if God had a unique plan for Manchester. Such reactions highlight a common Western perspective: the struggle to reconcile the existence of pain and suffering with the nature of God. This viewpoint often overlooks the reality that the life-threatening dangers of bombs, bullets, poverty, and persecution are the normal, everyday experiences of most Christians in the world today. The truth is, those of us in the West are the exceptions.

Despite a few wealthy individuals, many descriptions of the New Testament church suggest that God was largely revealing his identity not simply to the spiritually poor but primarily to the socially, politically, and economically poor. For these early Christians, marginalization and powerlessness were the norm.

After all, Mary was a young, unmarried peasant girl from an occupied people in an occupied country, chosen to bear a child out of wedlock. And Jesus was the Palestinian Jew,[21] who grew up with the stigma of being conceived out of wedlock and had to flee as a child refugee to Egypt in the face of political violence.

God's promise to his people was never a promise of "power over," as we understand it. The nature of their leadership in the world was not meant to be about dominion, as they never experienced power in this way. God's promise is not about being in charge but about being agents of change and having power "in," "with," and "for" rather than primarily "over" others. The Magnificat illustrates that metamorphic world-transforming contributions often emerge from what seems foolish by worldly standards. The friendship between Mary and Elizabeth may not have seemed like much to human eyes, but it serves to exemplify the power of relationship across difference to progress God's purposes against all the odds.

In contemplating our connections with others, we must resist the temptation to disqualify ourselves or those around us, especially the "least of these," because God has a way of taking the most powerless and marginalized in the eyes of the world and working his wonders in, through, and for them. This, it seems, is God's modus operandi.

Amidst it all, our challenge is to make an impact against the odds, both because of and in spite of who we are. Jesus reveals that metamorphic transformation is possible only when we make a friend and become the kind of friend who empowers others across differences. We must dare to be the kind of friend who faces challenges, embraces risks, and makes the necessary spiritual, emotional, psychological, and physical journeys to uplift others. This friendship should not compete with but rather celebrate and endorse one another's strengths. Ultimately, we are ready to create an impact when we facilitate the metamorphic, world-changing contributions of others, and perhaps also make our own contributions with the support of our many wonderful friends.

FOR PERSONAL REFLECTION OR GROUP DISCUSSION

Facing the Challenges and Experiencing the True Power of Friendship

1. How do *you* define true friendship, and how does it compare with the relationship between Jesus and his disciples or between Mary and Elizabeth?
2. Do you have a "full-disclosure" friend (i.e., someone from whom you hold nothing back)? If so, how did your friendship develop? If not, what barriers prevent you from forming such a deep connection?
3. Who confides in you about their experiences of the supernatural, divine intervention, being misunderstood, facing injustice, and their most challenging and most triumphant moments?

Crossing Boundaries in Your Relationships

1. Is there a "loneliness epidemic" in your church, neighborhood, team, or workplace? What *one* action could you take to make it a friendlier place?
2. What actions will you take to empower your friends, particularly those from different ethnic, cultural, social, or faith backgrounds?
3. How can you better acknowledge and celebrate your diverse friends' unique talents, traits, and challenges?

Creating Metamorphic Impact "Against all the Odds"

1. How do you support and uplift your friends through their spiritual, emotional, psychological, or physical challenges?
2. What specific steps can you take this week to encourage and facilitate the efforts of your friends who are engaged in transformative and world-changing activities?
3. What metamorphic change do you feel compelled to pursue, and how can your friends support you this week toward achieving it against the odds?

TIME FOR PRAYER

Take a moment for personal or group prayer. If part of a discussion group, lift up each member, asking for guidance, strength, and clarity as they navigate through their challenges and seek growth in their personal and leadership journey to discover the many ways in which *together is better*.

6

THE APOSTLES
JUST LEADERSHIP

Developing Radical Empathy to Break Systemic Strongholds

[Doing justice] is not about fixing things or solving problems, it's about reorienting creation back to its original intent.
SANDRA MARIA VAN OPSTAL

Could sin be better understood as a refusal to accept needed change, a refusal to grow, a resistance to the arc of transition that bends toward justice?
BRIAN D. MCLAREN

A gospel message that doesn't try to change the world only works for those who don't need the world to change.
JIM WALLIS

The tragic killing of George Floyd in Minneapolis, Minnesota, on May 25, 2020, shocked the millions who witnessed it through the media and those who learned about it indirectly. The implications of what had been caught on camera were so appalling that it triggered massive protests across the US, the UK, and the rest of the world. Some referred to it as a pivotal moment of racial reckoning,[1] while a number of Christian groups recognized it as nothing short of a kairos moment: God's opportune time for tackling racial injustices being perpetuated within workplaces, ministry spaces, and beyond.[2]

For me and many other Christians of color, reaction to Floyd's death and its aftermath exposed the painful realities of a church fraught with the same racially and culturally charged tensions on display in media outlets. It also brought to light the stark lack of genuinely diverse Christian congregations in Europe, the UK, and the US.[3] Some Christian leaders were surprised to learn for the first time that congregational worship was, in Martin Luther King Jr.'s words, still "the most segregated hour of the week,"[4] including *in* churches that considered themselves multiethnic or intercultural.[5]

So, it came as no surprise when organizations, institutions, and churches alike, nationally and internationally, Christian and non-Christian found themselves faced with the same challenge of what it means to lead effectively in a world divided by race. The George Floyd moment seemed to serve as a "great awakening," prompting many to commit to doing all they could to tackle racial inequality. In fact, by the end of May 2020, just days after Floyd's death, fifty-five CEOs of global corporations, along with leaders of smaller entities, publicly pledged change through statements and detailed action plans posted on social media.[6]

MAKING THE "INVISIBLE" VISIBLE

While some corporations were quick to respond, similar recognition and a commitment to act were notably slower to come from churches, denominations, and Christian organizations in the UK, Europe, and the US. Justin Welby, the Archbishop of Canterbury in the UK, openly referenced the "hostile environment" endured by people of color within the Church of England. His language was unequivocal: "When we look at our own church, we are still deeply institutionally racist. Let's be clear about that."[7] Ben Lindsay, founder and CEO of Power The Fight, highlighted the deep-seated racial disparities within UK church leadership in his timely publication *We Need to Talk About Race*, in which he describes the "Guinness effect"—a term used in the Black community to denote white-dominated leadership over a predominantly Black congregation or workforce.[8]

In his insightful paper "Europe 2021: A Missiological Report," Jim Memory examines the health and future of mission work in Europe. He makes a critical observation: "The future of the church in Europe may well depend on the emergence of a truly European Intercultural Christianity."[9] However, Memory identifies significant obstacles to achieving this vision, noting that many native European churches have either been unwilling or unsure how to assist diaspora churches (Memory's preferred term for ethnic or migrant churches).[10] He later adds, "In some parts of Europe, church leaders have simply not woken up to the potential of collaborating with diaspora churches. To do that, European church leaders may need to face up to their unconscious racism and colonial attitudes."[11]

On June 15, 2020, Rick Warren, the renowned author of *The Purpose Driven Life* and founding pastor of Saddleback Church in the US, made a poignant statement on his social media: "Racism is not some minor issue to God. It's at the heart of the gospel." Following this, Saddleback Church outlined steps they were taking to confront the root causes of racial inequality.[12] However, the very next day, on June 16, *Christianity Today* published an article revealing that only 62 percent of US churches acknowledged that churches had a responsibility to denounce racism in the wake of George Floyd's death. The same *Christianity Today* article also reported that a disheartening 20 percent of US pastors (one in five!) believed the church had no role in responding to the country's history of racism.[13] So, although there were some Christians who recognized the church's role in combating racial injustice, it became increasingly clear that many churches were willingly minimizing the pain experienced by people of color and exacerbating their anguish by failing to address or even acknowledge racism adequately.

And for those leaders who understood the church's role in addressing racial injustice, it soon became clear that they didn't necessarily know how to respond. Many who felt guilty as they became aware of the full extent of the challenge took to responding with default commitments and platitudes to "think and pray" about the issue. Those who sincerely wished to do better often focused on individual efforts, while overlooking the need to challenge and change the underlying theologies and structures in their churches and wider society that perpetuated the injustices and disparities in the first place.

Consequently, the wave of eloquent statements and promises made by churches, workplaces, and organizations in the aftermath of George Floyd often lacked follow-through in terms of measurably tangible results. There was so little consistency that the following wry remark fast became commonplace, "When all was said and done, there was a lot more said than done!"[14]

Evading Racism

While Christians have ample reasons to excel in matters of justice and have responded accordingly in some areas, the response to racism within many Christian communities has been disappointingly lackluster.

In the realm of public discourse, where various forms of discrimination are increasingly being highlighted, the issue of racial injustice has frequently been the most evaded and least addressed, even in the post-George Floyd era. Groups and organizations, including those with Christian affiliations, have often acted on diversity and inclusion measures while conspicuously sidestepping issues related to racism and racial inequality. This has led some (including me) to surmise that they either consider racism the most daunting "ism" of all or the least relevant by far.[15] All the while, anti-Black sentiment continues to insidiously intersect with and exacerbate the challenges faced by every other socially marginalized group or "protected characteristic" in society.[16]

In a section entitled "How to Talk About Race When—eek!—it is so Hard!" author Kelly McDonald addresses the difficulties surrounding race discussions, especially for many white people. She points out,

> Unlike other issues at work that you have to resolve and work through, this is about people ... For most White people, the subject of race is incredibly uncomfortable to talk about because we have no skills in this area. We weren't taught how to do it. In fact, most of us were probably taught not to discuss race.[17]

Unfortunately, the reluctance to engage in conversations about race historically also extends to church and ministry settings where racial tensions have either been ignored or rationalized with spiritual and theological justifications,[18] and silence over racial matters has, in some cases, been elevated to a spiritual virtue.[19]

The aftermath of George Floyd's death made it clear that racial barriers are not simply confined to Western Europe or the US. Part of the reason the protests were worldwide is precisely because race-related barriers are a global issue.[20] *The Guardian* columnist Ahmed Olayinka Sule underlines this:

In today's Brazil, black people are still treated as second-class citizens; while in India, students of African origin are persecuted. In South Africa, a majority Black country, 72% of the country's private farmland is owned by white people, who make up 9% of the population. During the apartheid era there was a clear racial hierarchy with whites at the top, Indians and "coloureds" in the middle, and Black people at the bottom.[21]

Out of Sight, Out of Mind

As I mentioned earlier, much like the rest of the world, the initial response of white church leaders in the UK to the killing of George Floyd was painfully and frustratingly slow. There were, I believe, several underlying reasons for this.

First, many leaders, while appalled, perceived the incident as an individual and isolated event and therefore as personal rather than systemic racism. Second, there was a prevailing belief that racism, as highlighted by the incident, was a problem confined to the US and not relevant to the UK. Third, many churches in the UK were convinced they were wonderfully happy families because racial issues were not openly discussed. Fourth, churches lacking racial diversity did not see racism as *their* issue because their congregations were homogenous—the people around them looked, believed, sounded, and acted like them. Therefore, they didn't consider themselves overtly exposed to the challenges of racial diversity. Yet, as I have often said, this lack of exposure doesn't necessarily equate to an absence of racial biases or prejudices. Anyone who reads the national media or watches the daily news is already forming opinions and developing a mindset about "race" that is seldom informed by biblical principles or shaped by biblical values, leading inevitably to unbiblical attitudes, behaviors, and responses whenever the occasion arises. Finally, like many white people in the UK, there are church leaders who struggle to believe racism is an issue for them because they don't feel *they* have a personal problem with it as it doesn't manifest in US-style issues.

Although it's true that the British media doesn't frequently report racially motivated violence, overt racial discrimination like the "n-word" is rarely used anymore, and police brutality isn't generally reinforced with firearms, this does not imply an absence of racism in the UK. The shooting of Chris Kaba—a twenty-four-year-old, unarmed soon-to-be father—by a police officer in London on September 5, 2022, starkly illustrates this point.[22] This tragic event occurred over two years after George Floyd's death and serves as a reminder that generalizations about the absence of racial issues can be misleading, especially considering Mr. Kaba had been followed by a police car without lights or sirens and was not a suspect when he was shot and killed. A simple internet search reveals numerous other heartbreaking examples of racial injustice in the UK.

Britain's history of slavery also might feel distant in comparison to America's, primarily because the brutality of the plantations did not take place in Britain itself but in the West Indies and other British colonies. This geographical distance often masks the true extent of Britain's pervasive and extensive involvement in and profiting from slavery.

So, for many, the last few years have been partly about getting to grips with the realities of a racism that, for them, has simply been "out of sight, out of mind."

SYSTEMIC DISCRIMINATION IN THE EARLY CHURCH

In Acts chapter 6, frustrations associated with "overlooked" systemic discrimination, not unlike racism, erupted in the early church. The chapter introduces us to five distinct groups: the Greek-speaking believers (the "Hellenistic Jews"), the Hebrew-speaking believers ("Hebraic Jews"), the apostles (who were also predominantly Hebrew-speaking), the broader church community, and the seven individuals appointed to address the significant fallout.

The Hellenistic Jews were "foreign" Diaspora Jews who had grown up in Greek-speaking regions outside of Israel. They had assimilated Greek culture, including language and dress. Conversely, the Hebraic Jews were native to Israel, speaking Hebrew and Aramaic, and adhered closely to traditional Jewish customs, including the way they dressed. Despite being followers of Jesus, they still harbored deep-seated cultural biases regarding the Hellenists. The Hebraic Jews often viewed their approach to Judaism and, subsequently, their Christian faith as a more "pure" or authentic expression. This sense of superiority and entitlement, ingrained in their majority culture, inevitably spilled over into discriminatory practices within the early church.

Various translations of Acts 6:1 highlight the issue at hand: The Hellenist widows were being "overlooked" (NIV), "discriminated against" (MSG), or "neglected" (NKJV). In other words, the situation was sufficiently dire, systemic, and negative that the Hellenists were unhappy enough to raise strong objections and make their voices heard regarding what was being witnessed and experienced by their community.

The way discrimination spilled over in this situation is noteworthy because, in Jewish law, widows without male relatives to support them were particularly vulnerable. The church's initiative to provide for these widows led them to pioneer an early form of social welfare. Yet it was precisely as the church was trying to do something right that they discovered that something was very wrong ... systemic discrimination, not unlike racism, was alive and well in the church.

Caste Aside

Racism affects different so-called "races" in different ways. There is anti-Black racism, anti-Asian racism (which affects East and South Asians differently), anti-Arab racism (which often combines with Islamophobia[23]), and multiple other types of racism. Each racism is also usually accompanied by varying degrees of xenophobia.[24]

Ellen E. Jones, journalist, broadcaster, and author of *Screen Deep: How Film and TV Can Solve Racism and Save the World*, helpfully clarifies a common misunderstanding:

> In colloquial English we use the same inadequate word—"racism"—to describe two distinct, but connected, phenomena. 1) Racism is interpersonal prejudice or bigotry based on skin colour or other racially coded physical traits. But 2) Racism is also the pervasive and deeply embedded disadvantage that people of colour experience as a holdover from European colonialism and transatlantic slavery, and the way in which it is produced, condoned and perpetuated by a multiplicity of social systems and structures. This is often referred to as "structural racism" or "systemic racism" but, just as often, simply as "racism".[25]

To effectively combat all forms of racism, we must recognize that the idea of "race" itself operates similarly to a caste system, binding and compelling even those oppressed by it to sometimes perpetuate the cycle of oppressive practices by competing for scarce and questionable "rewards." The system bears a striking resemblance to the apartheid regime in South Africa mentioned earlier, where the distinction of skin color—both literal and symbolic—defines the boundaries of separation.[26]

I sometimes get asked, "What makes racism different from simple ethnocentrism?" It is this racial hierarchy that partly distinguishes the two.

Ethnocentrism is a prejudice in thought or action that ranks ethnic and cultural groups against one another, but it is mutable and transferable, whereas racism acts as a ranking of inherited human value and usage and positions the perceived "superior" race at the top and the "inferior" one at the bottom. Just as caste systems rely on the stigmatization of those deemed inherently inferior based on their birth, racism does the same. I often have to remind people that racism is never primarily about personal feelings or morality. It is always about *power*—which groups get to make the decisions and which do not; *resources*—which group gets to acquire, control, and distribute them; and *legitimacy*—which groups are considered worthy of being heard, respected, deemed competent and worthy of authority, and why. The distorted image of whites as superior is so globally pervasive that even if Black people are prejudiced or ethnocentric against whites, they don't usually have the social power to act on those feelings in ways that can impact the futures of white people. The reverse, however, is simply not the case.

Similar to the caste system, racism is a process by which systems and policies, actions and attitudes create unequal and inequitable opportunities and outcomes for people based on their so-called "race." As such, it has been a tool for oppression with socioeconomic motives, as exemplified during the transatlantic slave trade and even today continues through the global arrangements marked by neocolonialism. Historically, it has usually been Black or darker-skinned people who have been relegated to the lowest rung of this racial hierarchy. There are multiple and complex reasons for this. However, the sale of almost ten million Africans to Arabia and the Indian subcontinent by Arab slave traders between 650 CE and the 1800s and the transportation of at least twelve million Africans across the Atlantic by European slave traders between the sixteenth and nineteenth century have undoubtedly contributed to a lasting global legacy that continues to affect Black and darker-skinned people even today.[27]

Before the development of racialized hierarchies, slavery was practiced widely across a variety of civilizations but was rarely linked to notions of inherent racial inferiority. Instead, it was often viewed ethnocentrically or as the unfortunate consequence of being on the losing side of battle and ancient warfare.

Today, Black and darker-skinned people "inherit" a perceived racial inferiority and thus experience a range of disparate outcomes in virtually every sector of every society around the globe. This racial bias is evident in the continued use of pejorative terms for Black people in virtually every geographic context imaginable. Ahmed Olayinka Sule notes,

> The Arabic word *abeed*, which means "slave," is still used to describe Black people in countries from Algeria to Yemen. In the US, they are called "nigger," in Brazil they are termed *macaco*; in South Africa, they are nicknamed *kaffir*; in India, *bandar*; in China *hak gwai*.[28]

The Race for Truth

The irony of all this is that despite its prevalence, the modern category of "race" is grounded in neither biology nor in any reputable science.[29] Biologically speaking, all people living today belong to one species: Homo sapiens, and this species has evolved together without branching off into different human species. Likewise, the concept of "race" is not a biblical construct. The Bible acknowledges only one human race and addresses issues of diversity, not by starting with the differences in the human family but with the oneness of humanity created in the image of God. One of the first things we learn about God's intentions for humanity is that we are created to be like him and, in some way, to reflect who God is and what God is like. Genesis 1:26 states, "Let us make humankind in our image, according to our likeness" (NRSV). This directive establishes God, not humanity, as the ultimate reference point for all reality. To put it another way, both diversity and distinctiveness are not only part of God's design, but they are also characteristics of God himself, and it is God who "sets the bar" for their meaning and value.

At the very beginning of the biblical narrative, we discover God as a collective "we" rather than a solitary "me." In theological terms, this is expressed through the doctrine of the Trinity, where three distinct persons—coequal and coeternal—exemplify perfect unity amidst diversity. However, we should note that God values unity in diversity characterized by equality just as much in the human family too, including cultural and ethnic differences. This fact is reflected throughout the Bible in texts such as Revelation 7:9, "After this I looked, and there before me was a great multitude that no one could count, from every nation, tribe, people and language, standing before the throne and before the Lamb." Exodus 12:38 describes the exodus of God's people from Egypt as a "mixed multitude" (ESV), so their identity wasn't grounded in the concept of "race" as understood today. Instead, their distinctiveness throughout their developmental journey was their worship of the one true God.

The modern notion of "race" emerged in the late sixteenth century as a social construct and attempt to categorize people into different "types" based on their physical and cultural traits.[30] By the mid-eighteenth century, this misguided notion had been conveniently solidified by white Europeans, particularly the British, into a means of justifying the cultural and economic domination of other groups through mechanisms like slavery, indentured servitude, and oppression.[31]

While the term "race" lacks biological or scientific validity, the ideology of race wields significant and often destructive power. Worse still, it has acquired a seemingly tangible and common-sense-like quality. As a result, systems of racial hierarchy have thoroughly co-opted our consciousness, language, and behavior and continue to be knowingly and unknowingly perpetuated today, even among Christians worldwide, from Africa to India and Europe to China.

It is therefore more important than ever for Christians to reject the concept of racial hierarchies and to proactively oppose all attempts to reassert them all over the world.

A Diversifying World Needs a Diversifying Church

While "race" is a human construct, increasing diversity is a growing reality. The twenty-first century, in particular, has been characterized by a significant increase in global diversity. However, contrary to popular opinion, the most culturally diverse nations are not in Western Europe or the Americas but in Africa. At the time of writing (2024), Uganda, Liberia, Chad, Cameroon, and Togo are among the top ten most culturally diverse countries in the world, as confirmed by the multiple methods used to measure them.[32] According to the World Population Review, Canada is the only Western country in the top twenty most culturally diverse countries,[33] with both the US and the UK ranking significantly lower.[34]

This surge in diversity has been driven by political, social, environmental, and economic factors that have led to displacement, forced migration, and large-scale movements of people across borders. The extent of this global mixing is expected to increase significantly in the coming years, but the US and

Western Europe will experience a relatively small amount of this, despite the inflammatory rhetoric suggesting otherwise.

These rapid demographic changes and advances in communication have led to unprecedented levels of interaction among different ideologies, philosophies, and religions. People are increasingly encountering diverse perspectives in their own homes, workplaces, and educational establishments in ways that were previously unheard of. We are living at a time in history where vastly different worldviews—with all their associated opinions, distinctives, values, and beliefs—not only coexist but also sometimes clash … violently.

In the UK, projections already indicate that by 2061, over 35 percent of the population will be of non-white English or Irish descent, a significant increase from 13 percent in 2011.[35] This demographic will include individuals identified as "Black," "Asian," "UK minority," or "global majority," depending on the terminology adopted. In the United States, people of color are expected to constitute around 54 percent of the population by around the same time.[36] Europe is also expected to be a whole shade darker. Notably, UK, European, and US churches are witnessing these demographic shifts much faster, partly because people of color are far more likely to be involved in faith communities.[37] This should come as no surprise, given the center of gravity of Christianity has shifted decisively from the Global North to the Global South and from the West to the East. Christianity is growing substantially within these regions and among these people groups all over the world.

As we look to the future, whatever the context, it will inevitably become more diverse and thus more complex over time. This escalating diversity and complexity will require Christian leaders to employ biblical wisdom in leading and guiding their churches, workplaces, and wider society through the massive cultural transitions that will accompany them.

Even if "race" is not an issue in the classic sense, every society, including those plagued by colorism,[38] will need to engage in some kind of soul-searching, as each community likely harbors some form of insider/outsider dynamic informed by racial legacies. Many churches and Christian organizations are still coming to terms with the reality that racism functions in every society, community, and church context—albeit in slightly different ways. This means we all have our own version of a racialized world,[39] and the way it shows up in your church or organization is likely to reflect how it shows up in your wider society and community. In reality, as people come to Christ, they inevitably bring with them attitudes, habits, and practices all in need of a metamorphic transformation. Given our history of valuing some bodies over others—men over women, rich over poor, Christian over Jewish, and white over Black and brown—it's no surprise that these biases are reflected in our churches. The UK home-grown variety of racism may look different to varieties found elsewhere, but just because it is often wrapped up in a politer package doesn't make it any less destructive, systemic, or soul-destroying! All this raises the question of what will be required of leaders and leadership in diversifying contexts, a question that will become increasingly critical.

JUST ... JUST LEADERSHIP

As noted throughout this book, leadership is increasingly defined by its capacity to influence rather than by titles, and hinges more on trust than on a hierarchical position. In diversifying and racialized landscapes, trust is often scarce due to historical misuses of spirituality, pseudoscience, and bias (conscious or not) in ways that uphold existing power structures. In low-trust environments, recognizing and achieving breakthroughs can be particularly tricky. So, the concept of "just leadership" is even more critical.

When we think about "justice," it is often in the context of retribution or punishment aimed at those who cause harm or make people suffer. The common cry for "justice" usually means seeking one's rights, often from a specific individual or legal system. However, the biblical concept of justice is far deeper and wider, and punishment is not even its primary concern. In the Old Testament, the Hebrew word for justice, *misphat*, is frequently paired with *tsedeqa*, translated as "righteousness." Together, these terms often appear as "justice and righteousness" and encompass the ideas of corrective/restorative justice (i.e., putting things right) and distributive justice or impartiality and fairness (i.e., doing things right). An example of this is Isaiah 1:17: "Learn to do right; seek justice. Defend the oppressed. Take up the cause of the fatherless; plead the case of the widow."

In the New Testament, these concepts are encapsulated in the Greek word *dikaiosune*, which encompasses both aspects of correction and fairness. It is clear from this that God's focus is not primarily punishment but on fostering right relationships, actions, and order. This holistic view of justice emphasizes the importance of fairness and restoration in leadership, particularly in contexts where trust needs to be rebuilt and historical injustices addressed. As leaders, embracing this broader, more restorative notion of justice is key to navigating and leading effectively in diverse and complex environments. It is often why churches and Christian organizations that show little interest in corrective practices are regarded with suspicion by marginalized communities.

The kind of "justice" the Bible has in view has no limit or boundaries and applies in private as well as in public life. It also encompasses personal, interpersonal, and systemic aspects of our relationships. Essentially, justice is relevant wherever God has interests, which means absolutely everywhere!

Removing the Veil of Blindness

There are no easy ways to rid the world of the evils of race-related thinking and oppression, but it will demand nothing less than a metanoic change of mind and a metamorphic display of transformation. Both suggest that the church not only has a part to play but also an opportunity to lead this change.

Yet, our pivotal role cannot be realized if we fail to confront the truth of our own historical involvement in the creation and perpetuation of racial categories and oppression in the first place. 2 Corinthians 3:18 provides the crucial reminder: "And we all, who with unveiled faces contemplate the Lord's glory, are being transformed into his image with ever-increasing glory, which comes from the Lord, who is the Spirit." This verse suggests that the transformation we seek for our churches, Christian organizations, and daily lives is a profound journey that requires divine intervention. But we must first be willing to remove the veil that blinds us to our own biases and shortcomings, especially when it comes to race-related thinking, and earnestly seek God's transformative power.

We can, of course, try to bury our heads in the sand and pretend that everything in our churches and organizations is wonderful, but there is no getting around the fact that it is always and only "the truth that sets us free!" Conversely, self-deception is very costly, and denial of the truth only keeps us stagnating in unresolved issues for even longer. The metamorphic transformation we long for and that takes us from "glory to glory" is only possible when metanoia is embraced as an ongoing daily practice of unlearning and relearning and not merely a one-off event.

There is a misconception among Christians that merely sharing the same space, beliefs, and practices, and attending the same church along with those who differ from us actually changes things. It rarely does. There really is no substitute for intentionality when it comes to catalyzing metamorphic change. Just because we live, work, and even worship alongside diverse others doesn't mean we have learned how to relate effectively, navigate faith, or even worship authentically together.

Recent years have demonstrated how painful it can be for people to work or worship together across the barriers of "race," ethnicity, and culture without understanding what is really at stake. In her article "Why Developing Intercultural Management Skills Is Essential in Today's Complex World," independent global executive coach and intercultural leadership consultant Myriam Callegarin spells it out:

> Most people interact with others across cultures without being aware of the communication breakdowns and the invisible conflicts they unintentionally create. They are unaware of the unwritten rules and the invisible codes that are valid in the other culture. Most interactions are careless and clueless, not due to bad intentions, but rather because of a lack of knowledge and self-reflection.[40]

We seldom notice that the low engagement of particular communities within our institutions, organizations, churches, and even our neighborhoods and networks has less to do with their disinterest in our vision, mission, community, or Jesus and more to do with our lack of awareness and cultural sensitivity. The need for racial sensitivity and cultural competence has never been more pressing than it is today.

Ironically, Christians are the custodians of the unique narrative, practices, and resources so crucial for both effective communication and community building in racially and culturally diverse spaces. Yet, all too often, it is Christians who are the most hesitant to engage and the least willing to change.

The Desperate Need for Radical Empathy

I believe that a lack of empathy lies at the core of this failure. Likewise, it is radical empathy that lies at the core of our much-needed metamorphic transformation, just as it always has. Empathy is embodied in the scriptural principle found in Romans 12:15, which encourages believers to "Rejoice with those who rejoice; mourn with those who mourn," and in 1 Corinthians 12:26, which states, "If one part suffers, every part suffers with it." This captures the essence of what it means to be part of genuine community. The New Testament and church history provide compelling evidence that it is strong communities that ignite potent and effective mission. But now I'm getting ahead of myself and into the final section of this book devoted to metamorphic mission! My point, however, is we desperately need leaders who are capable of leading in radically empathetic ways.

In her insightful book *Radical Empathy*, political scientist and entrepreneur Terri E. Givens offers a transformative perspective. She defines empathy as,

> The ability to see the world from another person's perspective, in order to understand their feelings and life experiences. "Radical empathy" takes this a step further, encouraging each of us not only to understand the feelings of others, but also to be motivated to create the change that will allow all of us to benefit from economic prosperity and develop the social relationships that are beneficial to our emotional wellbeing.[41]

In my work, I often draw parallels between "radical empathy" and the concept of "incarnational practice." Although incarnation is a concept found in various religions, such as Buddhism and Hinduism, it acquires a unique dimension in Christianity and is exemplified by Jesus Christ. Incarnation in the Christian context involves a deep commitment to fully understanding and sharing in the experiences of others. It means standing in their shoes, hearing with their ears, and seeing through their eyes. Jesus not only epitomized this approach but also went beyond simply imagining the pain of others to actually experiencing and transforming that pain. Philippians 2:5–7 exhorts believers to emulate this attitude:

> In your relationships with one another, have the same mindset as Christ Jesus: Who, being in very nature God, did not consider equality with God something to be used to his own advantage; rather, he made himself nothing by taking the very nature of a servant, being made in human likeness.

Radical empathy and incarnational practice remind us to go beyond *exploring* how *we* feel about *their* struggles to actually *experiencing* how *they* feel about their struggles too.

Effectively addressing racial challenges requires an understanding of the lived experiences of marginalized groups. Engaging with what they see, hear, and feel in their everyday lives can be the revelation that enables organizations, businesses, churches, and individuals to reassess and modify their actions and approaches toward them. However, empathy rooted in a profound belief in the power of connection is crucial for today's leadership practices for reasons that extend beyond effectively engaging with marginalized groups. Julia Middleton, founder of Common Purpose, acknowledges, "If for no other reason than that today's world is full of trauma, primary and secondary, empathy feels ever more essential to leading."[42]

It's important to recognize that the discipline of "incarnational practice" is not necessarily a reciprocal exercise. Historically, people of color have been expected to understand and adapt to the perspectives of white experiences for the sake of their well-being, economic advancement, and even physical survival. They are constantly expected to see through white eyes, hear with white ears, and modify their actions to suit white sensibilities.[13] Sharing her own personal experience in her book *Our Unforming*, Cindy S. Lee explains,

> As an Asian American growing up in the United States, I am trained to put the white experience at the center. As I learned history and literature, the white experience was the center. As I watched TV and movies, the white experience was the center. As I work in predominately white institutions, the white experience is the center.[44]

As a result, white people, and white Christians in particular, will need to get used to making a conscious effort to engage with perspectives outside their own racial experiences. This can happen through deliberate exploration or indirectly through relationships, such as marriage, friendships, growing up, or simply becoming immersed in multicultural environments. Such experiences can significantly broaden a person's perspective and reveal aspects of life they may not have previously considered.

Indeed, the discipline of radical empathy or engaging in incarnational practice is necessary for any majority group who normatively wields power. I practice it when I am in marginalized Global South environments. The challenge of justice, as exemplified by Jesus, involves actively choosing to understand and empathize with the experiences of the minority or less powerful groups we encounter. Emulating this approach requires stepping out of our own comfort zones to embrace and learn from perspectives that differ from our own, hopefully fostering a deeper sense of empathy in our interactions and decision-making as we do. Jesus also exemplifies this, reminding us that actions are the primary way we express empathy rather than just through words, thoughts, and prayers.

> ## JOSEPH: A METAMORPHIC AWAKENING
>
> Several years had passed since I had last seen Joseph, and I found our last interaction particularly challenging. I had felt compelled to distance myself from his organization for the sake of my own well-being. Joseph was a dynamic leader and sincere believer but had unfortunately mishandled the rising racial tensions amongst his leaders and church members. His approach of stifling debate and labeling dissenters as "woke" only exacerbated the situation. It was only a matter of time before it would all erupt, and erupt it did. The situation reached boiling point, and leaders and members alike began to vote with their feet by leaving and resigning.
>
> However, when I met Joseph again, I could see the change in him. Amidst this turmoil, something remarkable had happened—Joseph had a notable shift in disposition, a new humility, and an openness to change. Joseph had clearly been working on his "stuff" since our last interaction and had undergone a profound transformation.
>
> He spoke of mentoring a young Black man, a relationship in which he found himself becoming something of a father figure. Through this experience, Joseph noticed the biases and judgments the young man faced in his interactions with others. He saw how people regarded the young man when they were out together, how they often assumed the worst if he was boisterous and having fun, and how they judged the nature of the relationship without asking or waiting to be informed.
>
> Joseph's eyes were now open to realities he had previously ignored or even denied. And now that he had seen, he couldn't unsee. Joseph admitted that much of the learning in this mentoring

> journey was happening on his part, a humbling revelation that marked his journey toward greater awareness and empathy.
>
> I expressed how heartening it was to see the work God was doing in his life. As we hugged, I encouraged him to continue this path of growth and understanding. Joseph's response was one of gratitude, tinged with relief. He hugged me again, and this time his smile reached his eyes.
>
> "I thought you would judge me," he said. "Thank you."

JUST LEADERSHIP IN THE EARLY CHURCH

Recognizing what we might be missing in our understanding and perception of racism is invaluable. Adopting incarnational practice or a radically empathetic approach humbles us and reminds us that no one has it all, and no one knows it all, including in matters pertaining to God.

In the Christian context, every gathering for prayer, worship, Bible study, or fellowship in our workplaces or churches presents us with both discipleship opportunities and prophetic moments. The early church only gradually came to understand this, and in Acts 6:1–7, we meet them at one of many kairos moments in the biblical text and in their own version of a diversifying yet racialized environment. It is here we discover how their discipleship opportunity and prophetic moment became a key turning point for both strengthening and maturing their community, as well as fueling and accelerating the growth of the early church itself. Essentially, it is only leadership infused with justice and radical empathy that can facilitate this process. The following reveals some of the critical leadership principles that emerge from their story.

Raise Awareness

It's noteworthy that in Acts 6, it was the Hellenists, *not* the Hebrews, who noticed the persistent pattern of discrimination. And even as hard feelings and resentment began to arise, it was the Hellenists who had to make their voices heard.

This pattern reveals a common reality: Those who are least affected by structural discrimination are often the most unaware of its existence. This phenomenon is what some describe as the "curse of privilege." Father Richard Rohr said in an interview, "We largely do not recognize the structural access we enjoy, the trust we think we deserve, the assumption that we always belong and do not have to earn our belonging. All this we take for granted as normal. Only the outsider can spot these attitudes in us."[45]

This lack of awareness was evident during the racial justice protests following George Floyd's death. Many church leaders in the UK who were not directly impacted by the racial injustices being protested expressed surprise and confusion about the extent of the issues. They had *no* idea how bad things were for people of color, even within their own congregations. In fact, many church leaders contacted people within their congregations to find out if the media reports were accurate or exaggerated. Some found themselves on the receiving end of very broken and angry church members and revelations about the presence of racial injustices within their own church communities. One wise church leader I know asked the right question when he said, "How did I not know?"

Christians of color have long had to wrestle with the historical reality of who God has been for white Christianity and with the fact that the faith of white people has often been complicit with white patriarchy, slavery, colonization, and the genocide of indigenous communities. Many white Christians have yet to fully acknowledge or wrestle with that history or to ask themselves the question, "How could this have happened?"

It seems that the Hebrew-speaking believers in Acts 6 were also initially unaware of what was happening in their midst. Even the apostles, Hebrew-speaking believers themselves, were ignorant of the dynamics until the moment the Hellenists brought it to their attention. They could, of course, have dealt with it in much the same way as some church leaders continue to do to this day: "Oh, the Hellenists are imagining it. They always 'play the Hellenist card.' I think it's a foreign thing. I can't see what they're going on about, can you? Don't they know we love them? This is not a 'gospel' priority. Let's ignore it, and maybe it'll go away." But that's precisely the problem … these things don't go away. They go underground, smolder, create resentment, distrust, and deep-seated conflict. They damage the credibility of our witness and compromise the sense of genuine community we're seeking to model as followers of Jesus.

Prioritize Impact Over Intention

While it may not have been intentional, the actions of the Hebrew-speaking believers in the early church had introduced the ugly ethnocentric, xenophobic, and elitist behaviors so prevalent in their wider society into their own church behaviors and structures. This is why it is so important to distinguish between intention and impact.

Much of what needs addressing in our churches and organizations goes beyond the realm of what people *feel* about each other. While I rarely question the sincerity of people's love or good intentions, there is good reason why God asserts, "The heart is deceitful above all things!" (Jer. 17:9). Sin is not just what we *commit*; it is also what we *omit*, and although the Bible recognizes *personal sin* and individual actions, it also acknowledges *social sin* and structural oppression. The Bible consistently highlights the plight of certain groups who are regularly denied power, resources, respect, and authority. These groups are disproportionately vulnerable to injustice and disproportionately victims of injustice. Some scholars refer to them as the "quartet of the vulnerable." They include widows, orphans, immigrants, and the poor. These groups are systemically excluded from economic opportunities and social justice, as well as persistently exploited and marginalized both physically and materially.

Theologian Nicholas Wolterstorff, who popularized the term "quartet of the vulnerable," points out that God is constantly reminding his own people, as well as the surrounding nations, that widows' lives matter, orphans' lives matter, immigrants' lives matter, and poor people's lives matter, because unfortunately, sometimes both Israel and the nations behaved as if those lives didn't matter at all.[46]

We may *feel* that we aren't personally sinning against others intentionally, but if we are doing things (committing) or failing to do things (omitting) in ways that effectively reinforce or maintain social structures that preferentially impact one group of people over another, we are still "implicated subjects,"[47] and it is still sin. Much of what both white people and people of color have learned about each other is rooted in a systemic racialization that keeps reproducing itself at a level most of us are unaware of. Some refer to this underlying dynamic as "unconscious bias," a term that highlights how these ingrained beliefs and attitudes can influence our thoughts and actions without our conscious awareness.

Therefore, in Acts 6, the discriminatory challenges can be seen as embedded in structures, not just in individuals, and we must recognize the themes of power, resources, and legitimacy (mentioned earlier in this chapter). Just like the early church in Acts 6, many churches and organizations that have good intentions don't necessarily recognize these dynamics at play until the boiling point is reached.

Merely intending to do the right thing is not the same as *actually* doing the right thing (righteousness), and an intention to put things right is not the same as *actually* putting things right (justice). Metamorphic transformation always has an outward manifestation; if there is no evidence of this, we cannot assume any actual internal change has occurred.

Thankfully, in an effort to address the difference between intention and impact, more and more church and organizational leaders are choosing the route we find in Acts 6. Some describe this as the practice of "allyship." I prefer the term "radical solidarity." Because, although I appreciate the willingness of others to enter into what I may be feeling and experiencing (radical empathy), I'd much rather they did something concrete that prevented me from having to feel and experience it in the first place!

From Radical Empathy to Radical Solidarity

The difference between *feeling* like taking action and *taking action* on what we're feeling is reflected in the difference between incarnational practice and structural repentance. Radical empathy or incarnational practice is a necessary beginning that gets us oriented and motivated, but without the restorative steps of radical solidarity, what we have is aspiration rather than transformation.

The apostles in this story apply radical solidarity. They belong to the dominant group, but once the matter is brought to their attention, they respond by using their influence and their privilege to rectify the discrimination. They move beyond unproductive feelings, relinquish claims to control, refuse to prioritize the interests of their own group, and act in concert with the desires and needs of the marginalized group. Their actions affirm that "Hellenist lives matter"—not to the exclusion of Hebrew lives but in recognition that in this specific instance, it is the Hellenists who are experiencing injustice and vulnerability.

When the dominant group works on diversity and justice issues, it's crucial to move beyond feelings of guilt, shame, or fear. Although these emotions are important to acknowledge and reflect upon, they can become a huge distraction to actually getting anything done and creating necessary change. The way to acknowledge and move beyond feelings of guilt, shame, and fear is through structural repentance, similar to what follows.

The apostles call the entire church to participate in the process of repentance. Unlike an apology, as already intimated, repentance is not just a one-off event but a continuous and ongoing process. They demonstrate that followers of Jesus aren't called to pretend everything is okay or to even avoid feeling bad at all costs. Discipling moments, with all their pain and discomfort, are designed to return us to God's ways and the pursuit of his purposes. This is how the apostle Paul speaks about it in 2 Corinthians 7:11: "See what this godly sorrow has produced in you: what earnestness, what eagerness to clear yourselves, what indignation, what alarm, what longing, what concern, what readiness to see justice done."

Those who are radically empathetic initiate and engage in acts of biblical repentance that are both personal and structural because they are eager to take actual steps to put things right. This empathy leading to solidarity is the essence of "just leadership." I once overheard a church leader remark, "Romans 12:15 instructs us to 'weep with those who weep' not 'justify why we aren't weeping' or 'correct those who weep.' To weep with, we need to feel the pain. To feel the pain, we need to understand. To understand, we need to be informed. To be informed, we need to listen [read/watch/learn]."

The responsibility for our re-education ~ about racism and its impacts should not fall on the shoulders of those who experience it. Expecting our diverse friends or colleagues to provide all the answers or insights into racism places an unfair burden on them. What's more, they may or may not know the answers! No one is born with this knowledge, even if they have to live with its reality.

Listening is only one part of the journey toward understanding. Do your own work, as this will also enable you to stay aware of the evolving narratives around race and racism and will free your friends or employees of color to focus on their own well-being (and sanity!) and to volunteer rather than feel obliged to offer their contributions.

It's only as we listen, read, watch, and learn that we become better equipped to use our influence to change things where needed, especially if we are senior decision-makers and members of dominant groups. Unless radical empathy finds expression in radical solidarity, it is of little use to anyone.

Take Bold Action and Avoid Quick Fixes

The tendency of many UK church leaders has been to look for quick fixes that enable them to continue with business as usual. Yet, it is "business as usual" that got us here in the first place!

Acts 6 provides a model for addressing such challenges in a more profound and effective way that expresses radical solidarity.

1. ***Bring issues into the open.*** The apostles didn't try to suppress or ignore the concerns raised by the Hellenists. Instead, they acted in concert by bringing the issue to the attention of the entire church. This openness allowed for collective recognition, repentance, and understanding of the problem and avoided defensiveness, shame, or guilt.
2. ***Move beyond performative gestures.*** While declarations, lamentations, and discussions are important starting points, they must lead to substantive action. The apostles didn't settle for symbolic gestures or expect the Hellenists to settle for them either; they proposed a concrete solution that addressed the core issues while ensuring their continued focus on prayer and preaching.
3. ***Address power, resource, and legitimacy inequalities.*** The solution proposed by the apostles involved a redistribution of authority and resources. They empowered the church community to nominate individuals who would address the inequities, ensuring that the solution was community-driven and involved the best candidates.

Interestingly, all those chosen to address the inequities had Greek names, suggesting that the church entrusted the welfare of all the widows to the Hellenists, the ones who had been wronged! Nicolas, the last to be named, was not merely a Hellenist but a gentile convert to Judaism from paganism (Acts 6:5). Perhaps this approach demonstrated the church's commitment to rebalance the power dynamics and to validate the concerns of the marginalized group.

Unfortunately, in our politically correct environment, we would opt for parity. We'd say, "Let's make the team half Jews and half Greeks, half traditionalist and half new church, half men and half women, half young and half old." The politically correct option seldom solves the problem and is often simply another way of perpetuating the existing inequalities. It assumes a "level playing field" that doesn't actually exist. Transformation is only possible when such facades are swept away. Radical solutions are necessary precisely because those who have been used to power and privilege do not suddenly give them up simply because they and their less advantaged colleagues are represented in equal numbers. They have been socialized to believe they know better and will default to taking control and driving the agenda unless they are committed to sustaining their awareness and dying daily to self-interest and self-preservation.

The entire church responded so radically that fifteen years later, the leadership of the new center of church activity, Antioch, was more diverse than any before. According to Acts 13:1ff, there were Hellenistic and Hebraic Jews and gentiles from Africa, Asia, and southern Europe who spoke Aramaic, Greek, and many other languages.[48] In an unusual move, Luke details their ethnicities alongside their roles and gifts, highlighting the significance of their diversity, which was crucial given Antioch's own history of ethnic tensions and "race riots."[49] In all likelihood, the events of Acts 13 makes the mixed-gender leadership teams of Romans 16, including Phoebe, Prisca, and Junia, a future normal too.

Antioch's diverse community was so unique that some suggest the term "Christians" was coined there by Roman authorities (probably pejoratively) to describe a group that didn't fit into any of their existing ethnic categories (Acts 11:26; Acts 26:28).[50] It is the Antioch church's example of nonconformity, marked by its radical diversity, that became the model for the expansion of the early church, and we need to reclaim it.

The transformative journey from Acts 6 to the diverse leadership in Acts 13 demonstrates that radical, faith-filled action can significantly alter structures and cultures. Diversity consultant, author, speaker, lawyer, and corporate executive Vernā Myers powerfully and visually encapsulates this transformational journey. The following is an evolved version of Myers' insightful observation: "Diversity is being invited to the party. Equity is making it possible for you to get there. Inclusion is being asked to dance, and belonging is dancing as if you don't care who's watching!"[51]

In other words, when all our diverse leaders, organizational or church members, youth and children feel invited to the party … when we've employed the necessary means and resources to get them there … when they've been asked to dance … and when they're dancing as if they don't care who's watching, we are ready to engage with the ultimate principle of just leadership.

TRANSFORM COMMUNITIES, TRANSFORM MISSION, AND TRANSFORM YOUR WORLD

The story of Acts 6 is often used to illustrate the need for robust church structures, distributed leadership, or the importance of serving the poor. But we should also note that although Acts 6:1 shows "the disciples were increasing in numbers by leaps and bounds" (MSG), by the end of verse 7 we learn "the word of God prospered. The number of disciples in Jerusalem increased rapidly." We see how, as justice was being done in ways their society had never seen before, the church experienced further significant growth and expansion.

However, this was more than the numerical expansion described in Acts 6:1. What is described in 6:7 is exponential growth and an ever-widening circle of influence as their understanding of God's Word grew. They were now seeing the gospel spread to people groups, systems, and structures they had not succeeded in reaching before, such that even "a large number of priests became obedient to the faith" (Acts 6:7).

Individual churches and organizations can grow to a certain size by ignoring socially and culturally destructive patterns and unjust practices like racism. They can grow even larger by simply remaining homogenous. But they eventually begin to lose their credibility, as well as their spiritual and moral authority, because they seem to reinforce the status quo. Only time will tell if churches and Christian organizations today can embrace justice in their attempts to build equitable communities that transform their mission.

As mentioned earlier, missionary endeavors that value some bodies over others inevitably adopt colonial approaches that seek to conform one "inferior" community to the standards of a "superior" community, rather than embracing an incarnational, missional posture. The Holy Spirit had to confront the apostle Peter's personal biases through a dream before sending him to a gentile who wanted to be saved. Peter had to hear Cornelius's description of God's activity in his life (Acts 10) before Peter was able to confess to all present, "I now realize how true it is that God does not show favoritism but accepts from every nation the one who fears him and does what is right" (Acts 10:34–35). According to the chronology of Acts 8:26–40, Philip needed no such intervention for his encounter with the Ethiopian eunuch on the desert road that turned into a pivotal moment in the spread of the gospel into gentile territory. In both cases the gospel was advanced firstly into Ethiopia and then among the Romans. However, it's unsurprising that Philip was unencumbered by the same prejudices as Peter; he was one of the Hellenists chosen to serve the widows in the Acts 6 scenario. In biblical terms, justice is the imperative to do what is right in a manner that is fair and impartial. Philip extended this equity without question when sharing the gospel with a gentile, while Peter followed suit only after considerable soul-searching and being put to sleep for a Holy Spirit tutorial! As long as leaders and leadership are being transformed and transforming, the route to the desired destination is less important.

When the apostle Paul sought guidance from the Council of Jerusalem in Acts 15 about whether gentiles should follow Jewish customs to become Christians, it was the transformed Peter who supported him. Peter declared,

> "[God] did not discriminate between us and them, for he purified their hearts by faith. Now then, why do you try to test God by putting on the necks of Gentiles a yoke that neither we nor our ancestors have been able to bear? No! We believe it is through the grace of our Lord Jesus that we are saved, just as they are."
>
> ACTS 15:9-11

Thankfully, the Council agreed with Peter and Paul, and the gospel was able to advance unencumbered among the gentiles, and the early churches became an ever-more powerful expression of God's kingdom.

Church leaders and leaders of Christian organizations can become overly preoccupied with multiplication and numbers to the detriment of spreading gospel influence. Improved structure, distributed leadership, and service to the poor undoubtedly advance and expand the reach of the gospel. But so does overturning racism and ethnocentrism and promoting justice (not just social welfare) among the people of God. Developing irresistible Acts-13-type churches and organizations is a far more compelling mission than maintaining a theology that celebrates our numbers while explaining away our homogeneity, indifference, and inaction.

If the simple (but not easy) act of addressing racism within our churches, organizations, and missionary endeavors removes barriers to the diversity God loves and the expansion of the Great Commission Jesus gave, we should not hesitate to lead justly, to act with empathy and in solidarity with marginalized people. Only applications of biblical justice, as seen in Acts 6, can overturn racialized hierarchies in ways that further advance and expand the reach of the gospel and release the diversity of leaders required for our increasingly diversifying churches. As my friend Dele Okuwobi recently shared with me, "Diversity does not solve injustice, but where there is justice, diversity thrives. The Christian church has confused the order."

Expecting the world to change when we are little more than a mirror image of our own society is an exercise in futility. We *have* an answer, but we must also *be* an answer. The early believers transformed their version of a racialized world and renewed their mission by transforming their version of a racialized church! There are no quick fixes to racisms that have been hundreds of years in the making. But if we are prepared to invest our time, energy, and resources into developing the kind of compelling communities Jesus died for, there is no telling what might be possible.

FOR PERSONAL REFLECTION OR GROUP DISCUSSION

Racial Dynamics and Challenges

1. What racial dynamics and challenges exist *around* your neighborhood, network, work, or church environment, and why do you think this is? (Choose one.)
2. How are these mirrored *within* your church, work, or organization?

Factors Hindering or Overshadowing Action

1. Identify three factors that hinder or overshadow actions that your church or organization wish to take to bring about racial justice.
2. How could these be set aside or resolved?
3. How do individuals who aren't negatively impacted by them demonstrate their lack of awareness of racial inequalities in your context?
4. In what ways could your church or organization actively nurture radical solidarity in addressing these challenges?

Radical Empathy and Solidarity

1. What would radical empathy (incarnational practice) look like, practically speaking, in the meetings, planning, and budgeting of your church or organization?
2. What would radical solidarity (structural repentance) look like, practically speaking, in the meetings, planning, and budgeting of your church or organization?
3. What actionable steps, if implemented, could bring about a fundamental transformation in the mission of your church or organization?

TIME FOR PRAYER

Take a moment for personal or group prayer. If part of a discussion group, lift up each member, asking for guidance, strength, and clarity as they navigate through their challenges and seek growth in their exercise of *radical empathy* in their personal and leadership journey.

PART FOUR

TRANSFORMING MISSION

7

ESTHER
LEADING ON PURPOSE

Discerning Your "Whys"

> *The two most important days in life are the day you are born and the day you discover the reason why.*
> MARK TWAIN

> *Purpose connects us to the why that lies beyond our comfort and security zone.*
> SUSAN BEAUMONT

> *I don't know any other way to live but to wake up every day armed with my convictions, not yielding them to the threat of danger and to the power and force of people who might despise me.*
> WOLE SOYINKA

Although it is tempting, leaders cannot simply become all things to all people, nor can they realistically cater to everyone's needs. This is why author and organizational consultant Susan Beaumont rightly advises that the main responsibility of a leader is to clarify "how we intend to make a difference and be useful in the world moving forward."[1] Being an effective agent for change ultimately rests on our ability to establish what is and isn't ours to do. We must also aim to identify what realistically lies within our scope of influence, as it's quite possible to be a great leader in one situation and a poor leader in another. Unfortunately, the journey toward such clarity can be anxiety-inducing, leaving individuals, groups, and organizations stuck in revolving doors of crafting and re-crafting purpose statements while fretting over whether they genuinely align with God's intended purposes.

This concern is perhaps less surprising when we consider that purpose not only explains the motives behind our actions but also gives meaning to our very existence. According to the Collins Dictionary, purpose is "the reason for which something is made or done."[2] And, in discerning it, we invite God to show us who we are called to be in this world. Purpose is much more than a role, a project, or a task. Although it sometimes seems elusive, God's gift of purpose is very much alive and well within every single one of us.

In the lives of biblical figures like Peter, purpose shows up in their everyday activities. Initially a fisherman, Peter is ultimately *called* by Jesus to "fish" for people.[3] Similarly, Moses, at one time a shepherd of sheep, becomes a shepherd of people and, ultimately, the shepherd of an emerging nation. Deborah, known for dispensing wisdom and counsel, directs her purpose through her divinely appointed role as leader of Israel during the era of the Judges, which included leading the military campaign with Barak in Judges 4:9. Although purpose and calling remain unchanged, how we live out our purpose changes according to place, people, and time.

Since everyone and everything has a purpose, even churches and church movements have one too. As important as finding purpose is for individuals, communities, and organizations, it is equally critical for the vision and mission we choose to participate in, contribute to, or learn from. In the next chapter, we will see more clearly how church movements have discernable purpose alongside that of bringing people to faith in Jesus. Finding their purpose can protect movements from being hijacked and co-opted into serving merely human interests or even malevolent forces. In his book *Movements That Change the World*, Steve Addison refers to purpose using the language of the "founding charism" of a movement—a gift that's intended to benefit both recipients of that purpose and the wider church:

Monasticism modeled a deep devotion to Christ in the face of growing nominalism in the church. The Franciscans' gift to the church and the world was God's heart for the poor. The Reformation upheld the authority of Scripture and restored the truth of salvation by grace through faith. The Anabaptists emphasized the importance of discipleship and the believers' church. The Moravians were an inspiration as the first Protestant missionary order. The Methodists and Salvation Army combined evangelistic zeal and holiness with a heart for the poor. The Pentecostals rediscovered the untamed power of the Holy Spirit.[4]

Ultimately, discovering purpose depends far more on discernment and revelation than it does on invention or improvisation. Therefore, movements, organizations, communities, and individuals cannot create their God-given purpose; they can only uncover it and learn how to live it out wherever they find themselves. Thankfully, as incomprehensible as it sounds, our ability to uncover our purpose actually means more to God than it does even to us, presumably because God's own investment in progressing his overarching purpose always exceeds our own.

THE IMPORTANCE OF ASKING GOOD QUESTIONS

You may have realized by now that I have at least three great passions in life. First and foremost, I am dedicated to leadership, especially women's leadership. Second, I am committed to mission in its narrowest and broadest sense—men and women following Jesus for themselves, and I also believe we are called to proactively "earth" God's purposes by seeking to reshape our broader culture after God's own heart. My third passion relates to diversity and justice. I have written for journals and books on many aspects of this over the years while taking practical action to embody it wherever I can. However, I feel most alive when all three passions converge. Ironically, these instances of overlap are also among the most challenging and discomforting moments of my life. But I've come to realize that embracing these intersections is more rewarding, despite the discomfort, than actually trying to evade them. It is precisely when I find myself within these "tight" places that I truly express who I am and what God has called me to be in the world.

As a result, I have come to understand that my ultimate driving force is geared toward the development and empowerment of change-making leaders who understand their *own* calling and purpose. As I reflect on my youth, I realize I was engaged in this even while I was working on a factory production line selling bread and doughnuts and, much later, Elvis Presley memorabilia, and filing pension reports and eye test results. Long before I considered myself a leader or follower of Jesus, the seeds of purpose had been sown by God and were in the process of being revealed. I also practiced developing leaders as a student by leading a pioneering drama group while I was at university. Again, I did this without really thinking about it when I pastored churches in London and then again in Birmingham, UK. I continue to do it today and imagine I'll be developing change-makers every day until God calls me home.

My commitment to metamorphs, those who lead both from and for transformation, means I invest a significant amount of my time and energy in coaching and mentoring leaders in a variety of settings—be it churches, communities, or the marketplace. I am therefore acutely aware that asking good questions—and asking them well—is an essential skill for coaches and mentors. I've discovered that gaining clarity on "purpose" comes far more easily when we proactively ask critical questions of God and of ourselves because good questions help us engage in the kind of internal dialogue that encourages matters of purpose to bubble up to the surface. When this happens, we discover that our answers to questions we have in common reveal the exclusive and specific nature of purpose. Purpose is indeed the unique "why" of every leader, organization, and movement that makes them and their contribution to the world very different from anyone else's.

However, the kind of questions capable of mining such depths have characteristics that are worthy of brief exploration. First, most are open-ended and cannot be answered with a simple yes or no. This means the best questions are textured as "what, why, when, where, how, tell me about, what are your thoughts on …?" questions. Second, good questions are perceptive and intuitive, in that they pay attention to what is explicit and evidently visible but also to what is implicit, not being said, and therefore "hidden" between the lines. Third, good questions are often direct and cut to the heart of whatever matter is in the spotlight. Fourth, good questions invite helpful introspection in others and encourage a degree of self-awareness and self-management. Finally, great questions safely, but often "unexpectedly," uncover hidden fears and reveal deeper issues that might also need exploration or confrontation.

In my journey of leadership and ministry, I've been incredibly blessed to be on the receiving end of many such thought-provoking questions. Some of the most extraordinary women and men I've ever interacted with have posed them precisely for my benefit. I've been grateful for the way each one of them has brought their own distinctive perspective to the table while serving as an exceptional mentor or coach. They have had the (sometimes unnerving) knack of knowing exactly what to ask, when to ask it, and even how to ask in ways that both disturb and enrich my life and leadership simultaneously. They have been masters of the art of bringing both comfort and discomfort, a skill very much needed in today's leadership environment. I'm grateful that many of them continue to do this for me, even today. With God's help, and despite myself, they have managed to steer me toward becoming the leader I am today and the leader I aspire to be tomorrow.

Even if there was no more to questions than this, the mere experience of being on both the receiving *and* giving end of such interactions has deepened my appreciation for the profound impact a well-timed, thoughtful question can have. This is particularly true when it is posed by a caring yet critical friend (with the emphasis on "caring" and "friend"). Even so, I've never encountered transformative questions quite like the questions God asks, and there are valuable lessons to be learned from these too.

LEARNING FROM GOD'S QUESTIONS

There are at least 300 questions attributed to God in the Old Testament, and Jesus is recorded as asking 307 questions across all 4 Gospels. Yet, of the 183 questions asked *of* Jesus in the Gospels, he answers only 3 of them directly. It appears that God is far less interested in answering our questions than he is in asking a few of his own. Unfortunately, we can be so preoccupied with the questions we have for God that we are probably missing the very crucial questions God has for us. Since God asks questions for many different reasons in the Bible, it would be a shame to miss the significance of even one of them.

We witness God using questions as a means of establishing, nurturing, and advancing relationships—both with individuals and with his entire community. For instance, in Genesis 16:8, as Hagar flees through a perilous wilderness to escape the mistreatment and indifference of her masters Sarai and Abram, God inquires, "Where have you come from, and where are you going?" In the exact moment she is most likely to feel abandoned, invisible, and forgotten, she has an encounter with God that leads her to do something no man or woman has ever done before or since in the biblical narrative: Hagar names God as "*El Roi*," on the basis of her interaction with him: "The God who sees me" (v. 13).[5]

God also poses questions designed to prompt introspection, self-correction, redirection, and restoration within individuals, families, and nations. For instance, in Exodus 4 (examined in chapter three of this book), as Moses wrestles with his overwhelming sense of inadequacy and perhaps even his own indifference, God asks him, "What is that in your hand?" (v. 2). In that crucial moment, Moses realizes that, aided by God, he possesses greater potential and is meant for a far more significant destiny than he has ever imagined.

At pivotal moments in salvation history, some of God's inquiries directed at key individuals mark significant turning points in the trajectory of God's people—for better or worse. In Ezekiel 37:3, the prophet is caught up in a vision of a valley strewn with dry bones that depicts both the dire circumstances of God's people as well as their profound possibilities. In this moment God inquires of Ezekiel, "Can these bones live?" Amid the sensory overload and what must appear to be an obvious impossibility, the prophet somehow finds faith enough to trust that God still has all the answers. "You alone know," Ezekiel responds.

But make no mistake, God does not pose questions in search of information he lacks. In fact, what is taking place seems more akin to a teacher calling on a student to gauge their understanding and to discover what the student knows. (Again, see Moses in chapter three.) "Where are you?" God asks the man and woman who hide from him in Genesis 3:9, inquiring into more than their mere physical whereabouts. Having eaten the "forbidden" fruit in the Garden of Eden, they are nowhere to be found, and it soon becomes abundantly clear that our first parents are in a decidedly poor place, emotionally, psychologically, and even spiritually.

Whenever God asks a question, it is intended to unveil truth to *us*. He wants *us* to see the answer he already knows. "Where is your brother?" God demands after Cain murders Abel and conceals the act (Gen. 4:9). Cain famously retorts with a counter question, "Am I my brother's keeper?" To which the underlying answer from outside the text seems to be "Yes, you are."

Isaiah 46:10 declares that God knows "the end from the beginning." In other words, nothing is hidden from him. God doesn't ask questions because *he* needs answers. God asks questions because *we* need answers! This is particularly evident in the interaction between Jesus and his disciples in Matthew

16:15–17, where Jesus asks them what people have been speculating regarding his true identity. He then asks directly, "But ... Who do you say I am?" Simon Peter responds, "You are the Messiah, the Son of the living God." To which Jesus acknowledges, "Blessed are you, Simon son of Jonah, for this was not revealed to you by flesh and blood, but by my Father in heaven."

Leadership development is itself shifting from the expectation that leaders will provide the right answers to empowering them to ask better questions. This includes practicing inquiries like, "What haven't I considered? What requires my engagement or disengagement? Who haven't I heard from? When is it appropriate to say yes or no? How do I navigate the specific challenges or conflicts facing me right now? Why am I invested in this? Does this align with my purpose and calling?"

However, the principle of asking, listening, and learning is just as important for fostering a meaningful relationship with God. Regrettably, our communication with him is frequently characterized by a barrage of one-way traffic of unfiltered thoughts, words, asks, and demands. Rarely do we consider whether God has something to say or even ask first.

As we have seen, God's questions possess a powerful ability to provoke transformative change in those they are directed toward. So, we should learn to emulate their intent and emphasis when formulating our own prayerfully considered questions. We should ask questions with transformation at heart rather than a quest for information, focusing on what others need to discover rather than what we want to know. Of course, God's questions also carry the weight of God's creative presence, but Proverbs 18:21 states that "Death and life are in the power of the tongue" (ESV). So, if handled well, our questions can also carry the weight of God's presence in ways that lead others and ourselves from where we are to where we really need to be.

ASKING QUESTIONS ON PURPOSE

As intimated in chapters three and six, we live in a world where even the most well-intentioned Christian leader can become an "implicated subject" by consciously and unconsciously promoting convictions and carrying out actions that lead to the potential destruction of God's kingdom purposes.[6] These actions could include making it more difficult for people to hear and respond to the gospel, concentrating more and more wealth into fewer and fewer hands, exacerbating rather than healing divisions within and between communities, leading communities toward the brink of environmental crisis, and promoting the multiplication of weaponry with greater killing power than ever before. You may wish to add your own examples to this list. The point is, we should be cautious about promoting the popular notion of "effective" leadership when some leadership is clearly misguided, misleading, and downright ungodly.

Just because a leader *can* do something doesn't mean they *should* do it. We must always be ready to question what we are doing, how we are going about it, and, more importantly, why we are doing it in the first place. If the task of a Christian leader is to focus on the singular goal of advancing God's purpose and extending God's kingdom (which I believe it is), everything is not open to us. True effectiveness can only be measured by its alignment with God's purposes. Whether we can make things happen is irrelevant; whether we can make godly things happen, however, is beyond critical. Phil Thomas, founder and director of Transformations, frames this concern beautifully:

> The type of leadership principles which are biblical are those which are more pertinent to purpose rather than effectiveness. This is because for Christians, the most important leadership questions are "why am I doing this?" and "how will it further God's kingdom?" Contrastingly, the mainstream leadership literature mostly focuses upon effectiveness and asks the question "how do we attain certain outcomes?"[7]

Any achievement that strays from God's purposes or that lacks a leader's commitment to being both responsible and accountable to God's Spirit and community should be approached with caution.

Clearly the Holy Spirit can bring about transformation with or without our help, so our "effectiveness" is unlikely to explain why God continues to involve us in his change processes. Instead, our willingness to redirect our potentially destructive tendencies into purposefully transformative ones while embracing God's metamorphic intent is more likely to lie closer to the truth.

If we are to experience transformation personally and facilitate the transformation of others around us "from glory to glory," the questions that should guide us must be fundamentally purpose-driven and always aimed at the "why" of all we do and not just the "what." We should also be concerned with whether we truly aspire to Christlikeness in all our dealings with others or whether we are indifferent and willing to run rough-shod over them.

In order to consistently lead with purpose and make purpose our guiding force in all our decision-making, we must ask four fundamental purpose-driven questions. These questions are surprisingly simple and yet deeply profound. They also all begin with the word "why": Why me? Why here? Why this? and Why now?

These questions are wonderfully personified in the biblical story of yet another metamorph: Esther. Her narrative, which revolves around her sudden elevation to a position of significant leadership, evokes each of these inquiries. Her journey also sheds light on some of the essential themes every leader should ponder when navigating both challenging and uncertain times.

Our four questions—Why me? Why here? Why this? and Why now?—will reveal how Esther came to realize her God-given purpose. When we consider them in the context of Esther's story, we are immediately struck by the truth that not only does every person have a unique story to tell but also that God is purposefully working something of significance in and through every precious life story.

Much like Esther, every person needs an opportunity to understand their unique purpose in the world. Esther was about to discover hers, and if we take these questions seriously, we could also discover what it means to lead toward rather than away from our God-given purpose and mission. These simple yet powerful questions are as relevant today as they've ever been.

WHY ME? EXPLORING MY UNIQUENESS

If you're like me and have ever wondered, "Why me?" then Esther's journey could well provide points of resonance with yours. The first point is that Christian leadership can emerge from anyone and anywhere.

Like so many of the biblical figures we talk about, admire, and learn from, Esther was far from being a "religious professional." From Abraham to Deborah and Jesus to Paul, few were priests, Levites, Sadducees, or Teachers of the Law, or what we would consider "ordained" religious professionals today. Instead, many were ordinary people with regular jobs, playing typical roles within their respective communities. They demonstrate that, although formal religious leadership may be intended for a select few, anyone can exercise the kind of spiritual leadership each one of them displayed.

Abraham was a businessman, Deborah a prophetic civic leader, David a military man and songwriter, Isaiah a politician, Amos a shepherd, Nehemiah a civil servant, Peter a commercial fisherman, and even Jesus was a carpenter (and I suspect no one had cause to complain about his work!). Paul too was a religious scholar and a tentmaker.

Each exercised profound spiritual leadership wherever they were in life, and each knew how to pray, influence, and bless their respective communities. We too are called to influence our environments by serving as spiritual leaders within God's community and contributing positively to wider society. However, to be truly effective by God's measure, we must first understand the nature of our purpose and the primary sphere of our impact.

The story of Esther should motivate each of us to serve God to the best of our ability in whatever circumstance we find ourselves. Any position can enable us to influence the lives of others for good, be it within our family, community, church, business, or other sphere, and to fulfill some crucial leadership role.

Esther was called upon to exhibit spiritual leadership during a pivotal time for her family, people, community, and even the known world. However, she had no idea of God's intentions and certainly no personal understanding of her own purpose, so it took some time for the nature of what she was being invited to do and who she was invited to become to fully dawn on her. In one sense, she stumbled upon her destiny and the realization she could serve God and her people best within the sphere of governance (albeit of an empire). Even then, her path to purpose was anything but straightforward. Like so many of us, she needed both the questions and the challenge of those closest to her before she was willing to embark on her metamorphic journey.

Esther's story offers us hope and insight into how we sometimes find ourselves in the most unexpected roles, engaged in activity we'd simply rather not engage in, and sometimes with people we'd simply rather not know. It also points to what we should be doing with even the little influence we have been entrusted with. In other words, Esther has prophetic significance in helping us address the "Why me?" question for ourselves.

At first glance, it seems as if Esther's outstanding beauty was responsible for her eventual role as Israel's "savior." After all, she found herself among all the local beauties when the palace rounded up prospective brides for no less than the king. But in truth, we and Esther discover she was far more than just a pretty face. A compelling purpose, a calling to lead, and ultimately an assignment to "save" her people from potential genocide activated gifts and skills she may never have known she possessed.

A Woman of Substance

For women called to leadership at an extraordinary time in history, there's an undeniable resonance with Esther's journey. Many of us, like Esther, find ourselves thrust into roles and positions we didn't necessarily choose and navigating leadership paths we didn't necessarily seek. My own journey mirrors this, and I'm certain that some of you, male or female, can relate.

Esther was called to lead in an era when women lacked substantial power or authority. The fate of Queen Vashti—her predecessor who was unceremoniously removed from her position—set a stark precedent. Esther's position in the king's court was equally precarious. She understood that even as queen, one misstep could cost her everything. Her success hinged on her ability to please the men around her. From her cousin Mordecai to those in the king's inner circle, including Hegai (who had charge of the king's harem), Shaashgaz (the king's eunuch in charge of the concubines), and finally the king himself.

Although globally, some women continue to live close to this reality even today, for many others the situation has thankfully evolved since Esther's time. Yet, despite the progress that's been made, women continue to face significant resistance and negativity toward their leadership—within both church and society. In other words, although so much has seemingly changed, in fundamental ways, so very little is different. A 2023 LinkedIn data survey report based on figures from the US and Canada begins:

> Despite years of continual efforts to promote gender equality in the workplace, women remain underrepresented in leadership positions. This lack of diversity not only limits organizations' potential to thrive but also reinforces gender biases.[8]

The creation story of Genesis makes it clear that without woman, God's image in creation is incomplete. The mandate to rule is given to both male and female, not just to the male. This means there are unique contributions God intends to make through you, not *despite* you being a woman (or indeed a man) but precisely *because* of it!

Research indicates that a purpose-driven ethos, although recently becoming more appealing to men, resonates strongly with women in leadership roles.[9] It is women who seem to pursue and increasingly secure leadership roles in what are now known as purpose-driven sectors.[10] These include education, healthcare, NGOs, and government—in other words, environments that have goals beyond profit and that have a mission focused on uplifting and assisting others through their products or services. Therefore, we shouldn't be surprised that more and more women are leading within churches and Christian organizations (whether in acknowledged or unacknowledged ways).

Women recognized as being purpose-driven are particularly celebrated for their empathy, sensitivity, and inclusiveness. They are often entrepreneurial trailblazers who challenge the norm and disrupt global industries. With the growing consensus that women excel in leadership roles, often outperforming men,[11] it raises a critical question: If women are excelling in leadership, especially in purpose-driven roles, why aren't they being invited to lead more often and in more places?

The Genesis narrative suggests that women are intended to stand as co-stewards alongside men. In fact, it is my conviction that until this becomes the norm across business, public sectors, community groups, voluntary organizations, and yes, even the church, God's grand purposes for this world will ultimately remain unfulfilled.

We need women's leadership more than ever before as we stand on the cusp of an extraordinary moment in history. If the church hesitates to lead, the fulfillment of God's purposes may "arise from another place" (Esther 4:14). (Balaam's ass comes to mind! [Num. 22:21–38].) Even Jesus said that if his disciples are silenced, the "stones will cry out" (Luke 19:40). God's purposes will always be fulfilled ... the question is simply "how?"

In this story, Mordecai recognizes the limits of his own influence to change things. It is Esther's wisdom that rallies her people, earns the king's empathy, and eventually elevates Mordecai to a governmental role. Whether or not we have truly grasped the full extent of our influence, particularly as women who lead, identifying with Esther's prophetic significance could profoundly shape our understanding of who we are and what we bring to leadership. With this understanding, we would be more likely to embrace what it means to be driven by purpose, and perhaps even reclaim our unique gifts while confidently establishing God's purposes in ways that make sense to us.

An Outsider on the Inside

Esther has even more to teach us on the question of "Why me?" because, much like her, we do not always fit into what's considered the norm.

Esther was living under Persian rule, yet, despite having resided in Persia for many years, Esther's people were perceived as outsiders by the Persian Empire. They were considered outsiders not just on the basis of their faith (as we shall soon see) but also on the basis of their culture and ethnicity.

The subtle accusation that accompanied Haman's assertions sounds oh-so familiar in today's world: *They are outsiders, unassimilated and segregated; they pose a threat; we cannot afford to tolerate them.* Haman's specific words to the king were: "There is a certain people *dispersed* among the peoples in all the provinces of your kingdom who keep themselves *separate*. Their customs are *different* from those of all other people, and they *do not obey* the king's laws" (Esther 3:8, emphasis mine).

If you have ever felt like an outsider, ethnically, socially, or because of your ability, appearance, or speech, Esther's story mirrors this sentiment. Yet, as she embraced her call to leadership as an outsider on the inside in challenging times, her people would be established in ways that no one could have imagined.

God, it seems, frequently uses outsiders—those seemingly out of place—to achieve great things. He uses the second or last born instead of the first. David, the one who didn't initially get invited to the anointing party … Joseph, the one none of the others liked and ended up left for dead down a well … Ruth, a Moabitess rather than a Hebrew. From the Old Testament to the New, the Bible is full of the "out of place," the somewhat different, and the downright odd!

This resonates with me on all sorts of levels, as I've shared in earlier chapters. I too struggled in this way as the lone Black woman UK Baptist minister until I recognized my differences were positively shaping the nature of my influence. I saw that I could offer distinctive perspectives that blessed others and furthered God's purposes. It isn't just the uniqueness of our "why" that is an intentional part of God's design. Who we are uniquely and what we have to offer, specifically as women and as outsiders, is all part of God's design too.

There's a prophetic correlation between Esther's exile leadership and your own distinctiveness. Your background, your story, your challenges, your joys, and your breakthroughs are all part of God's plan. There's a wonderful resonance and a prophetic correlation with Esther.

Why you? Why ever not?!

Once we understand and accept our unique contribution to fulfilling God's purposes, we can ask the next purpose-full and crucial question Esther's narrative raises for us.

WHY HERE? UNDERSTANDING MY CONTEXT

Whether we believe that God intentionally places us in specific situations to work through us or that he uses the circumstances we already find ourselves in doesn't really alter what it means to be purposefully located. Attempts to pin God down to some formulaic way of working when it comes to where we find ourselves are ultimately futile. His ways seldom, if ever, conform to any human logic and, as John 3:8 suggests, "the wind [still] blows wherever it pleases."

We might believe that we arrive at a particular set of circumstances due entirely to coincidence and therefore attribute our specific role or current position to "chance." Or we attribute it to having been selected for the job, a partner's career move, or because it fits in with the school run or our other daily routines. Or we're convinced that it's because someone noticed us and gave us an opportunity, or because we demonstrated proficiency in certain skills, or there was alignment with a role that suited us. Whatever the factors are that have played a part, they do not fully explain the "why" behind our presence in a particular role or place.

Mordecai said to Esther, "Who knows but that you have come to your royal position for such a time as this?" (Esther 4:14). If we are open and willing, God can and will work in us and through us wherever we find ourselves because God's overarching purpose and God's purpose for our individual lives will always find a way. The important factor here is that purpose is never hindered or derailed, regardless of the circumstance in which we find ourselves.

The story of Esther suggests that we should always look beyond the surface-level explanations of life's circumstances and seek a more profound understanding of our purpose and place in the world.

Here for a Purpose

In some way or another, location is always a part of the divine plan. Esther is one of the most intriguing books in the Bible because God is never mentioned. Yet the text of Esther reveals a tale of intricately woven behind-the-scenes activity. For example, we are permitted to know Esther's true identity when no one other than Mordecai knows. We are permitted to know that Mordecai uncovers a plot to assassinate the king. We are permitted to know that the king forgets how Mordecai saves him and is later reminded for some mysterious reason. We are permitted to know of the king's intention to honor Mordecai and that simultaneously, Haman is secretly plotting to annihilate Mordecai together with all the Jews.

But we are not permitted to know what God is up to or indeed where God is at work. Instead, we get to witness the events unfolding at the same time as Esther, Mordecai, Haman, and everyone else! All the while, nothing presents itself as mere coincidence in the book of Esther. Every event in the narrative bears the hallmarks of an orchestration—yes, even the toughest and most challenging events of all.

As a theologian, I know I'm expected to uncover some deep and profound meaning in the fact that God's name isn't mentioned in the text and to either assume the absence of God or a lack of faith in those who suffer. Yet, I've encountered too many individuals who are confident of God's presence and faithfulness despite their experiences of torture, war, poverty, loss, and terror. So I do not believe that the absence of God's name in this text suggests the absence of God or a lack of belief and faith on the part of those who suffer. Only those confident of God's existence and engagement in their affairs would pray and fast, as Esther and her people did. For me, the omission of God's name underscores the mystery of the way God works. It signals God's covert activity rather than his total absence.

The book of Esther describes a people displaced by exile, dealing with the reality of multiple wounds as well as multiple griefs. At one time, they too may have believed they knew exactly how God was "supposed" to work in the world. Perhaps they had even boxed God in, as we sometimes do. Sometimes, multiple question marks, wounds, and losses are the journey we take before finally handing back the reins of control and acknowledging there is much more to God than we know or have ever experienced before. Perhaps they also needed to discover the God they did not know and that God is, after all, an utter mystery.

In our own narratives, amidst our struggles and challenges, we also slowly learn to recognize that, even when it appears otherwise, God is always present, intricately weaving his influence throughout it all. In such seasons, we are urged to seek out the fingerprints of God, particularly when we find ourselves preoccupied with the bootprints of the enemy!

The nature of our location and the circumstances of our lives are not unknown to God. In a sense, where we are in this current season of life is not random in the way we might expect, for we are always intentionally drawn into the overarching purpose of God, who has the ability to select anyone yet specifically chooses us. I used to joke with my friends that the job I wanted I didn't get, and the one I didn't want was the one I ended up with! I was, of course, being totally serious!

When God is working out his purpose through our purpose, our narrative becomes part of his much larger story. Indeed, it has never been solely ours to write. The place you're in, the community you serve, the family you're from, and the workplace you're part of are all woven into God's overarching plan. You might yearn for a different scenario, but God is working out a purpose right where you are, and there are no accidents in God's final design. Whether you wish you were elsewhere, long for a different family, or dream of a different job, God is actively working in and through your current circumstances at this specific time. Just like Esther, you may find yourself in your current situation for such a time as this, as God works out his purpose through yours.

Like Esther in a foreign land, you might not feel exactly as if you belong, but there's something special you can accomplish because your unique location offers opportunities that are unavailable elsewhere. Embrace it, for it holds a purpose beyond what meets the eye. Stick with it, for such a time as this! And when you finally get a clear sense that God is calling you to move on, whatever you do, please do not overstay or hang on for longer than is needed. Your task is done, and it is time for you to pass on the baton.

Esther didn't just end up in exile in a foreign land; she found herself within the palace walls. She wasn't just anywhere in general; she was somewhere in particular. Esther occupied a specific and significant position right at the heart of the empire with her location, granting her unique opportunities no one else could or would have.

If our location is neither incidental nor accidental, then it has implications. It is more than an address or a set of circumstances; there's an assignment, there's a calling, and there's a purpose. Our specific contexts present us with unique challenges and responsibilities. Mordecai's words to Esther echo this sentiment: "And who knows but that you have come to royal position for such a time as this."

Standing Out Where You Are

In addition to being exiled in a foreign country, Esther was part of a faith community. Unbeknownst to her, part of her purpose was to influence and represent that community.

We have already seen that, despite having resided in Persia for many years, Esther's people were viewed as being different. They had some distinct laws and unique customs and lived by what were often a very different set of values. The fact that they stood out in this way may have created friction from time to time within the empire. Haman, the antagonist of the story, was enraged that Mordecai would not bow to him like all the others. When he learned of Mordecai's Jewish identity, Haman aimed to exterminate all Jews by highlighting their differences to the king, noting their unique customs and alleged non-compliance with royal laws.

Along with all the Jews, Esther found herself at a critical juncture where her identity and conviction would be tested. She now had to know who she was, what she was about, and what she stood for. Unexpectedly, and somewhat ironically, instead of wholly agitating, disturbing, and destabilizing the Jews as Haman had intended, his actions seem to have created an opportunity for them to take stock and reaffirm their faith, their values, their principles, and even their priorities.

Esther's story is a reminder that although faith has the power to make a difference, it can also court significant danger. It is also a reminder that faith is not an optional extra, a set of traditions, comforting rituals, and practices, or even some kind of leisure activity that Christians "do" in their spare time. On the contrary, faith in Jesus is central to who we are and what we do. This faith should always guide our actions and affect what we choose to do and not do. It should influence what we stand up for or choose to sit out, what we promote or don't promote, and what we champion or don't champion. Faith should shape what we endorse or reject. For faith sits at the center of the compass called purpose and guides our choices, our decisions, and our actions, even in the face of our adversities and moral dilemmas.

Esther exemplifies a leader having to navigate the conditions of exile. She finds herself surrounded by those who do not share her values, her faith, or her convictions. She is a member of the people of God thrust into chaotic conditions where her convictions and commitments are severely tested.

We are currently living through some of the most testing times for Christians in the Western world. While these difficulties are not new to Christians who constantly face persecution, war, and poverty in other parts of the world, they are unfamiliar territory for many of us. Whether engaged with work, sharing the gospel, offering prayers, or standing against injustice, we often face growing criticism. We find ourselves being noticed but not always in the ways we would like. It's not that people mind us being Christians; they often willingly applaud our efforts and good deeds, but they would prefer it if we avoided discussing certain, um … sensitive topics, like … what it means to follow Jesus!

Amidst the charged protests for racial justice following George Floyd's tragic death, I discovered that standing up for what's right can cost and invite strong opposition. By its very nature, leading puts us out in front. It exposes us and leaves us both visible and vulnerable. In the same way, leadership also draws attention and inevitably attracts hostile opposition from the "usual suspects," like the Hamans of the world. These individuals, institutions, or organizations benefit from the way things are, so will often proactively resist anyone who dares to rock the boat.

However, and perhaps surprisingly, opposition can also arise from the least expected places, such as those who would ultimately benefit from any potential change itself. When Christians attack other Christians, it is sometimes referred to as an exchange of "friendly fire," a military term used when shots fired by one's own side accidentally hit an ally instead of the enemy. Despite Christians sharing the same faith, their "exchange of fire" is often far from friendly or even accidental! I remember being deeply shocked when reading some of the lesser-known stories of the civil rights era. While today, many celebrate the activism and courage of people like Dr. Martin Luther King Jr., only a tiny fraction of church leaders and their congregations marched alongside him or even supported his efforts. There was expected and significant resistance from white church leaders and their communities. In 2018, the editors of *Christianity Today*, a well-known evangelical publication with a global reach, went on record as formally apologizing for their opposition to Dr. King and the civil rights movement.[12] However, what many may not know is that many Black churches and their leaders also opposed King, his methods, and even the fight for civil rights itself. Historian Barbara Dianne Savage remarks that "Black churches, their members, and their ministers were crucial to what the [civil rights] movement achieved, but it never involved more than a small minority of Black religious people."[13]

We often imagine ourselves immune to the toxic fumes of, in this case, racialized atmospheres, as if we could never personally suffer its ill effects, be impacted by its presence, or implicated in its evils. Instead, we imagine ourselves always in step with God and on the right side of history as if this were a "fait accompli" simply because we claim to be followers of Jesus. However, history tells a different story of how even "committed" Christians can act tribally, potentially against their own best interests, or refrain from stepping forward, fearing backlash, condemnation, ridicule, or indeed change itself. Of course, like the editors of *Christianity Today*, some eventually realize that it is Jesus they've been "persecuting" all along, much like Saul on the road to Damascus in Acts 9:4, and they take steps to repent publicly. However, many do not. It's important to note that believers, both white and Black, who now honor and benefit from the achievements of the civil rights movement, might not have been advocates at the time. Worse still, we might even have been among the antagonists.

Part of the correlation we face as we consider Esther's narrative is not whether we are legitimate members of the people of God but what kind of Christian we are choosing to be. If others, including the Hamans of our time, would hesitate to "accuse" us of being Christian or would struggle to identify the distinctive telltale signs of our commitment to Jesus in moments of much-needed social change like the civil rights era, then we have our answer. Metamorphosis is, of course, open to all, but some will resist, misunderstand, or even willfully mislead, resulting in the degeneration and deformation discussed in chapter one. If Esther initially resisted the call to act courageously, it is very possible that we might do so too.

Although Christians must inevitably reinterpret the gospel for each new era and generation, there are some things about us that should never change. We are always called to be salt and light, even when few others step forward and some strongly disagree. Our values, ethics, commitments, and priorities should diverge from the world around us whenever necessary. Even if we fail at everything else, the one thing we really cannot afford to fail at is being Christlike. Indeed, if we claim to follow Jesus, this is the one thing everyone in and beyond church circles will hold us accountable to.

Over the years, I've been privileged to preach at the political party conferences of both the UK Labour and Conservative parties (our two main political parties) for their opening services. In those moments, I found myself reminding political leaders that churches and Christian organizations aren't simply *moved* to do good for others; they are *led* to do good. We are not simply following our hearts when we engage in our various activities; many Christians would categorically say they are seeking to follow Christ's example. We are following our leader, Jesus, and as his followers, we do not primarily exist to serve a government's interests; we follow another higher order of governance and authority, and sometimes our King guides us to counter or even challenge a government's wishes.

For Esther, this would eventually mean standing up, being countercultural, and going against the flow of even her own inclinations. The challenge for us, at such a time as this, is to rise up and be counted—to be metamorphs who lead both from and for transformation.

Esther's narrative is a reminder that we will sometimes be the minority voice "standing in the gap" on behalf of entire communities, whether Congolese, Ukrainians, Afghanis, Palestinians, Jews, Syrians, the impoverished, widows, or immigrants. Even when the Hamans of this world "spin" their narratives of fear and reprisal, we will refuse to be co-opted and led toward God's kingdom truth instead.

Although we must understand both our unique contribution to fulfilling God's purposes and why we find ourselves in a specific place, we must ensure that we are grounded in a steadfast faith and followship of Jesus … which sometimes calls us to stand up and stand out. And when that happens, and conflict inevitably arises, we must simply ask, "Why this?" the very next question that follows.

WHY THIS? IDENTIFYING MY CALLING

Your location has specific implications for your calling—and there is a divine assignment God is entrusting to you. It's not merely about your occupation, role, or job description; it transcends that. Your work, wherever it may be, is also a ministry—and an opportunity to manifest the kingdom of heaven on earth.

The language of calling isn't limited to those training to be ministers, pastors, and clergy; it has purpose way beyond this. It extends to anyone who understands their work as a sacred ministry and a place where the kingdom of heaven can open up into the earth through them.

Esther was born into a Jewish family. Her Hebrew name, Hadassah, is based on the root word for "myrtle tree." But her Persian name, Esther, although meant to conceal her true identity and heritage, also means "star," adding an ironic twist to her story.

Leaders can't do everything, but each of us is crafted to shine at something. Mordecai's reminder to Esther echoes this sentiment: "For if you remain silent at this time, relief and deliverance ... will arise from another place" (Esther 4:14). In other words, although relief and deliverance may come from elsewhere, no one can do what you're called to do in quite the way that you can.

This is partly why I dedicate most of my time to mentoring leaders, whether men or women. It's why we established Next Leadership,[14] to draw out remarkable influence by encouraging individuals to shine in their unique ways and to hold them accountable to their God-given possibilities. Your opportunities will always be shaped to fit you, so as a mentor and coach, my task is not to hold people accountable to what *I* think they should be doing but to what *they* believe God is asking of them.

MEERA: METAMORPHICALLY REPURPOSED

As Meera and I sat down together for the first time in ages, her heavy sigh hinted at an underlying anxiety; for some reason, she was especially burdened today.

"What's on your mind?" I inquired gently, sensing something was amiss.

"I think I might be called to pastor a congregation," she said, her tone heavy with despair.

Curious, I probed deeper, "What's brought this on?"

Meera was at a crossroads in her life and currently pondering a number of options that could lead her down any number of different pathways. Perhaps something new had been thrown into the mix.

Meera had previously held powerful senior roles in global business and possessed a deep passion for integrating God's purposes into that realm. She also actively contributed to her local church's boards and committees and had helped them navigate their way through some very "sticky" projects. It turned out that this was partly the source of her current discomfort. She explained that recent "suggestions" from some committee members about doing more for the local congregation were weighing heavily on her.

"Could you do more?" I asked.

"I thought I was doing my best, given my other commitments. You know me, I like to do church wherever I am. But the other day, someone suggested I should train to become a pastor ... I've been feeling awful ever since, and now I'm dreading going to church in case others start saying the same thing."

"What do you sense God is asking of you?" I questioned.

"Well, I'm still passionate about steering businesses toward greater social and environmental responsibility ... but I guess God must be asking me to do the church thing. But I'm really struggling with it ..." Her last few words were barely more than a whisper.

"Has anyone ever said you'd make a great pastor, even the person who suggested it?" I inquired.

"No," she replied. "I'm not great with people in that way, and everyone kind of knows it."

As a pastor myself for many years and knowing Meera's heart, I knew she was willing to follow God's call, even if it contradicted her own desires. I looked long and hard at her and wondered how I was going to shape the thought that was making its way to my mouth.

"Meera, not everything is a nail in need of a hammer, even if others think so. In all honesty, I think you'd make a terrible pastor! Besides, you're awesome in business, and you have vision for making it more like God's kingdom. Unless God redirects you, assume you're on the right path," I advised.

Visibly relieved, a glimmer of hope spread across her face. "Really?" she grinned. "You think I'd make a terrible pastor?"

This, it seemed, brought her the most comfort, and she beamed the broadest smile I've seen from anyone in a very long time.

Spiritual Dimensions of Calling

Esther engaged her calling spiritually, as seen in her direction for fasting and (presumably) prayer. What God entrusts to you is always going to be *you-shaped*, but it will also be *God-sized*! It will always require God's involvement, such that without prayer, our efforts will ultimately prove futile.

Some of the forces we battle against do not have human origins.

Attempting to fight against spiritually inspired malevolence without spiritually empowered weapons is frankly asking for a whole other dimension of trouble. In Daniel 10:10–19, we learn that although God heard Daniel's prayer as soon as he had prayed, the angel (Gabriel) who came in response to that prayer said he would have been there earlier but had been detained for twenty-one days by "the prince of the kingdom of Persia" (v. 13). Whatever the precise meaning of this phrase, it is clear that forces beyond our human understanding seek to resist our prayers and God's intentions in ways we cannot begin to imagine. There is a spiritual dimension to leadership that we dare not ignore.

By calling for a three-day extended period of prayer and fasting, Esther acknowledged there was more at stake than was immediately accessible to human sensibilities. By encouraging everyone to engage together, Esther also empowered herself and God's people to become conscious of their shared common purpose and to pray together in a spirit of agreement. This act of leadership may even have enabled them to discover their individual purpose within God's wider purposes.

Fasting and prayer wasn't all that Esther called for. Otherwise, all the Jews would have died on the day appointed by Haman. But through prayer, as we invite God's perspective and intervention, amazingly, God often invites our participation in the course of answering that very same prayer. To fully establish God's purpose, starting with the spiritual dimension of calling is essential, but Esther would still need to engage in the ethical, political, and social aspects of her calling too.

Ethical Dimensions of Calling

Faced with this daunting task, Esther did what many of us would have done in her place ... she said no. In fact, she went further and tried to persuade Mordecai that what he was asking of her was impossible; it wasn't protocol or tradition, and she could lose her own life if she were to go ahead with it.

Strictly speaking, all of Esther's concerns were accurate. She would be going against custom; her life would be endangered. However, it didn't make her right, and Mordecai didn't hold back from telling her so: "For if you remain silent at this time, relief and deliverance for the Jews will arise from another place, but you and your father's family will perish. And who knows but that you have come to your royal position for such a time as this?"

(Esther 4:14). There is a reason that this is one of the best-known verses in the entire book of Esther.

Mordecai's words strike a chord, not just with Esther's story but also with ours: Esther's position was for such a time as this, and she was subject to a divine calling much bigger than herself, a purpose God would fulfill with or without her. In the same way, God can fulfill our calling, with or without us.

Ethically, Esther eventually ensured that her actions were principled. There were many things she could have done to offend the king and still lose her life. But she figured that if she had to go before him and possibly die as a result, it might as well be for all the right reasons.

People may criticize you because of your faith, your color, your sex, your ethnicity, your accent, your style, your clothes, your approach to leadership, or even your personality. But whatever you do, don't give them a reason to criticize your character. As is often said, there is already enough offense in the gospel, so, if you're going to offend people, offend them for the right reasons!

Political Dimensions of Calling

Esther navigated the political realm boldly, engaging the highest authority despite the potential consequences. She could have been sentenced to death for her part in this political engagement.

Today, challenging authority can mean ridicule, isolation, or even risking our lives. Subsequently, there are always dangers involved in becoming too closely aligned with the ruling authorities, whoever and wherever they are. Wisdom is always key, and sometimes taking the lead means stepping up when no one else will.

Like Esther, we must seek wisdom to engage with those in power and be ready to take the initiative. She didn't wait for the king to recognize her, agree with her, or invite her. Neither did she hope that he'd hear what needed to be said from somewhere or someone else. Sometimes we are the answer to the prayer someone else is praying, and sometimes we are the answer to our very own prayer.

What I love about Esther's unique solution to the problem is that it involved using hospitality to gain favor and access and therefore leveraging her identity as a woman (not that women were responsible for *all* food-related hospitality within the culture). Esther was learning to lead in the wisdom of God and in ways that made sense to her, even if they made little sense to others, such as Haman, who spectacularly misinterpreted his own invitation to Esther's feast.

Social Dimensions of Calling

Esther's calling extended into the social sphere, demonstrating the power of purpose in uniting and inspiring others. Her realization that inaction could spell destruction for her people underscores the importance of social engagement and the impact of individual actions on the collective. Esther's story teaches us that when purpose shines, it transcends titles or authority. It's about working with people, for people, and because of people.

Esther discovered her purpose and life's calling in the midst of a crisis that was larger than herself and her own family. What originally seemed to be about marriage and having children (preferably sons) or a pursuit of status and position transformed into a divine assignment to save her people and the empire.

Purpose is deeply personal, yet it is not solitary. It acts like a magnetic north, drawing others in and giving them the choice to align themselves with a shared vision. In Esther's case, her purposeful leadership not only saved her people but also left a lasting legacy that continues to inspire. This teaches us that our social calling is not just about fulfilling our own goals but also about contributing to the greater good and making a positive impact on the lives of those around us, sometimes for millennia.

Once we've asked, "Why me, why here, and why this?" we can finally ask, "Why now?" to unveil the significance of God's preparation for us en route to whatever calling allows our purpose to shine.

WHY NOW? EMBRACING GOD'S TIMING

One of the key leadership lessons we learn from Esther is that great leaders are not forged in a vacuum. They don't just appear on the scene; they all come from somewhere and emerge from a specific set of circumstances and history that can make or break them and even redirect the course of their leadership.

Life happens to everyone, whether we're committed to Jesus or not, whether we're ready or not, or even whether we want it to or not. Jesus' words apply to us all: "In this world you will have trouble" (John 16:33). Ironically, we often end up experiencing metamorphic change precisely because of our challenges and pain rather than despite them.

Yes, Esther gets to marry the king, but we never hear whether she's actually very happy to be sent to live in a palace and married off to the richest guy in the land. What we do hear is how she chose to live with what life had dealt her.

Esther's pampering with luxurious oils and perfumes for a full year until she was thoroughly purified and fragrant enough to be brought before the king is often romanticized or even coveted.[15] Although I love a good soak (in the bath), I have to confess that a year's worth, every day for much of the day, sounds more like a prison sentence than a relaxing spa-like experience!

What people sometimes fail to recognize is that Esther's preparation didn't begin when she entered the palace. She emerges from the tragedy of losing both parents, the challenge of being orphaned, and the dangers associated with and belonging to a marginalized group. Esther's outward preparation was nothing compared to the inward work she'd been forced to do. Her years as an orphan, being rejected for her faith and sex, and belonging to a despised group—this is where her real preparation took place. She was formed during those years of absolute obscurity as she faced all the challenges that life threw at her. These hardships honed her decision-making skills and revealed the prophetic nature of who she was, the value of where she was, and the opportunities embedded within her soon-to-be role in life.

When God calls, it transcends our abilities. In other words, we will not be able to do it without him. We're pushed out of our comfort zones into God's. Why was God calling Esther to act now? Because in the end, God had been preparing Esther her whole life to liberate her family, her people, and the nation.

If I were asked today whether I'd be willing to relive any of the toughest experiences from my many years of ministry and leadership, my answer would be a resounding, "No thanks!" I certainly wouldn't want to go through any of that again. But this doesn't mean I don't value the part these experiences played in my journey or value what I learned from them along the way.

Our unique experiences, struggles, and pressures prepare us internally to become all that God is asking of us when the moment arrives. This is the nature of the metamorphic journey every would-be metamorph must make. As John Maxwell aptly notes,

> Crisis doesn't necessarily make character, but it certainly does reveal it. Adversity is a crossroads that makes a person choose one of two paths:

character or compromise. Every time he chooses character, he becomes stronger even if that choice brings negative consequences.[16]

Many of our critical decisions are made in obscurity, in the dark, away from prying eyes, when nobody else is watching, and quite frankly, when nobody else really cares. Nevertheless, it is the decisions we make in the dark that mold our character for when God calls us into the light.

So, as you consider these four questions: "Why me? Why here? Why this? Why now?" perhaps God is calling you to put your gifts, your skills, your experiences, *and* your tears into Jesus' service, for such a time as this!

FOR PERSONAL REFLECTION OR GROUP DISCUSSION

Why Me? Exploring My Uniqueness

1. What aspects of your background, history, experiences, challenges, struggles, joys, and breakthroughs make you unique in your leadership role?
2. What insights has your unique leadership given you? How has this reflection helped you better understand your purpose?
3. When you listen to others, what can you learn from their experiences? How do their stories and insights augment your own understanding of purposeful leadership?

Why Here? Understanding My Context

1. Can you describe the specific context and environment in which you are leading?
2. What unique opportunities do you see, and what specific challenges seem tailored to your skills and abilities?
3. What ways might you have to stand up and stand out in your current context?

Why This? Identifying My Calling

1. What are your core passions, gifts, skills, and frustrations?
2. What issues or problems do you feel a deep drive to address or solve?

Why Now? Embracing God's Timing

1. What season is it for you? What stage of life do you find yourself in?
2. What recent life events or challenges have shaped you and prepared you for your current role or a future role you envision?

TIME FOR PRAYER

Take a moment for personal or group prayer. If part of a discussion group, lift up each member, asking for guidance, strength, and clarity as they navigate through their challenges and seek growth in their personal and leadership *purpose*.

THE 120
MULTIPLYING DISRUPTED DISRUPTORS

Embedding a Strategic Mission Mindset

There have been some who were so preoccupied with spreading Christianity that they never gave a thought to Christ.
C. S. LEWIS

Never doubt that a small group of thoughtful committed individuals can change the world. In fact, it's the only thing that ever has.
MARGARET MEAD

The kingdom of heaven belongs to the violent who lay hold upon it. But this violence is not accepted by God unless the person practicing it is ready himself to bear the shock in return. Whoever wrestles with God in prayer puts his whole life at stake.
JACQUES ELLUL

When a Christian magazine asked me what I felt the role of the church should be amid global challenges, dwindling congregations, and declining members, I was quick to point out that this picture was generally only true of churches in Europe and the West. Elsewhere in the world, Christianity has been experiencing substantial growth, most notably in the Global South. And wherever immigrants from Asia, Africa, and Latin America are engaged and involved, even Western churches are being transformed and revived. As for uncertainty and instability, they may be relatively new for the contemporary church in the Global North,[1] but they are a simple fact of life for the global church as a whole. In fact, the church has faced an eye-watering array of trials and challenges throughout its history to the current day, ranging from persecution, poverty, exile, and refugee crises to war, climate disasters, political oppression, and more.

Despite all this, the fundamental mission of becoming a disciple *of* Jesus and making disciples *for* Jesus has not changed. The church does not need a new job description because the "old" one is as relevant as ever. The task of what I will later refer to as multiplying "disrupted disruptors" among the multitudes who have never heard of nor encountered Jesus also remains as urgent as ever. There is, however, a question mark over the approaches, behaviors, and priorities we tend to adopt, as well as what we seek to achieve in making disciples.

I began this book by sharing how "out of love" I am with the church as I've come to know it. Without intending to be dramatic, I have reached a point where I am completely done with celebrity culture and Christian entertainment disguised as an authentic spiritual encounter. There have been too many times I have wondered whether anyone would even notice if God didn't show up to the meeting ... yet again. So, I'm done with worship that lacks intensity, vitality, community, or reality or that is characterized by the predictability and uniformity of thought, approach, and appearance that seems to dominate our Christian platforms and airwaves.

This critique isn't aimed at anyone in particular. (I actually love my local church.) The truth is, I've been part of the very churches I critique and have even led some of them myself. And although each has been a genuine blessing in its own way, I long for a truly authentic Revelation 7:9 worship experience, where the creative diversity of nations, tribes, peoples, and languages are gathered together around the throne of God, praising God for who he is and directing all the glory to where it rightfully belongs. I know I'm not the only one who feels this way. There's a new generation rising that craves authentic supernatural experience, resists any form of religious entertainment, and longs to participate in community where men and women are being discipled and changed daily from the inside out rather than professing what never truly impacts their lives or behavior. In many ways, this chapter is written for them. (And of course, it is written for me too!)

THE NEED FOR DISRUPTED DISRUPTORS

I've long believed that new moves of God, whether by revival or Jesus-movements, are sparked, spread, and sustained by disruptors who have themselves experienced significant personal and social disruption.[2] Given the current unprecedented and disrupted state of our world, followers of Jesus have an incredible opportunity to both multiply and become the kind of disruptors our churches and societies desperately need.

The critical question is whether we know how to become disruptors or even how to initiate disruptive change in others or in the world around us. Given the history of Jesus-movements and our preoccupation with reproducibility, easy solutions, and shortcuts, the short answer seems to be, not really. Our desire to engage in ways that appeal primarily to human ingenuity, manipulation, and marketability is at odds with what is actually required in practice. The journey of a disrupting Jesus-movement is therefore unlikely to align with any desire for a one-size-fits-all approach. There simply is no straightforward formula or five-step process for getting us from where we are to where we need to be.

What seems to be required instead is a much more challenging commitment to obedience, dependence on God, attention to posture, openness to correction, and a greater responsiveness to the Holy Spirit's guidance. Revival historian Michael McClymond describes how "Winkie Pratney compared revival to romance. Just as someone who has been in love before may find that being in love with a new person is a new experience, so too the romance of the Spirit will never be exactly the same on any two occasions."[3]

If we are committed to the romance of the Spirit, we cannot artificially contrive or reproduce the mission of disruption we so desperately need. That said, we can at least attempt to promote the conditions under which a desired romance could be ignited and even flourish over time. We can refer to this as our mission *before the* mission, and in the same way that metamorphosis has its own logic, there is a predictability about this mission *before the* mission too. This is largely because God makes no secret of what it takes to attract the Holy Spirit's attention and is eager to share the information with anyone willing to listen. This is great news! It means there are observations and lessons that can be learned and even a strategic mission mindset to potentially adopt. The rest, as they say, is entirely up to God!

CHRIS: METAMORPHICALLY EMPOWERED

When Chris told me what had happened when he stepped out on his own to pray for people in public, I was as thrilled as he was. He had been eagerly preparing for months, learning to surrender control completely, step forward boldly, and trust God fully. Witnessing others facilitate incredible transformations and firsthand commitments to Jesus on the streets had deeply inspired him. He didn't want to be a perpetual spectator but an active participant. He wanted to embrace the adventure with God, to confront his fears, and to personally witness people discovering Jesus. So, as he described how he had found himself on an unfamiliar block in an unfamiliar part of town with a strong Muslim presence, I applauded his courage and refusal to give in to his own fears regarding Islam. It was clear he had followed the promptings of the Holy Spirit, even though some of his friends had looked at him sideways for venturing where they dared not.

Apparently, he had been praying quietly in tongues when he became self-consciously aware of how the people moving around him were dressed. It occurred to him that perhaps he was unhelpfully and conspicuously out of place. While he was distracted by these thoughts, he nearly bumped into two men. After a quick apology on his part, one of the men, looking somewhat puzzled, asked him what he was doing. Chris swallowed hard and then replied candidly, "I'm learning to pray. Would you like me to pray for you?" To his surprise, the man agreed, asking Chris to pray for both him and his friend. Chris laughed as he remembered how startled he'd been by the ease of the situation. He then found himself praying for two Muslim men, probably in their forties, named Ibrahim and Naeem.

He hadn't felt anything extraordinary happen as he prayed, so he plowed on and tried hard to ignore his feelings. After finishing, Ibrahim thanked him and shared that he had been struggling with a heaviness for weeks and had asked God that very morning for relief from the weight of it. His candor about his personal struggles surprised both him and Chris alike. He said that Chris seemed to be an answer to his prayer, and his heaviness had evaporated. Chris also acknowledged that Ibrahim was an answer to his prayers and explained how God had led him to that very block and that particular part of town to pray for whoever God might bring along.

Intrigued, Ibrahim asked why Chris was doing this. Chris seized the opportunity to share about Jesus, explaining his faith, God's love for Ibrahim and Naeem, and the motivation behind his actions.

In a matter of weeks, both Ibrahim and Naeem began attending Chris's church, having wholeheartedly embraced Jesus for themselves. It turned out that Ibrahim was a leader at his local mosque. He was not only eagerly sharing his story of liberation from depression through Jesus with his friends and family, but he also regularly invited Chris to family gatherings to pray for any who were sick or distressed.

As more of Ibrahim's circle showed interest in following Jesus, it became clear that Chris's local church was at a crossroads. They had no idea what to do with Ibrahim and his friends as they were only really accustomed to guiding white Americans in their faith journey.

I asked Chris if he knew what needed to happen next. He looked at me thoughtfully and said nervously, "Not really, but I do know that whatever is coming, I want to be a part of it. There are so many who still don't know Jesus. Ibrahim suggested we ask the Holy Spirit for wisdom and guidance, so that's what we've been doing, and now we're waiting to see what God has for us."

"How do you feel?" I asked.

"Excited, afraid, and more alive than ever," he said. "Everything's changed. I don't mean just for Ibrahim, Naeem, and their community; it's changed for me too, and most of the time I don't want it to stop."

I looked at him and nodded with understanding. We sat for a few moments in complete silence before we both suddenly and audibly inhaled deeply. As we turned to look at each other, realization dawning, we burst into laughter and allowed the tension of the moment to ebb away.

The best place to find disrupted disruptors in the life of the early church is in the Book of Acts. It's generally agreed that Acts is not a separate or new departure from Luke's Gospel but more of an extension that intensifies the prophetic nature of Jesus' ministry while shifting the focus from Jesus himself to Jesus' earliest followers.

There are principles buried in the specific events of the book of Acts, particularly Acts 2, that continue to reverberate throughout Christian history. And although the events themselves are never repeated in exactly the same way again, we see similar themes emerging time and time again in the experience of Christian communities across millennia and all over the world. They not only reveal how the disrupted disruptors of the early Christian communities came to be literally transformed and powerfully transformative, but they also suggest how we could join in with them too.

WAIT FOR ENCOUNTERS YOU CANNOT DO WITHOUT

The main event of Acts 2 is, of course, the day of Pentecost, which describes the birth of the New Testament church. From a leadership perspective, the sequence of events can be distilled into foundational principles and a "strategic mission mindset." As we engage in the behaviors associated with our mission *before the* mission, we create an environment worthy of a love affair with the Holy Spirit. Acts chapter 2 begins, "When the day of Pentecost came, they were all together in one place. Suddenly a sound like the blowing of a violent wind came from heaven and filled the whole house where they were sitting" (Act 2:1–2).

However, Acts 1:4–5 explains how the disciples came to be gathered together in the first place, "On one occasion, while he (Jesus) was eating with them, he gave them this command: 'Do not leave Jerusalem, but wait for the gift my Father promised, which you have heard me speak about. For John baptized with water, but in a few days you will be baptized with the Holy Spirit.'" Jesus' command for the disciples to wait in Jerusalem for the Holy Spirit prepared them for the incredible events of Pentecost.

Embrace Disrupting Encounters

World-changing mission is possible whenever God's missionaries or sent ones (*apostolos*) are themselves profoundly disrupted in true metamorphic style by being broken down and reconstituted somewhat like our caterpillar en route to becoming a butterfly. The Holy Spirit is ultimately the one who initiates and facilitates this unsettling process of metamorphosis; and our role, as mentioned elsewhere, is simply to stay open, receptive, and responsive.

Metamorphosing into what and who we're called to be is always a collaborative effort between ourselves, God, and those whom God places in our lives. As those called upon to lead, it is vital to proactively seek out and create the conditions that foster these encounters. The kind of disruptive mission that leads to revival or to new Jesus-movements transcends the bounds of human possibility alone.

Our interactions with mentors, coaches, spiritual directors, church leaders, partners, and all those who inspire and motivate us can, of course, spark profound changes within us. Some even empower us to overcome our very human constraints, while others correct and realign our perceptions and perspectives. Still others dispel our fears, enable us to overcome our timidity, give us a sense of purpose, and even instill a sense of courage we may never have felt before.

Yet, at their best, they can only facilitate change toward our becoming well-intentioned humanists, striving to do good within the confines of our finite human knowledge, ideas, energy, and power. By ourselves, we could be good and perhaps even great at what we do, as humanists often are. But without Jesus and the Holy Spirit in the picture, human encounters can only take us so far.

The reality is that our most profound changes emerge primarily from our encounters with God. So, these encounters should never be considered optional extras but essential experiences we cannot do without. I have already addressed the difference between just "hanging out" and having a genuine encounter with Jesus in chapter 4, so please assume the same applies to our encounters with the Holy Spirit too. Indeed, both believers and non-believers alike need exposure to as many of these transformative encounters as possible. In a way, the environment we need to create is not unlike the chrysalis, where a caterpillar morphs into a butterfly. The difference is that humans are destined to re-enter these transformative spaces as often as it takes under the direction of the Holy Spirit. Our encounters with the Holy Spirit transform us into beings capable of achieving something of eternal value, something truly cosmic and quite literally "out of this world." These encounters continually transform us by bringing us face-to-face with God and ourselves.

Our encounters with God also offer us a vital reality check. They remind us that as leaders, we only ever lead with permission—not just permission from those we serve or the organizations and communities to whom we are accountable, but primarily permission from the God to whom we are ultimately accountable. Our commitment to Jesus reminds us that we are never simply working to grow our churches, make the world more just, our communities better, relationships healthier, hearts clearer, convictions purer, or our churches and organizations better equipped for the future. At the end of the day, our encounters with Jesus and his Holy Spirit are divine invitations to participate in a cosmic mission that advances God's purposes *in* and *beyond* this world. Outlining the nature of our commitment, theologian Jürgen Moltmann reminds us that the mission of the church "is not to spread the church but to spread the kingdom."[4] In the book *Church Actually*, pastor, poet, and missionary Gerard Kelly drives this home:

> The mission of God is for the will of God to be done, and our participation in that process is our missional calling. Anything, in this view, that moves some aspect of the created order from rebellion to obedience, from God's will not being done to God's will being done, is missional.[5]

Becoming truly effective disruptors means a fundamental commitment to personal and organizational disruption. All disruption brings some kind of change to church and organizational life and to structures, systems, and processes that may no longer be fit for purpose. However, far from passively awaiting disruption, leaders are called to be active agents of (healthy) ongoing disruption. This means going beyond the simple act of waiting for the Holy Spirit's arrival to learning to walk in step with the Holy Spirit. Inevitably, it calls for a willingness to embrace the ongoing change that is so characteristic of truly effective change-makers. In *Movements that Change the World*, Steve Addison writes:

> The most effective movements are prepared to change everything about themselves except their core beliefs. Unencumbered by tradition, movements feel free to experiment with new forms and strategies. Movements pursue their mission with methods that are effective, flexible and reproducible, which outlast and even surpass the influence of the first generation of leaders.[6]

If we are willing to embrace the discomfort accompanying our wait for the Holy Spirit, we too can become instruments of God's loving disruption in the lives of the many worlds we inhabit.

Practice Disrupting Prayer

When Jesus instructed his 120 disciples to "wait for the gift my Father promised" (Acts 1:4), we discover, "They all joined together constantly in prayer" (v. 14). In other words, they interpreted their "wait" in the upper room as an occasion for prayer rather than an excuse for passivity. Like them, we cannot afford to be passive as we wait. The openness, receptivity, and responsiveness we are seeking to cultivate for our anticipated romance with the Holy Spirit are possible only through prayer. Our wait must therefore be as active as theirs was and characterized by burdened, focused, and expectant prayer in anticipation of the one Jesus said would come.

Unfortunately, waiting is not often a "Zen-like" activity. The early believers were disrupted even before arriving in the upper room and experienced further upheaval through the prayers and events that followed. Having appeared to his disciples over a period of forty days after his resurrection, Jesus appeared for the last time before his ascension, just ten days before Pentecost, commanding them to pray and wait for the Holy Spirit. Then for ten days, they prayed without getting their answer. Subsequently, those final ten days of waiting were unlikely to be calm, composed, or free from fear and doubt![7]

Waiting isn't easy, even when we think we know what's coming. On the contrary, this kind of waiting is a thoroughly counterintuitive desperate measure. It is probably the hardest thing we can do, especially for activists who long to get the problem solved and the job done. Waiting forces us to stop our constant activities and simply look to God. The importance of seeking God and what he is doing, rather than what we or other people are doing, cannot be overstated. Without prayer, we are effectively left to our own devices, so it should never be considered an optional extra. It is only through prayerful waiting that we can truly acknowledge our limitations, brokenness, and the overwhelming nature of everything. We wait in the knowledge that God cares less about what we do or accomplish and more about the kind of people we are becoming. Prayer is the only way to experience the personal transformation and receive the resources we so desperately need for our mission. It is also a reminder that whatever God is up to, it will inevitably involve us. In this, we are again like the entombed caterpillar. But unlike the caterpillar, this aspect of transformation isn't just for ourselves; we are also praying new lives and new births into reality.

The notion of brokenness and desperation filling the early believers as they prayerfully waited for the Holy Spirit's arrival at Pentecost is echoed in the pre-revival experiences and the birth of Jesus-movements both historically and today. David R. Thomas, United Methodist pastor and executive director of New Room, goes as far as to say, "Tears are the church's prayer language."[8] This is especially true in parts of the world that experience constant persecution, brokenness, and desperation. May this be true for us too, as we engage in the kind of prayer that disrupts while waiting for our much-needed change.

Although not easy, the room where the disciples waited was formative. They experienced terror and release in that upper room. Everyone already knew everyone else in that room, all 120. How else could they possibly know that the person who suddenly appeared among them, who happened to be Jesus, had not been in the room with them all along? Some of their most powerful bonding experiences were taking place there. They not only encountered the resurrected Jesus in that room, but they also journeyed from the edge of despair to a place of hope. In John 20:21–22, we see how that room became the place where Jesus himself offered them peace and breathed holy breath on them, gifting them the Spirit for the first time. By Pentecost, that upper room would also become the place of their greatest "fired up" encounter with God's Holy Spirit.

That room was a special place, but it was also a dangerous place. Perhaps ironically, the place of their liberation, revelation, prayer, deep worship, and encounter also had the potential to become their prison due to familiarity or fear, as we shall see from what follows. Only the arrival of the Holy Spirit and the disciples' obedience to Jesus' instruction changed everything and perhaps even saved everything too. The first believers demonstrate in the most graphic terms possible what it means to be transformed by an "upper room encounter" and also break free from an "upper room" mindset.

BREAK FREE FROM AN "UPPER ROOM" MINDSET

Unfortunately, many church and organizational leaders, together with their communities, are still very much attached to their "upper room"—the site of their last success, the last paradigm, the last experience, the last significant encounter, and even the last place that Jesus sent them. We can be trapped in idealized memories of past times, waiting for "lightning" to strike with much the same effect as a previous special moment of brilliance.

Churches and organizations can live in the hope that they will get a repeat dose of the same results they had last time. But the odds of being struck by lightning twice in a lifetime are apparently one in nine million![9]

Jesus commanded in Acts 1:4, "Do not leave Jerusalem, but wait for the gift my Father promised." And then again declares in Acts 1:8, "You will receive power when the Holy Spirit comes on you; and you will be my witnesses in Jerusalem, and in all Judea and Samaria, and to the ends of the earth." In other words, although they were commanded to wait for the Holy Spirit in the upper room, they were never intended to *stay* in the upper room!

Whether your "upper room" is a geographical location, an ideological mindset, a way of doing things, a cultural framework, or an attitude of heart and mind, it is only ever intended to be an incubator, a temporary space of preparation, and never a permanent settlement for putting down roots and definitely not a prison. Just as the Israelites learned to follow the pillar of cloud and fire in the wilderness, we should be ready to move whenever God leads us on.

Unfortunately, familiarity, predictability, and maintaining the status quo are incredibly attractive to us as human beings. So, it's not surprising that we repeatedly encounter the same "upper room mindset" in need of the Holy Spirit's disruption throughout both the book of Acts and the history of the church to this very day. In a 1965 essay, Austrian psychoanalyst Theodor Reik captured it perfectly when he wrote, "It has been said that history repeats itself. This is perhaps not quite correct; it merely rhymes."[10]

Relinquish Geographical Captivity

Acts chapter 8 reveals just how much history rhymes. It appears that many of the Jewish visitors from regions like North Africa, Asia, and Europe who witnessed the extraordinary events of Pentecost in Jerusalem never actually left the city. This is understandable, given the magnitude of what had happened there, but it is also a cautionary tale of how quickly awe and gratitude can deteriorate into superstition. Just because something had happened in Jerusalem didn't mean that something as seismic couldn't happen elsewhere. We must never make the mistake of confining God by geography because God is always far bigger than we think.

In this case, the first believers had become "stuck" in the geographical comfort zone of Jerusalem. It literally took the force of persecution in Acts 8:1 to finally scatter them into spreading the gospel beyond Jerusalem into Judea, Samaria, and eventually beyond, just as Jesus had originally envisaged.

The Jewish followers of Jesus who resided in Jerusalem soon learned that their new faith was inherently multiethnic and polycentric, or according to the subtitle of author Allen Yeh's book *Polycentric Missiology*, "from everyone to everywhere."[11] As their faith spread to Samaritans and Greeks, Antioch became the new geographical center of their faith.

The geographical center of Christianity has subsequently shifted again and again throughout history. Christians from places like Rome, Alexandria, Carthage, and Constantinople all succumbed to geographical captivity. This was also true for Christians in the centers of the Reformation, such as Geneva, Zurich, Strasbourg, Tubingen, Paris, Leipzig, London, Oxford, Wittenberg, and Cambridge. All needed to be reminded that Christianity defies all attempts at being constrained to any one place or claimed by any one people group.

Today's shift of Christianity's numerical center of gravity from the Global North to Africa, Asia, and Latin America has created new centers of Christian growth, and geographical captivity may have to be countered once again.

These shifts should not surprise us. Christianity stands out as the only major religion without a geographical center or an ethnic majority. Its foundational texts were written in Koine Greek, a language different from its founder, Jesus' native Aramaic. Interestingly, it was this language choice that helped Christianity spread widely across the Eastern Roman Empire. You'd think Christianity was quite literally born to travel!

Whenever Christianity has escaped the bonds of geographical captivity, it has expanded and progressed again beyond even geographically confined people groups and into culturally shifting diasporas. Breaking free from the upper room of geographical captivity means letting go of the idea that *where we are is where it's at*. If we are to multiply disciples, we must believe that everyone everywhere matters equally to God and that the rejection of geographical captivity can lead to both internal growth and external multiplication.

Reject Ideological and Cultural Captivity

By Acts 15, the disciples and the gospel became "stuck" in a new way. This time, it was the ideological, cultural, and religious confines of Judaism. It's not surprising that Jews thought their beliefs and religious practices were superior, considering their long-held perception of having an exclusive connection with God. The challenge of gentile conversions ultimately liberated them from being trapped in ideological and cultural confinement, realizing that not everyone needs to conform to the same beliefs and practices to be Jesus-followers. With the apostle Paul and Peter's guidance, they overcame the debate on whether gentiles needed to adopt Jewish customs such as circumcision and become Jews in order to follow Jesus. This ultimately broadened the mission to include the non-Jewish world.

Acts 2:5 tells us, "There were staying in Jerusalem God-fearing Jews from every nation under heaven." And later, in Acts 2:11, the crowd declares, "We hear them [the disciples] declaring the wonders of God in our own tongues!" In other words, at the birth of the church, God didn't obliterate differences; identities were respected and embraced. Instead of forcing the crowd to use the one language they all knew, the common imperial language of empire (Koine Greek), the followers of Jesus developed the ability to communicate across differences, and the Holy Spirit empowered them to speak (or to at least be heard) in the different languages of peoples from nations in Africa, Asia, Europe, and, of course, Palestine. In other words, the Holy Spirit enabled them to speak in languages that were not their own and to understand each other despite their linguistic diversity!

Many believe Pentecost to be the reverse of Babel, which, like the empires that followed, sought to use its wealth and power to enforce uniformity, conformity, and assimilation on its people and to commodify and domesticate God. Babel was an empire ultimately destroyed when God multiplied their languages and scattered them into separate nations. By contrast, at Pentecost, God defeated the idea of empire by bringing the people together but *without* erasing their diversity or multiple languages. The Holy Spirit never models the church after "empire." Instead, God builds his kingdom by birthing a united church while preserving the diversity of people.

Interestingly, the rapid growth of Christianity in the non-Western world, coupled with the decline of Christianity in the West, has led to a sense of disorientation among Western Christians. Rather than celebrating this global shift and the rise of Christianity around the world, they find themselves grappling with their increasingly marginal position. Instead of adjusting, attempts have been made by Western Christians to monopolize and inappropriately influence global Christianity. Such attempts are likely to fail, as the West's claim to Christianity's universal primacy was perhaps a reality only during the first half of the second millennium.

The reality is that each people group brings back to God something that is missing from all the others. Freedom from ideological captivity acknowledges that different peoples come to God and mission with different questions. In the Two-Thirds World,[12] theological and missiological inquiries often focus on postcolonialism, the fate of ancestors, spiritual warfare, the relationship between poverty and faith, polygamy, and the complexities of religious pluralism, such as the concept of Messianic Muslims (e.g., can you be a Messianic Muslim in the same way that someone can be a Messianic Jew?).[13] Diaspora communities, living between worlds due to displacement or voluntary migration, grapple with issues like migration, trafficking, intercultural mission, multiethnic churches, identity, racism, globalization, and reverse mission.

In contrast, Western Christian concerns often mirror the West's dominant cultural values, like the role of the papacy, theological debates (e.g., Calvinism vs. Arminianism, egalitarianism vs. complementarianism, evangelism vs. social justice), denominationalism, and the validity of cessationism and dispensationalism. Western Christianity, shaped by enlightenment rationalism, leans toward individualism, dualism, and transactional spirituality, often simplifying salvation to a "me-and-Jesus prayer." In many other parts of the world, conversion is a household or even community affair.

No single person or group has a full picture of God; perspectives vary by cultural background. Europeans, Asians, Africans, and Latinos each have their unique viewpoints shaped by their history and interactions with God. All these perspectives hold elements of truth, but none are complete on their own. The idea that this is a form of relativism is to misunderstand what is taking place. Instead of giving us relativistic lenses, learning from one another's cultural insights provides us with greater clarity. While there is absolute truth, we must be humble enough to acknowledge that we only perceive that truth in part, not in full, and that we need the perspectives of others if we are to gain a fuller understanding of God's truth. To paraphrase Two-Thirds World theologian Allen Yeh, there is more than just orthodoxy or heterodoxy; there is also undiscovered theology (a subset of orthodoxy).[14]

Since no person or people group has a monopoly on discipleship, any attempt to tame, commodify, or domesticate Jesus' demands or the Holy Spirit's activities is always exposed as "empire" rather than "kingdom" building. We often interpret Jesus' command to make disciples as an invitation to reproduce ourselves. But this is clearly not the task. We are called to make obedient learners of Jesus and to invite them to imitate us only in as much as we imitate Christ (1 Cor. 11:1). Ultimately, the call to follow Jesus clashes at some level with every worldview, culture, and every human heart; we all have something to offer and something to surrender in yielding our hearts to him. If the gospel is to continue to captivate hearts and minds, we must be prepared to reject the idea that *the way we believe and do things is how everyone else should believe and do things*. To multiply disciples, we must believe there are other ways of being followers and doing life with Jesus that matter to God.

Refuse Gender Captivity

Christians are also just as prone to locking others, as well as ourselves, into upper rooms of our own making. This is particularly true when it comes to attitudes toward women in many Christian traditions, including those started by women themselves!

We must never overlook the fact that the Spirit was poured out on both women and men. In Acts 2:17–18, the point couldn't be clearer—the Spirit gave without regard for status, sex, or nationality. This passage, based on Joel's vision of a Spirit-soaked future, presents us with a tantalizing promise of diversity and wholesale gender equality for the first time in the biblical text. To a culture with little regard or esteem for children, youth, or women … and as for foreigners … what Peter was prophesying (eight centuries after Joel) was unimaginable. This was quite literally unlike anything they'd ever seen before!

A world governed by leadership based on a person's measure of testosterone is a very dangerous world indeed. However, the promise prophesied by Joel and then by Peter suggests a transformative "new normal" where gender no longer presents a barrier to leadership.

The book *Motus Dei: The Movement of God to Disciple the Nations*, edited by Warrick Farah, presents over thirty first-person accounts detailing indigenous church-planting movements worldwide. Several case studies report that many rapidly expanding movements emphasize the priesthood of all believers and the Holy Spirit's role in each disciple's life. The American debate on women's roles in the church, such as egalitarian vs. complementarian views, is largely irrelevant to these movements. Instead, many have women in leadership roles and embrace a countercultural approach that fosters social transformation.

It's clear that God doesn't share our hang-ups, so we should resist oversharing them with others! God seems quite happy to disrupt gender captivity right along with geographical, ideological, cultural, and any other kind we can possibly think of. While we may hesitate to empower both men and women in leadership, the Holy Spirit, far from waiting for our approval, is already disrupting women from the "upper room" to lead all over the world.

Be a Disruptive Disruptor: Pandita Ramabai

Pandita Ramabai was a pioneering South Asian social reformer, educationalist, emancipator, and evangelist. In his foreword to *India's Woman of the Millennium: Pandita Ramabai,* teacher, missionary, and professor of theology, Dr. Eddie Hyatt describes her as "one of the most remarkable Christians in the history of the church."[15] Not only did she make significant strides in disrupting societal norms in India, but she also models what it means to break out of upper rooms, including those others have prepared for us.

Born during British colonial rule in a caste-dominated society that viewed women as inferior, Pandita Ramabai faced early hardship at the young age of sixteen, with the loss of her family to starvation during The Great Famine (1876–78). Despite these challenges, she became a respected scholar and the first female to be awarded the prestigious title "Pandita," meaning "the learned one" (just in case you thought Pandita was her first name!) by the University of Calcutta.

She continued to disrupt cultural and societal norms by marrying someone from a lower caste and from a different region. Tragically, she was widowed at the age of twenty-three, left alone to look after their daughter, and experienced firsthand the harsh treatment of widows in India. This fueled her later activism, as did discovering a copy of Luke's Gospel and seeing how Jesus treated women. After converting to Christianity in England, Pandita faced relentless resistance and opposition but remained undeterred: "In Christianity I found a religion which gave its privileges equally to men and women; there was no distinction of caste, color, or sex made in it."[16] In this way, she awoke to her true mission in life. However, she faced disapproval and backlash from the Indian community for converting and becoming a follower of Jesus. At the same time, she encountered criticism from British Christians, particularly the Church of

England, for being "too Indian." She found much of the church's language and rituals confusing and resisted cultural assimilation. However, she refused the standard that each group attempted to impose on her of what a woman, Indian, Christian, and Christian woman should and shouldn't be. Instead, she went right ahead and disrupted just about every ideological, cultural, and religious norm she encountered, simply by being who she was.

Pandita refused to be marginalized, silenced, or erased from society. An extraordinary linguist and fluent in seven languages, including Greek and Hebrew, she eventually translated the Bible into her mother tongue. She also championed the rights of widows and child brides and led national campaigns to raise awareness of their conditions. She lobbied government ministers, testified before commissions, and traveled to the US, gaining support from like-minded Christian activists, including Harriet Tubman.[17]

Inspired by the news of the Welsh Revival in 1904, Pandita sparked a revival at Mukti Mission in 1905,[18] which spread across India, earning her the title "Mother of the Pentecostal Movement in India."[19] This revival would later influence the 1906 Azusa Street revival in Los Angeles, California.

Despite her amazing impact (and that of many others like her), there are still those who believe women should have been confined to the "upper room"! Thankfully, God is in the business of disruption, and in some of the most patriarchal societies today, such as Iran, China, Africa, and Southeast Asia, God continues to raise women to lead without the permission of their husbands, brothers, fathers, uncles, sons, or even Western theologians![20]

Stay Clear of the Upper Room

Whether someone attempts to lock us in an upper room of their making, or we end up doing it to ourselves, we should never underestimate our tendency to cling to our very own geographical, ideological, and cultural "upper rooms." Any one of us—regardless of our background or experience—can become attached to the "upper room" of where others think we belong, or our last encounter with God, his last act in our lives, our last revelation, our last experience of him, the last thing he said to us, or even the last place he sent us to.

Breaking free from an "upper room" mindset requires a multifaceted approach. It can't simply be wished away; it must be prayed out, taught out, reasoned out, inspired out, persuaded out, assured out, and drawn out. If we seriously want to see disciples multiplied and people becoming followers of

Jesus everywhere, then breaking free of our "upper rooms" means preparing for significant and metamorphic change.

The current challenges facing Western Christians are an opportunity for growth and expansion on a par with the early church. These difficulties could be the very disruption we need to scatter us into areas where Jesus longs to be at work. Instead of viewing our current struggles as the darkness of a *tomb* and, therefore, evidence of a definitive end, we could see them as the darkness of a *womb*—a place of hidden growth and development, an indicator of new life.

The leader's role in breaking free from the "upper room mindset" is that of a midwife who delivers or a guide who leads people beyond their biases and apprehensions, including any harbored by the leader as well. The leader seeks to remind everyone, "Change and transformation are what we're here for. They are part of our calling!" as they simultaneously hold out the hope that it will all be worth it in the end.

The question we must ask ourselves is whether we will be thanking God or lamenting the loss of our "upper room." We must simply learn to want what's coming more than we loved what we had before. If we seek to monopolize mission by geography, ideology, culture, or gender, we effectively constrain and slow down the progress of the gospel. But by acknowledging that everyone everywhere has a part to play, we allow the gospel to advance unhindered by our "hang-ups" and to multiply beyond our borders.

Regardless of whether we are planting churches, preparing for new growth, or structurally transitioning our churches, organizations, and leadership for new approaches, we neglect relinquishing an "upper room mindset" at our peril!

CLOSE THE GAP BETWEEN THOSE WHO DO AND DON'T KNOW JESUS

It's not incidental that all three synoptic Gospels end with a call to cross boundaries, beginning in "Jerusalem, and in all Judea and Samaria, and to the ends of the earth (Acts 1:8). Far too often, Christians create mission models and outreach strategies that don't really require the help of the Holy Spirit. Frankly, if we aren't crossing impossible boundaries like those mentioned earlier, we can do most of our mission through marketing and campaigns. In a kingdom filled with the miraculous, we often settle for far too little. Many of our models of church planting and mission follow colonial and imperialistic rules by encouraging people to become and stay Christians without crossing cultural, linguistic, or socioeconomic barriers.

Similarly, most of our resources focus on one cultural group and encourage others to assimilate, which is decidedly more empire than kingdom. Martin Luther King Jr.'s words are as relevant today as they were the first time he uttered them: "This hour in history needs a dedicated circle of transformed nonconformists. The saving of our world from pending doom will come not from the actions of a conforming majority but from the creative maladjustment of a transformed minority."[21]

Being disrupted disruptors means more than just leaving the comfort zones of our "upper rooms." We must also be willing to close the gap between those who have been introduced to Jesus and those who have not. In the Acts 2 scenario, the Holy Spirit's activity was not limited to the violent wind and tongues of fire among the disciples in the upper room; it was also active among the Pentecost crowds out on the streets.

The sound of the Holy Spirit's arrival and the disciples' speaking in various languages attracted a large crowd of over three thousand people, curious about the events that were unfolding in the city, leaving the disciples with the same choice to close the gap that faces us.

To close the gap between those who have been introduced to Jesus and those who have not, I propose we respond to the challenge to step out, stand out, and speak up.

Step Out

Just like the disciples, who stepped out to engage with the crowds stirred by the very commotion they had created, the first challenge is to venture beyond our comfort zones and try something new. The direction of flow is always outwards from our comfort zones to where others feel most at ease.

We should not expect our "crowds" to cross the vast chasm of our church cultures. It's up to us, like the disciples, to take the initiative and step into their world. Acts 2 doesn't detail how the disciples moved from their upstairs room to mingle with the crowds, in what many believe to have been the temple grounds. What is clear is that the Holy Spirit didn't simply sweep them out of the upper room against their will and inclinations; they likely used their feet in choosing to mingle with the crowds. In other words, here, as elsewhere, there's no point waiting for God to do what God is evidently waiting for us to do.

The first disciples took only a few physical steps out of the door to close the gap between themselves and their crowds. We may need a little more help with this, but there's usually someone on hand to offer valuable experience or guidance, and the Holy Spirit has a way of ensuring that we get to meet them. When Christians gather for worship and teaching, it can be an opportunity to share each other's resources and learn from each other's insights in ways that could save us from having to "reinvent the wheel." There are all kinds of inspiring stories, examples, frameworks, and principles that could help us literally step out of our buildings into the homes, workplaces, clubs, bars, cultures, and subcultures where our crowds are most likely to be found.

Stand Out

Closing the gap involves not just "stepping out" but also "standing out" and being visible. We know that there were at least two reasons the disciples were staying in the "upper room" to begin with. First, they were obediently "waiting" for the Holy Spirit to arrive, in line with Jesus' instructions. But second, they were quite literally hiding!

We sometimes face the same dilemma they did: On the one hand, we want the Holy Spirit to turn up and totally transform us, while on the other hand, we're not sure we want to be disturbed from the comfort and security of our upper room. The disciples, at least, had a valid reason to be hiding from the crowds and the authorities; they were known associates of a man executed for a capital offense whose body was still "missing."

However, what the Holy Spirit does next gives us pause to consider whether we really want to surrender at all. When the Spirit arrives, it totally blows their cover! In this, the Holy Spirit is a bit like the noisy friend who arrives late at night and wakes the entire family and neighbors while attempting to attract our attention. Except this Friend, the Comforter, wakes the entire city and makes so much noise that thousands hear. As if this isn't bad enough, the Holy Spirit stirs the disciples so much they end up creating the very commotion and attention they had been trying to avoid in the first place. Your mission, should you choose to accept it, isn't to boldly go where no one is likely to find you!

The problem with visibility is that it can be uncomfortable. When we're visible enough to be celebrated, we're also visible enough to be criticized or misunderstood, just like the disciples in Acts 2:13 whom some mocked and accused of being drunk. Ironically, in today's world, people often long to be noticed but are simultaneously afraid of standing out. Of course, it's possible to gain visibility for all the wrong reasons, and stories abound about Christians who have been anything other than Christlike in their dealings with others. However, we can also stand out by truly loving our enemies, sharing our resources, coming alongside the marginalized, and imitating Jesus in our dealings with the "quartet of the vulnerable" (widows, orphans, immigrants, and the poor) mentioned in chapter six of this book. If we are to be vilified, let's at least ensure it's because we have been identified as having "been with Jesus" (Acts 4:13).

Speak Up

To close the gap, we must also be ready to speak up and say whatever's necessary. If we discover nothing else from Acts 2, we should note it reveals an incredibly talkative bunch. Not only is the Holy Spirit's arrival marked by the sound of a violent wind, but there are also tongues of fire and other "languages." It's as if the power of communication and language is being thrust into the foreground. Here, God not only accepts different languages, but he also introduces a few more through the Spirit-inspired speech of the disciples.

In my city, where over 30 percent of the population is Muslim, there have been numerous accounts of Muslims experiencing dreams and visions of Jesus or angels. These individuals are consistently guided in their dreams to seek out Christians or "people of the book" for explanations. They are literally walking into churches in search of someone who can interpret their dreams.

It strikes me as incredibly odd that an angel would go to all the trouble of appearing to someone, only to direct them to seek further information from someone else. But then I'm reminded of the story of Cornelius in Acts 10. In verses 4–5, an angel appears and acknowledges Cornelius's prayers and charitable acts. But instead of providing direct guidance and information about Jesus, the angel instructs Cornelius to send for Peter, who still needs his prejudices challenged. Before disappearing, the angel simply provides an address, saying, "He [Peter] is staying with Simon the tanner, whose house is by the sea" (v. 6).

I believe that supernatural encounters like these will become more commonplace as we increasingly close the gap with our neighbors, but I also believe that God will not send an angel to do the *speaking up* that's intended for us!

In Acts 2, the crowd was amazed to hear Galileans praising God in their own languages (v. 7). Peter's sermon, inspired by the Holy Spirit, was filled with familiar imagery and references to connect with the Jewish audience and converts to Judaism in an ideological, philosophical, and religious language they could understand.

Scholars debate whether Pentecost was i) a miracle of language—with disciples speaking unknown tongues, ii) a hearing miracle—where everyone understood in their own language, or iii) a boldness miracle—where the disciples spoke with such conviction that the message simply resonated with everyone. We could, of course, debate all of this, but what is not up for debate is the miraculous occurrence that led to three thousand being added to the church in a single day!

Closing the gap is about more than a willingness to move across the physical boundaries of churches, organizations, institutions, or businesses. If we are to reach those wholly unfamiliar with Jesus' message, it will also involve bridging ideological, philosophical, emotional, and psychological distances. This includes engaging with people whose lifestyles we may not agree with and those we might prefer to avoid altogether. If we wish to be responsive to the Spirit, we must understand that the final choice of who we are sent to is rarely ours to make. We can, of course, decline to go. But the best leaders, churches, and organizations are multilingual. They not only appreciate the need to speak in languages others understand, but they also possess or develop the skill to make themselves understood.

Acts 2 also reminds us that God's work is not limited to the church; he's active in the wider world. The danger with all the talk of the Spirit's activity through the church is we can easily forget that God's Spirit had a job before we ever came along. The Holy Spirit is not a genie in a bottle waiting to be "rubbed up the right way" to do our bidding and grant us three wishes! As John 3:8 reminds us, we can't control its direction or understand its path.[22] The gospel has always advanced across boundaries and barriers of diversity from the earliest times until now. There is no reason to believe that the future will be any different.

When we intentionally locate ourselves among the people in our communities, we often find that the Holy Spirit has already been at work among them. When we step out of our comfort zones and into theirs, we discover we're not always met with resistance, hostility, or surprise. Often, we find openness among the curious and expectant, the uninformed, or the "ready and waiting." And like Peter in Acts 10:34, we often have something to learn from them too.

The Holy Spirit is already at work, so thankfully, it doesn't *all* depend on us. Thank God we've been entrusted with a dynamic gospel, and the Holy Spirit is not limited by the walls of our churches and organizations or the language of our worship. The Holy Spirit is just as eager and capable of healing not only individual hearts, minds, and bodies but also entire systems, communities, and nations.

Closing the gap means stepping out and trying something we've never done before, standing out and being uncomfortably visible, and speaking up *and* being ready to listen. In doing so, we become disrupted disruptors who multiply those who choose to follow Jesus!

EMBODY THE MESSAGE

Disrupted disruptors transform the world in ways similar to how they have been transformed themselves. In other words, they seek to embody the message they preach.

One of the reasons the early church was so successful in its evangelism is because it slowly dealt with its own collusion with worldly values and behaviors, openly repenting and calling them out. It genuinely cared for marginalized groups like widows, orphans (especially baby girls left exposed to die), and strangers and actively challenged societal prejudices and ethnocentrisms. They often learned, sometimes painfully, that following Jesus meant living counterculturally. In fact, the book of Acts often reads like the initiation of one social movement after another that ultimately transformed societies, including our own.

I sometimes hear of churches planted and movements growing without significantly crossing racial, social, or subcultural boundaries or even transforming relationships with kingdom possibilities. Rather than accept this as normative, we should question how sustainable and transformative they truly are and in what ways they embody the gospel message. Discussions about the unfinished mission frequently frame it as a numbers game, focusing on maximizing conversions and getting as many people "saved" as possible. However, rather than just increasing church attendance, the true essence of mission is revealed in Jesus' ultimate act of embodiment that we refer to as "incarnation." It is also about us embodying kingdom values in such a way that others choose to join, even if they fear the consequences of doing so, as they often did in the book of Acts. Experience shows that a church's size doesn't always correlate with its impact on fostering kingdom-like qualities within itself, let alone in the surrounding community. Believers need a far more radical commitment to crossing boundaries with embodied faith and sometimes forget that ministries aren't simply called to grow bigger. They are called to envision and incarnate another world in which they are agents of kingdom transformation.

Reclaim Lost Opportunities: Azusa Street

A year after the Mukti Mission revival in 1905, Los Angeles became the birthplace of the Azusa Street Revival, led by William Seymour, the son of recently freed slaves. Seymour was a self-educated Black preacher in his mid-thirties with vision in only one eye. His prior religious experience included the Methodist Episcopal Church, the Church of God, and, briefly, the Salvation Army. His time with the Salvation Army and the Evening Light Saints, in particular, shaped his commitment to evangelical, Pentecostal, and interracial Christianity.

On April 9, 1906, William Seymour experienced a significant spiritual event, which was his own "second blessing." He started his Apostolic Faith Mission at 312 Azusa Street, preaching "that tongues accompanied by the dissolution of racial barriers were the indisputable sign of the Holy Spirit."[23] It was here that Blacks, whites, Hispanics, and Europeans met and worshiped together, crossing formerly impossible cultural lines.

The Azusa Street Revival was groundbreaking in how it shattered racial, cultural, and economic barriers over fifty years before *all* women were "permitted" to vote,[24] and fifty years before the civil rights movement began.[25] People of color and women were actively involved in leading and preaching in the mission, with six out of twelve elders being female.

The services were unconventional, with no preset plans or structure. Seymour believed God directed the gatherings, which involved spontaneous preaching, prayer, and singing, often with extended periods of seeking God. Indeed, he seldom even preached.

This revival went global from the very beginning, and in just five months sent out thirty-eight missionaries. Within two years, it had reached over fifty nations, totally transforming global Christianity to this day.

However, by 1909, various factors sowed the seeds of its decline. Seymour had initially turned to Charles Parham, a Ku Klux Klan sympathizer, who ran

Bethel College, a Holiness Bible School in Houston, Texas, and who taught on the need for "the baptism of the Holy Ghost," leading to speaking in tongues. Despite Parham's views of Blacks, Seymour begged to be admitted into his school and was eventually allowed to listen to Parham's lectures from a chair placed outside an open window.

In their book *The Ten Greatest Revivals Ever*, authors Elmer Towns and Douglas Porter describe how,

> Parham shuddered to see blacks and whites praying at the same altar. When a white woman "slain in the Spirit" (that is, overcome by the power of God) fell back into the arms of a black man, he was horrified at what he called a "darkey revival." When he began preaching, he accused those gathered of practicing animism and rebuked them for their disregard for racial distinctions.[26]

Such criticisms of the racial integration at Azusa Street had a lasting impact, and the initial messages of equality and empowerment faded. Pentecostals lost sight of this message and, over time, reestablished conventional and largely segregated patterns of church.

The demise of the Azusa Street revival provides one of the clearest examples of an "upper room" of racism, sexism, and intolerance that grieved the Holy Spirit and quenched a movement of God. In "What Revivals Can Teach Us," revival historian Michael McClymond outlines the typical characteristics of revival: "People not previously given a voice or a chance to lead have been thrust into the limelight. Women, people of color, the young, and the less educated have all played major roles in modern Christian revivals."[27]

If we long for revival, the multiplication of disciples, and divinely inspired visitations like Acts 2, we must understand what we are asking for. If we want what looks and feels like Pentecost, we might well be asking for all the challenges that accompanied the culturally and socially diverse conditions that called for Pentecost. That means relinquishing dearly held mindsets that effectively ignore segregation, conformity, uniformity, and assimilation. Palestinian theologian Mitri Raheb writes, "The church born in Jerusalem was meant to counter the empire not by creating another, but by providing a new pluralistic Euro-Mediterranean vision. The spirituality so needed today, more than at any previous time, is one that embraces diversity and pluralism and celebrates it as strength."[28]

While Pentecostalism stands as one of the most diverse movements within global Christianity, it still faces issues of segregation all over the world (even in racially homogenous groups). It has not fully embraced Seymour's teaching regarding eliminating racial and ethnic divides.[29] Although Pentecostal and charismatic Christianity continue to be the fastest-growing groups within global Christianity, their expansion rate is already decelerating, dropping from quadruple to double the overall growth rate of Christianity.[30]

Walk the Talk: Show Them How It's Done!

Perhaps Pentecostalism was intended to recover more than the untamed power of the Holy Spirit, as proposed by Steve Addison,[31] or the shared interest in Spirit baptism, spiritual gifts, and spiritual experiences, identified by Gina Zurlo, codirector of Gordon-Conwell Theological Seminary's Center for the Study of Global Christianity.[32] What if it was intended to embrace something far more fundamental—something that segregationist Parham abhorred? What if Pentecostalism's main purpose was to establish the "miracle" of ethnic and gender equality and the equitable sharing of resources through the power of the Spirit, much like that of the New Testament believers?

One wonders what would have happened if Christians had embraced this embodiment of the gospel and demonstrated that a new kind of community was indeed possible. Would the women's movement, civil rights movement, Black Lives Matter, and the climate movement have been necessary? Have we largely missed the point and turned Pentecostal experiences into "light entertainment," dramatic displays with token expressions of signs and wonders? How many potential disciples might we have lost along the way?

The Pentecostal and charismatic movements rightly empower believers to see the supernatural everywhere and to believe in the Holy Spirit's unlimited, supernatural, and transformative power. Tragically, each could also become just another movement that once upon a time equipped followers to apply these truths to everything *except* systemic and structural sin. Once truly disruptive, but eventually "tamed" and emptied of transformative power, only time will tell if the Pentecostal and charismatic movements regain their heart for intercultural possibilities. One wonders what impact Seymour's emphasis on equality could have had on the tribal, ethnic, racial, socioeconomic, and even environmental challenges we face today.

Disrupted disruptors have always shared key characteristics and embraced the strategic mission mindset exemplified in people like Pandita Ramabai and William Seymour. They commit to breaking free from geographical, ideological, cultural, and gender "upper room" mindsets. They are compelled to close the gap between themselves and those not yet introduced to Jesus by stepping out, standing out, and speaking up whenever necessary. They transform the world not simply by talking about how things should be but by literally showing people what the kingdom looks like in practice and enabling others to embrace it too. In their introduction to *The Ten Greatest Revivals Ever*, authors Elmer Towns and Douglas Porter describe how people, systems, structures, and even animals powerfully reveal the fruit of revival:

> The First Great Awakening in England, for example, resulted in Sunday school and educational reform, changes to labor and child welfare laws, significant prison reforms, and the abolition of slavery. During the Welsh Revival, the culture was so transformed that new mules had to be secured to work in the coal mines: The old mules wouldn't respond to miners who no longer cursed and abused the animals![33]

Unless we are showing the world what we mean by the gospel in our personal, interpersonal, and systemic interactions, we must question whether we are truly engaged in the kind of metamorphic disruption envisaged in Acts 2. Disrupted disruptors make no attempts to control the Holy Spirit and no apology for the disruption it causes. Instead, they wait proactively and expectantly, believing that God's Spirit will arrive on time and in power to enact God's will.

Wherever there is a contradiction between what the church teaches and what it does in practice, it experiences both an erosion of credibility and an inevitable decline in every era. If we don't walk our talk, we should not be surprised when those who see what we are really like are repelled rather than attracted by us. Authentic faith in Jesus is always a call to transformation, not just information, education, or multiplication! Whenever disrupted disruptors embrace this strategic mission mindset and hold out a vision of God's kingdom touching earth, they inevitably multiply disciples who cannot help but become disrupted disruptors too. I invite you to join those seeking to embody and advance the metamorphic mission *before* the mission today and to be part of the rise of God's Spirit-inspired metamorphs.

FOR PERSONAL REFLECTION OR GROUP DISCUSSION

Rate yourself from 1–10 (where 1 = needs significant improvement and 10 = exceptional).

Waiting for the Holy Spirit

1. I am known for waiting for the Holy Spirit by habitually
   - Embracing disruptive encounters (1———————————————–10)
   - Praying disrupting prayers (1———————————————————–10)
2. How could you strengthen your own commitment to wait?

Living as a Disrupted Disruptor

1. I am free from an "upper room" mentality when it comes to
   - Geographical captivity (1———————————————————————–10)
   - Ideological and cultural captivity (1———————————————–10)
   - Gender captivity (1——————————————————————————–10)
2. Where have you gotten stuck, and why are you stuck there?

Seeking to "Close the Gap"

1. I am closing the gap by
   - Stepping out (1————————————————————————————————–10)
   - Standing out (1———————————————————————————————–10)
   - Speaking up (1————————————————————————————————–10)
2. What do you think separates you from the people you've been called to serve?
3. Are your barriers linguistic, physical, or invisible (e.g., your own fears)?

Embodying the Message

1. I am embodying my message by walking my talk and doing what I say and saying what I do. (1———————————————————————–10)
2. My Christian community walks our talk and does what we say and say what we do. (1————————————————————————————————–10)

3. In what ways is the message you/your community speak(s) and your life/the life of your community inconsistent?

Identify one actionable change for each area that could significantly impact your effectiveness. Feel free to share your insights and discoveries.

TIME FOR PRAYER

Take a moment for personal or group prayer. If part of a discussion group, lift up each member, asking for the grace to *embed a strategic mission mindset*. Ask for wisdom to take every necessary step to align ourselves, our churches, our organizations, and our communities in ways that invite God to multiply the disrupted disrupters among us and through us in the world around us.

If your actions create a legacy that inspires others to dream more, learn more, do more and become more, then, you are an excellent leader.
DOLLY PARTON

She [He] Who Learns, Teaches
ETHIOPIAN PROVERB

THE METAMORPHIC JOURNEY CONTINUES

Congratulations! You've reached the end of the book, but your transformation journey is just beginning.

As a fellow metamorph, I am cheering you on and encouraging you to keep moving forward to unleash your full potential as a transformative leader!

Wondering what's next? Here are some ideas:

- **Form a book club or study group:** Discuss the book with other leaders and deepen your learning.
- **Use it as a teaching tool:** Share your insights with organizational leaders or create a sermon series based on the book's themes.

Ready to connect? Visit us at www.nextleadership.co.uk and share your ongoing journey.

ACKNOWLEDGMENTS

Where do I begin, when "acknowledgments" is such an inadequate word to express what I owe to those who have "been there" for me throughout my writing journey? I want to thank and honor the many wonderful women and men in my life, without whom this book would never have been completed. Special thanks go to Christine Caine for your foreword. You have an unmatched ability to truly see and "get" people. You also ask the best questions! Thanks also to Alan Hirsch for your staunch support throughout and for your foreword, which is, as always, perceptive.

Love and appreciation go to my sister by birth, Grace Owen, and my sister by choice, Cham Kaur-Mann—both of whom spent hours listening to me, rereading, questioning, and strengthening the content while also challenging, encouraging, and strengthening me when I most felt like giving up (which was far too often). Thanks especially to Cham, who had to live with me talking it through, day after day after day after day after ... (I think you get the picture.) I now understand Shakespeare's sentiments about friendship from *Hamlet*, which I paraphrase here: "Hold tightly to the friends you have, whose loyalty has been proven, and keep them close to your heart as if bound by unbreakable bonds." I am so grateful to God for you both. This would definitely not have been possible without you.

A shout out to my first group of readers: John Chaldecott, Oneya and Dele Okuwobi, Michelle Nunn, Sarah Whittleston, Grace Owen, and Cham Kaur-Mann. Thank you for helpfully critiquing the earliest version of the book and seeing something of value even then.

There are many others who also contributed and commented on content, covers, and planning every step of the way, together with endorsers who made time to read the manuscript amid busy schedules. Please accept my heartfelt appreciation for the part you all played in shaping this offering.

I should also thank my wonderful prayer partners, many of whom regularly cheered me on and kept me going throughout the major upheavals of this project, especially Kay and John Chaldecott, who shared some of my lowest and highest moments along the journey. Unfortunately, I can't mention you all by name without writing a whole new chapter! The same could be said of the many men and women I have mentored, coached, and interacted with over the years who have allowed me to represent aspects of their stories in these pages. May God continue to take you all from strength to strength. You are amazing metamorphs!

And nearly last (but certainly not least!), my thanks to Anna Robinson—our connection was clearly a divine appointment—and the rest of the editorial team at 100 Movements Publishing. It has been a privilege.

Needless to say, without God, I wouldn't have been here to write at all! There really are no words to express my gratitude for him … *Gye Nyame*!

NOTES

FOREWORD: CHRISTINE CAINE

1. Although many attribute this quote to Albert Einstein, there is no evidence to support this.
2. See page 17 of this book.
3. See page 16 of this book.

1 METAMORPHIC LEADERSHIP

1. The origins of this insightful and compelling morality tale are somewhat shrouded in mystery. A variety of versions exist in which the key sentiments are expressed by a "young man" ("Legacy story: Findings of a man who decided to change the world," Purpose Focus Commitment, accessed May 13, 2024, https://purposefocuscommitment.com/legacy-story-findings-man-who-decided-change-world/); an unknown Monk, in CE 1100 (Byron Pulsifer, "I Wanted To Change The World," Wow4u, September 24, 2017, https://www.wow4u.com/change-world/); and a Chinese general (emerging from ancient Chinese folklore), "The Man Who Wanted to Change the World," Eden Sunshine, accessed May 13, 2024, https://www.edensunshine.com/the-man-who-wanted-to-change-the-world/. Some consider the story to be an expanded version of a comparable and better-known declaration made either by Rumi, a thirteenth-century Persian poet, Hanafi faqih, Islamic scholar, Maturidi theologian, and Sufi mystic originally from Greater Khorasan in Greater Iran: "Yesterday I was clever, so I wanted to change the world. Today I am wise, so I am changing myself." Others attribute its roots to English philosopher and writer Aldous Leonard Huxley (1894–1963), writer of nearly fifty works of fiction and non-fiction. The following statement is said to have been recorded two years before his death in 1963 at the age of sixty-nine: "I wanted to change the world. But I have found that the only thing one can be sure of changing is oneself," *The Observer*, Section: Weekend Review, Sayings of the Week, quote page 32, column 2, London, England, July 2, 1961 (Newspapers.com). Whatever the case, the sentiment continues to challenge and inspire leaders everywhere.
2. Including our institutions, organizations, networks, communities, churches, etc.
3. In Genesis chapter 1:28, God chooses not to be the only being who has or exercises creative power and makes it quite clear that both male and female are called as co-stewards of the earth: "God blessed them and said to them, 'Be fruitful and increase in number; fill the earth and subdue it. Rule over the fish in the sea and the birds in the sky and over every living creature that moves on the ground.'" In other words, God shares his power from the very beginning.
4. Including mental, social, cultural, structural, environmental, organizational, emotional, etc.

5   The transcendence of God means that God is outside of humanity's full experience, perception, or grasp. The immanence of God means that he is knowable, perceivable, or graspable.

6   As well as skill, talent, social, generational, cultural, and beyond.

7   Ease of access means that "ordinary people" can influence decision-making and amass followers regardless of experience, credentials, or the recognition and accountability that is often (but not always) provided by the more institutional routes to authority. They can influence decision-making simply by amplifying and exacerbating preexisting social and political divisions in disturbing and destructive ways or they can educate and raise peoples' awareness on things that really matter to them in pursuit of community transformation or justice in ways that was simply not possible before. As some traditional leadership tasks and decision-making are being delegated to artificial intelligence (AI), this raises questions about what leadership truly is, where, what, and how humans should be involved as well as heightening the need for more human-centered leadership. See AI use in Job Mwaura, "Kenya protests: Gen Z shows the power of digital activism—driving change from screens to the streets," *The Conversation*, June 22, 2024, https://theconversation.com/kenya-protests-gen-z-shows-the-power-of-digital-activism-driving-change-from-screens-to-the-streets-233065.

8   Richard Rohr, "Praying With Nature," Center for Action and Contemplation, October 30, 2023, https://cac.org/daily-meditations/praying-with-nature/.

9   See the section entitled "Our Spiritual Postures," in Cindy S. Lee, *Our Unforming: De-Westernizing Spiritual Formation* (Minneapolis, MN: Fortress Press, 2022), 11–13.

10 See Part 1, "Orientation Cyclical," in Lee, *Our Unforming*, 11–13.

11 Richard Rohr, "Other Ways of Knowing," Center for Action and Contemplation, August 7, 2018, https://cac.org/daily-meditations/other-ways-of-knowing-2018-08-07/.

12 Humility involves recognizing one's limitations, acknowledging dependence on God, and treating others with respect and dignity. Humility includes a willingness to serve and a posture of openness to learning and growth. This is particularly emphasized in the increasing commitment across businesses to what is lauded as agile leadership (see "Leading Agile Transformation: The New Capabilities Leaders Need to Build 21st-Century Organizations," McKinsey & Company, October 1, 2018, https://www.mckinsey.com/capabilities/people-and-organizational-performance/our-insights/leading-agile-transformation-the-new-capabilities-leaders-need-to-build-21st-century-organizations) and in the field of Christian missions as polycentric leadership (see Joseph W. Handley, "Polycentrism as the New Leadership Paradigm," accessed February 7, 2024, https://lausanne.org/content/lga/2021-05/polycentrism-as-the-new-leadership-paradigm).

13 An interesting example of this has been in disaster management as climate change makes more notable inroads into the West, and as Europe is identified as the fastest warming continent and woefully unprepared for climate disaster. See Peter Yeung, "As Extreme Heat and Wildfires Hit Europe, Experts Look to Bangladesh for Climate Change Advice," *Telegraph*, July 18, 2023, https://www.telegraph.co.uk/global-health/climate-and-people/bangladesh-climate-change-early-warning-system-weather/.

14 See Eric Helleiner, "Economic Globalization's Polycrisis," *International Studies Quarterly: A Publication of the International Studies Association* 68, no. 2 (2024): 1–20, https://doi.

org/10.1093/isq/sqae024. A polycrisis is a cluster of disparate crises and shocks that interact, entangle, and mutually reinforce one another.

15 Lois Frankel highlights how "leadership in the twenty-first century is different from leadership in the mid-twentieth century is different from leadership in the pre-twentieth century. What makes leadership different through the ages are the needs of the followers…. Today's followers are similar to the followers of past centuries in that they want strong leaders. The difference is that they also want to participate in the decision-making process, want to be recognized for their accomplishments and want autonomy in how they achieve organizational goals." Lois P. Frankel, *See Jane Lead: 99 Ways for Women to Take Charge at Work* (New York, NY: Warner Business, 2007), xviii.

16 Vaughan S. Roberts and David Sims, *Leading by Story: Rethinking Church Leadership* (London, England: SCM Press, 2017), 26.

17 Ruchika Tulshyan and Jodi-Ann Burey, "Stop Telling Women They Have Imposter Syndrome," *Harvard Business Review*, February 11, 2021, https://hbr.org/2021/02/stop-telling-women-they-have-imposter-syndrome.

18 Tyler Kleeberger in "Ecological Entanglement: A Preferential Option for Creation" in *Red Skies: 10 Essential Conversations Exploring Our Future as the Church*, ed., L. Rowland Smith (Cody, WY: 100 Movements Publishing, 2022), 94.

19 Influence can be defined as *the power to change or affect someone or something: the power to cause changes without directly forcing them to happen*, whereas popularity is effectively *the state or condition of being liked, admired, or supported by many people*. Christians can also mistake the potentially far-ranging benefits of one for the temporary and fleeting impact of the other. We too can settle for the narrow gains of popularity at the expense of world-changing influence. Yet Jesus never settled for popularity but ended up changing the world anyway.

20 Richard Rohr, *The Wisdom Pattern: Order, Disorder, Reorder* (Cincinnati, OH: Franciscan Media, 2020), 84–85 (emphasis original).

21 In reference to Hahn (2006), quoted in Ingo Gildenhard and Andrew Zissos, eds., *Transformative Change in Western Thought: A History of Metamorphosis from Homer to Hollywood* (Oxford, NY: Routledge Legenda, 2013), 47.

22 Latin: pupa, "doll"; plural: pupae is the life stage of some insects undergoing transformation between immature and mature stages. The metamorphosis from a caterpillar into a butterfly occurs during the pupa stage. During this stage, the caterpillar's old body dies and a new body forms inside a protective shell known as a chrysalis.

23 Josh Davis, "Metamorphosis is Helping to Explain Salamander Skull Diversity," Natural History Museum, June 22, 2020, https://www.nhm.ac.uk/discover/news/2020/june/metamorphosis-is-helping-to-explain-salamander-skull-diversity.html.

24 Marshall Scott, "Transformation or Transfiguration?" MT Tabor Presbyterian Church, February 11, 2018, https://mttaborchurch.net/transformation-or-transfiguration/.

25 In other words, humans who metamorphose are still physically recognisable unlike the caterpillar to butterfly.

26 Jim Wallis, *Seven Ways to Change the World: Reviving Faith and Politics* (Oxford, England: Lion Hudson PLC, 2008), 49.

27 Alan Hirsch and Rob Kelly reminds us that meta ideas are essentially foundational ideas

that other ideas are or can be built upon. Alan Hirsch with Rob Kelly, *Metanoia: How God Radically Transforms People, Churches, and Organizations From the Inside Out* (Cody, WY: 100 Movements Publishing, 2023), 145.
28   Hirsch and Kelly, *Metanoia*, 61
29   In Christian thought, genuine faith is demonstrated through habitual good actions that reinforce, deepen, and transform our faith and way of thinking. See, for example, Tom Wright, *Virtue Reborn* (London, England: SPCK, 2010), 223.
30   Steven Croft, "A Theology of Christian Leadership," in *Focus on Leadership: A Theology of Church Leadership*, Church Leadership Foundation, London, 2005, 13.
31   See Ingo Gildenhard and Andrew Zissos, "Metamorphosis – Angles of Approach," Institute of Advanced Study, Durham University, *Insights* 3, no. 12 (2010): 6. They say, "Metamorphosis plays a key role in Judeo-Christian monotheism, both in the Bible and beyond." See also Gildenhard and Zissos, eds., *Transformative Change*.
32   Franz Kafka, *The Metamorphosis* (New York, NY: Project Gutenberg, 2002), www.gutenberg.org/ebooks/5200.
33   Kafka, *The Metamorphosis*, Kindle loc., 787.
34   See https://innerdevelopmentgoals.org/. The following can be found on their website: "In 2015, the Sustainable Development Goals gave us a comprehensive plan for a sustainable world by 2030. The seventeen goals cover a wide range of issues that involve people with different needs, values, and convictions. There is a vision of what needs to happen, but progress along this vision has so far been disappointing. We lack the inner capacity to deal with our increasingly complex environment and challenges. Fortunately, modern research shows that the inner abilities we now all need can be developed. This was the starting point for the 'Inner Development Goals' initiative."
35   Whereas transformation leads to a complete change in nature, condition, or function, deformation leads to a loss of form or shape brought about by some external force or pressure. The external forces that act on leaders include VUCA (volatility, uncertainty, complexity, and ambiguity), sin, and temptation.
36   See Cal Newport, *Deep Work: Rules for Focused Success in a Distracted World* (London, England: Little Brown Book Group, 2016), 100. Discipline requires that we exercise our willpower and self-control. We "have a finite amount of willpower that becomes depleted as [we] use it." Alternatively, we appear to have a hard time fighting desires and deep longings of any kind. We can also develop practices and habits that support our desires.
37   Knowledge is an awareness of facts, a familiarity with individuals and situations, or a practical skill. Knowledge of facts, also called propositional knowledge, is often characterized as true belief that is distinct from opinion or guesswork by virtue of justification.
38   Particularly in terms of deepening levels of consciousness.
39   Nahum Ward-Lev, *The Liberating Path of the Hebrew Prophets: Then and Now* (Maryknoll, NY: Orbis Books, 2019), 140 and 144. Rabbi Nahum Ward-Lev leads Beit Midrash of Santa Fe, a multifaith sacred learning community. It is worth noting here that all leadership involves failure, and God supports falling forward. The earlier, more often, and more cheaply we fail, the better. However, when a woman or person of color fails, the stakes tend to be higher, they are less likely to be supported, and the tables are more likely to be turned against them.

40 Faithfulness refers to being trustworthy, reliable, and committed. It involves fulfilling one's responsibilities and obligations with diligence and integrity. Faithfulness includes being faithful to God, to others, and to the calling and tasks entrusted to individuals.

41 Richard Rohr, *Things Hidden: Scripture as Spirituality* (Cincinnati, OH: Franciscan Media, 2008), 103–104.

42 Pastor Rick Warren, "There is no success without growth," Facebook, August 28, 2016, https://www.facebook.com/pastorrickwarren/photos/a.414149010902/10154337532830903/?type=3.

43 Richard Rohr asserts that when it comes to human development, "the way up is the way down. Or, if you prefer, the way down is the way up." The concept of "falling upward" suggests that the descent into suffering and failure is actually an ascent into a more profound and authentic self. True growth comes from embracing life's difficulties and learning from them. Richard Rohr, *Falling Upward: A Spirituality for the Two Halves of Life* (San Francisco, CA: Jossey-Bass, 2011), 24.

44 "Shalom is the stuff of the Kingdom. It's what the Kingdom of God looks like in context. It's what citizenship in the Kingdom of God requires and what the Kingdom promises to those who choose God and God's ways to peace." See Lisa Sharon Harper, *The Very Good Gospel: How Everything Wrong Can Be Made Right*, (Colorado Springs, CO: Waterbrook Press, 2019), 12–13.

45 Harper, *The Very Good Gospel*, 12.

46 David Brooks, *The Road to Character* (New York, NY: Penguin Books Ltd, 2015), 12.

47 Leadership specialist Jeanne Porter King writes, "We bring all of ourselves—spirit, soul and body—into our leadership role. And if our spirit, our emotions, our minds, and our bodies are hurting, we will hurt those who follow us…. Becoming the leader you were meant to be starts with your innermost self." She adds, "Defensive, over-controlling and insecure people make defensive, over-controlling and insecure leaders—who in turn, create rigid, overly structured, and competitive organizations, businesses, ministries, or agencies. The leader who has not sufficiently worked through her own issues will bring those issues with her into her leadership role." Jeanne Porter, *Leading Lessons: Insights on Leadership from Women of the Bible* (Minneapolis, MO: Augsburg, 2005), 31.

48 Henri J. M. Nouwen, *Bread for the Journey: A Daybook of Wisdom and Faith* (New York, NY: HarperCollins, 1997), 77.

2 TRANSFORMING WISDOM

1 John C. Maxwell, *The 21 Indispensable Qualities of a Leader: Becoming the Person Others Will Want to Follow*, 2nd ed., (Nashville, TN: HarperCollins Leadership, 2007), 7. Maxwell is sometimes referred to as America's leadership expert.

2 Marshall Goldsmith, "If They Understand, They Will Do," Marshall Goldsmith Library, accessed June 26, 2024, https://marshallgoldsmithlibrary.com/cim/articles_print.php?aid=227.

3 Laura Heaton, "Sensemaking in a VUCA World: Applying Vertical Development to Enhance Learning Agility," in *The Age of Agility: Building Learning Agile Leaders and Organizations*, eds., Veronica Schmidt Harvey and Kenneth P. De Meuse (New York, NY: Oxford University Press, 2021), 17.

4   It doesn't matter if you consider ours a VUCA (Volatile, Uncertain, Complex, and Ambiguous), BANI (Brittle, Anxious, Non-linear, Incomprehensible), RUPT (Rapid, Unpredictable, Paradoxical, Tangled), or TUNA (Turbulent, Uncertain, Novel, Ambiguous) world. If we look at the explanations, the essence is not very different; they all point to extreme and rapid changes in the external environment that cause uncertainty for all of us as organizations, communities, and individuals.

5   1 Sam. 16 tells of the prophet Samuel's search for a "replacement" leader for Israel. He is sent off by God to anoint one of Jesse's sons, and when Samuel arrives at Jesse's house, he is dazzled by the "usual suspects" for leadership because all of Jesse's invited sons look like a great match for the job! So, God has to interrupt the prophet Samuel's deliberations with the words, "The LORD does not look at the things people look at. People look at the outward appearance, but the LORD looks at the heart." In other words, "Samuel, the stuff you're focusing on in this job search is the least important thing of all."

6   Strong's Exhaustive Concordance of the Bible cites that the heart is referred to 826 times throughout the Bible.

7   Often translated in some Bible versions as "pure."

8   The things we tell ourselves about ourselves and our circumstances. Individuals hold internal scripts and use them to guide the way they process tasks and whatever else they may be faced with, but these internal scripts may be inaccurate and flawed.

9   What we really believe, and not just what we say we believe.

10 Not just who and what we are but also who and what we want to become.

11 Suzi Skinner, *Build Your Leader Identity: A Practical Guide to Leading Authentically from Any Position* (Haberfield, NSW: Longueville Media, 2015), 164–165.

12 James M. Kouzes and Barry Z. Posner, *A Leader's Legacy* (San Francisco, CA: John Wiley & Sons, 2006), 90.

13 See Michel Ferrari and Nic M. Weststrate, *The Scientific Study of Personal Wisdom: From Contemplative Traditions to Neuroscience* (Dordrecht, NL: Springer, 2014). They emphasize how the concept of wisdom is elevated particularly in Eastern cultures (Chinese and Indian), Middle Eastern cultures (including Islamic), Ancient Greek cultures, Judeo-Christian traditions, and African cultures. We could add to these Aboriginal and First Nations peoples.

14 Richard Rohr, *The Wisdom Pattern: Order, Disorder, Reorder* (Cincinnati, OH: Franciscan Media, 2020), 84–85.

15 Ferrari and Weststrate, *The Scientific Study of Personal Wisdom*, 5. They explain: "Personal wisdom refers to individuals' insight into their selves, their own life. Analogous to the third-person perspective, general wisdom is concerned with individuals' insights into life in general, into life from an observer's point of view, that is, when their own life is not directly concerned."

16 Ferrari and Weststrate, *The Scientific Study of Personal Wisdom*, 5.

17 Albert Einstein, "We cannot solve the problems using the same kind of thinking we used when we created them," quoted in FBIS Daily Report: East Europe, April 4, 1995, 45, as cited in Paul Arden, *It's Not How Good You Are, It's How Good You Want to Be* (London, England: Phaidon Press, 2003), 60.

18 Will Storr, *The Science of Storytelling: Why Stories Make Us Human, and How to Tell Them Better* (New York, NY: HarperCollins Publishers, 2019), 211.
19 Ivan Illich, "Ivan Illich Quotes," AZQuotes.com, accessed December 31, 2023, https://www.azquotes.com/quote/726324.
20 This involves interpreting the Bible story through a specific interpretive lens that expands on background, context, and method in ways that highlight particular themes. Jesus liberally employs this interpretive approach. I use it here to highlight whatever is able to emphasize the leadership themes within a particular text.
21 Vaughan S. Roberts and David Sims, *Leading by Story: Rethinking Church Leadership* (London, England: SCM Press, 2017), 44.
22 Roberts and Sims, *Leading by Story*, 44.
23 Alan Hirsch, *The Forgotten Ways: Reactivating the Missional Church* (Grand Rapids, MI: Baker Publishing Group, 2006), 221.
24 "A griot is a West African storyteller, singer, musician, and oral historian. They train to excel as orators, lyricists and musicians. The griot keeps records of all the births, deaths, marriages through the generations of the village or family." For more information, see Hakimah Abdul-Fattah, "How Griots Tell Legendary Epics through Stories and Songs in West Africa," The Metropolitan Museum of Art, April 20, 2020, https://www.metmuseum.org/perspectives/articles/2020/4/sahel-sunjata-stories-songs.
25 Storr, *The Science of Storytelling*, 155, 211.
26 Hirsch, *The Forgotten Ways*, 55.
27 See Roberts and Sims, *Leading by Story*, 60.
28 Stanley Hauerwas and William H. Willimon, *Resident Aliens: Life in the Christian Colony* (Nashville, TN: Abingdon Press, 1989), 21.
29 Ferrari and Weststrate, *The Scientific Study of Personal Wisdom*, 149.
30 Jennifer Butler, *Who Stole My Bible?: Reclaiming Scripture as a Handbook for Resisting Tyranny* (Washington DC, CO: Faith in Public Life, 2020), 7–8.
31 Cheryl Bridges Johns, "Grieving, Brooding, and Transforming: The Spirit, the Bible, and Gender," in *Grieving, Brooding, and Transforming: The Spirit, the Bible, and Gender*, eds., Cheryl Bridges Johns and Lisa Stephenson, *Journal of Pentecostal Theology Supplement* 46 (Leiden, NL: Brill, 2021), 11.
32 Midrash is a method of biblical interpretation found in Jewish tradition that seeks to uncover deeper meanings, draw out implications, and explore the applications of biblical texts. The term "midrash" itself comes from the Hebrew root "darash," which means "to seek" or "to inquire." Midrash encompasses both the process of interpretation and the body of literature produced by this interpretive method.
33 This is known as "narrative transportation," where listeners or readers become so absorbed in a story that they feel as if they are a part of the narrative's world. See Storr, *The Science of Storytelling*, 207. Storr writes, "We can become so replaced by the storyteller's simulated model-world that we miss our train stop or forget to go to sleep. Psychologists call this state 'transportation'. Research suggests that, when we're transported, our beliefs, attitudes and intentions are vulnerable to being altered, in accordance with the mores of the story, and that these alterations can stick. Research has demonstrated that the transported 'traveller' can return changed by the journey."

34 See section entitled, "Cause and Effect: Literary versus Mass-Market Storytelling," in *The Science of Storytelling*, 48–56. Storr examines how stories literally condition our minds. They can have lasting cognitive and emotional effects, enhance memory, influence our mood, and sometimes even affect our worldview. However, long-term engagement with complex narratives has been shown to change the structures within the brain, enhancing areas involved in language comprehension and processing, as well as improving our ability to empathize with others and understand their motives and feelings.

35 Harvey Cox, *When Jesus Came to Harvard: Making Moral Choices Today* (Boston, MA: Houghton Mifflin, 2004), 155, 159.

36 Chimamanda Ngozi Adichie, "The Danger of a Single Story," filmed July 2009 at TEDGlobal, Oxford, UK, video, 18:49, https://www.ted.com/talks/chimamanda_adichie_the_danger_of_a_single_story.

37 Liz Shercliff, *Preaching Women: Gender, Power and the Pulpit* (London, England: SCM Press, 2019), Kindle locs., 299–302.

38 James H. Cone, *God of the Oppressed* (Maryknoll, NY: Orbis Books, 1997), 36.

39 Deepa Purushothaman, *The First, the Few, the Only: How Women of Color Can Redefine Power in Corporate America* (New York, NY: Harper Business, 2022), Kindle locs., 299–302.

40 Liz Shercliff further clarifies this through the storytelling tradition of preaching, remarking, "One of the wonders of preaching is not that God speaks through human lips, but that God speaks through human personalities." Shercliff, *Preaching Women*, Kindle locs., 242–243. Hence, our telling of God's story, our theology, is never neutral. It inevitably reveals, mirrors, and perhaps exposes our gender, history, values, ethics, traditions, and culture even as it shapes and informs us. In the words of Tom A. Steffen, "No-one comes to God's sacred story book storyless." Tom A. Steffen, *Reconnecting God's Story to Ministry: Cross-Cultural Storytelling at Home and Abroad* (Centre for Organizational and Ministry Development, USA, 1996), 15.

41 The use of all white Euro-American casts in biblical epics and stories designed to convey a world that was both culturally and visibly Afro-Asiatic is a case in point and has contributed to the unhealthy racialized dynamics within churches and led to erasure and false self-understandings of Black, brown, and white populations everywhere.

42 Shercliff, *Preaching Women*, Kindle locs., 262–263.

43 See Alice Walker, *In Search of Our Mothers' Gardens: Womanist Prose* (London, England: Weidenfeld & Nicolson, 2011).

44 Rachel Held Evans, *A Year of Biblical Womanhood: How a Liberated Woman Found Herself Sitting on Her Roof, Covering Her Head, and Calling Her Husband Master* (Nashville, TN: Thomas Nelson, 2012), 296.

45 Here we return to the principle outlined by Jesus, "By their fruit you will recognize them" (Matt. 7:16).

3 MOSES

1 Storr, *The Science of Storytelling*, 17.

2 Knowledge is understood here as facts, information, data, and skills acquired through experience or education and the theoretical or practical understanding of a subject.

3 The preoccupation with the uncertainty of the existence of God and of malevolent or good spirits that is characteristic of the Post-Enlightenment European worldview is not a feature of the African or Afrocentric worldview. Just ask a continental African or Caribbean

person the question, "How do you know that God exists?" Unless they have been steeped in European culture and values, you are likely to be greeted with the following response, "What kind of foolish question is that?" They may differ on the precise manifestation of God but rarely on whether God exists.

4   Some religious scholars have drawn analogies between the name of God, YHWH (often pronounced "Yahweh"), and the act of breathing in (YH) and out (WH), reminding us that God is in every breath. See Chris Lacy, "YHWH: His Breath in Our Lungs," Medium, April 8, 2023, https://chrislacy1990.medium.com/yhwh-his-breath-in-our-lungs-21c2bc60571b.

5   In individualistic cultures, the primary agent of control is the individual. In collectivist cultures, it is the group. The entire aim in collectivist cultures is to ensure the group rather than the individual is successful. Thankfully, it is at least clear that in both instances, Moses was attempting to act in the interests of God's people.

6   These three major religious traditions are Judaism, Christianity, and Islam.

7   See page 22 of this book.

8   There are two kinds of identities—inherited and acquired. Inherited identities are almost fixed and are fairly well defined, e.g., race, color, region, society, etc. Others see us through this identity. An individual has different levels of affinity to different identities. Acquired identities are what you think you are. Identities such as liberal, conservative, secular are, in a way, values too. These values help you go beyond the constraints of inherited identity. A widely practiced religion, a political party, or an association of people that transcends the boundaries of inherited identities are some examples. Unlike inherited identities, these identities are self-certified or certified by the association.

9   Peter Burke, "Identity," in *The Cambridge Handbook of Social Theory: Volume 2: Contemporary Theories and Issues*, ed. Peter Kivisto (Cambridge, England: Cambridge University Press, 2020), 63–78 (emphasis added).

10 Blind spots are the specific area on the retina of each eye that lacks photoreceptor cells (rods and cones), making it insensitive to light. This area corresponds to the location where the optic nerve exits the eye and leads to the brain. They obscure a lemon-sized area of our vision in each eye. In addition, blinking also leaves us momentarily blind. Although our brains fill in the gaps, this is not always accurate. See Storr, *The Science of Storytelling*, 22. This is why the perspectives of others are critical.

11 For more on this, see Kate Coleman, *7 Deadly Sins of Women in Leadership: Overcome Self-Defeating Behavior in Work and Ministry*, Updated edition (Grand Rapids, MI: Zondervan, 2021), 106–108.

12 See Natalie Collins, "We Are All Implicated Subjects," God Loves Women, May 27, 2023, https://mrsglw.wordpress.com/2023/05/27/we-are-all-implicated-subjects/.

13 Collins, "We Are All Implicated Subjects."

14 Exod. 34:29–35.

15 See https://www.myersbriggs.org, https://www.gallup.com/cliftonstrengths, https://www.enneagramtest.com.

4   THE WOMAN AT THE WELL

1   For those who are interested, the biological factors that impact development include genetic influences, brain chemistry, hormone levels, nutrition, and gender.

2   About 330 billion cells are replaced daily, equivalent to about 1 percent of all our cells. In

80 to 100 days, 30 trillion will have replenished. This is the equivalent of generating a brand new you! See Mark Fischetti and Jen Christiansen, "Our Bodies Replace Billions of Cells Every Day," *Scientific American*, last modified February 1, 2023, https://www.scientificamerican.com/article/our-bodies-replace-billions-of-cells-every-day/.

3   These words are most commonly attributed to Swiss Roman Catholic theologian and priest Hans Urs von Balthasar, considered one of the most important theologians of the twentieth century.

4   This quote is often attributed to Frankl but is not found in any of his published works. The quote was popularized by motivational author Stephen R. Covey; however, Covey disclaims authorship.

5   This usual route circumvented Samaria by crossing the Jordan River and traveling northward along its eastern side before re-entering Galilee.

6   When King Rehoboam of Judah (in the south) gathered an army with the expressed intention of reunifying the two nations through warfare (1 Kings 12:21–24), the news is not received well in Israel to the north. This prompts Jeroboam, the king of Israel, to ensure that inhabitants of the northern kingdom no longer have to travel to Jerusalem for worship. Jeroboam establishes alternative worship sites in Bethel and Dan, introducing golden calves for worship to prevent his people from going to Jerusalem (1 Kings 12:25–33). Judah later witnesses the fall of the northern kingdom of Israel to the Assyrians in 722–721 BCE. The Assyrians, in line with their imperial tactics, attempt to erase Israel's identity, culture, and religion by deporting many Israelites to distant regions of their empire. They then repopulate Samaria with people from other parts of the Assyrian empire, who eventually intermarry with the remaining Israelites and adopt a syncretized form of the Jewish faith. A century later, Assyria's power wanes, and Babylon becomes the dominant regional power. In 587 BCE, Babylon conquers Jerusalem, destroying the city and the temple, and exiles the Judean elite, skilled craftsmen, and other prominent individuals to Babylon. Many years later, the exiled Jews begin to return to their homeland in Judah, after being liberated by the Persians in 538 BCE. Upon their return, the Jews view the people who had remained in the region, including many of the "mixed" Samaritans, not as long-lost family members but as inferior outcasts. When these Samaritans express a desire to help rebuild Jerusalem, they are rebuffed and sent away. In response, the Samaritans build a rival temple on Mount Gerizim and no longer regard the Jerusalem temple as the proper place of worship. They establish their own religious practices based solely on the Pentateuch. This animosity develops into a long history of hostility and prejudice between Jews and Samaritans. See Christopher Naseri-Mutiti Naseri, "Jews Have no Dealings With Samaritans: A Study of Relations Between Jews and Samaritans at the Time of Jesus Christ," *LWATI: A Journal of Contemporary Research*, 11, no. 2 (2014): 75–88.

7   D. A. Carson, *The Gospel According to John* (Nottingham, England: Apollos, 1991), 216.

8   Eva Catafygiotu Topping, "St. Photini, The Samaritan Woman," Orthodox Christian, accessed July 1, 2024, http://www.orthodoxchristian.info/pages/photini.htm, adapted from *Saints and Sisterhood: The Lives of Forty-Eight Holy Women* (Minneapolis, MN: Light and Life Publishing Company, 1990).

9   Ironically, she is said to have been martyred by being thrown down a well.

10 Robin J. Ely, Herminia Ibarra, and Deborah Kolb, "Taking Gender into Account: Theory and Design for Women's Leadership Development Programs," *Academy of Management Learning and Education* 10, no. 3 (2011); D. Scott DeRue and Susan J. Ashford, "Who

Will Lead and Who Will Follow? A Social Process of Leadership Identity Construction in Organizations," *Academy of Management Review* 35, no. 4 (2010): 627–47.
11   Herminia Ibarra, Robin J. Ely, and Deborah M. Kolb, "Women Rising: The Unseen Barriers," *Harvard Business Review*, September 1, 2013, https://hbr.org/2013/09/women-rising-the-unseen-barriers. They state, "Integrating leadership into one's core identity is particularly challenging for women, who must establish credibility in a culture that is deeply conflicted about whether, when, and how they should exercise authority."
12   Whereas a biography is a person's published life story, a hagiography (based on the Greek words, *hagios*, meaning holy, and *graphia*, meaning writing) is a written account of a saint's life or the study of saints. (In this case, it applies to St. Photini.)
13   See, for example, "Why Did The Samaritan Woman At The Well Have So Many Marriages?" Dust Off The Bible, June 26, 2016, https://dustoffthebible.com/Blog-archive/2016/06/26/why-did-the-samaritan-woman-at-the-well-have-so-many-marriages. See also "Was the woman at the well a 'bad girl?'" Bible.org Blogs, January 2, 2015, https://blogs.bible.org/was-the-woman-at-the-well-a-bad-girl/.
14   See examples in Ruth Tucker and Walter L. L. Liefeld, *Daughters of the Church: Women and Ministry from New Testament Times to the Present* (Kentwood, MI: Zondervan, 2010), and Halee Gray Scott, *Dare Mighty Things: Mapping the Challenges of Leadership for Christian Women* (Grand Rapids, MI: Zondervan, 2014).
15   Asset-Based Community Development (ABCD) was developed in the early 1990s by John L. McKnight and Jody Kretzmann at Northwestern University Il, US.
16   Bruce Milne, *The Message of John* (Leicester, England: Inter-Varsity Press, 1993), 83.
17   Babylonian Talmud, *Niddah*, 44b.
18   The New English Bible (NEB) is similar: "Jews and Samaritans, it should be noted, do not use vessels in common." See also Carson, *The Gospel According to John*, 218.
19   It was much later that Peter and John eventually preached voluntarily and extensively in Samaritan towns in support of Philip's pioneering mission in Acts 8.
20   This phrase has been variously attributed to Aristotle, Walter Lippmann, and Winston Churchill. However, the closest version on record was penned by biographer James Boswell, who authored *The Life of Samuel Johnson* and records him as saying, "Courage is reckoned the greatest of all virtues; because, unless a man has that virtue, he has no security for preserving any other." James Boswell, *The Life of Samuel Johnson, LL.D.: Comprehending an Account of His Studies and Numerous Works, in Chronological Order*, vol. 1 (London, England: Henry Baldwin for Charles Dilly, 1791), 473, https://babel.hathitrust.org/cgi/pt?id=uc1.31175035193740&seq=491.
21   Individuality refers to all the characteristics that make a person unique—and refers to only one person. Individualism, on the other hand, is a set of beliefs, ideas, practices, and assumptions that emphasize the liberty and autonomy of individuals. It isn't something that just belongs to one person.

5   MARY AND ELIZABETH

1   John 13:23.
2   Diana Butler Bass, *Christianity After Religion: The End of Church and the Birth of a New Spiritual Awakening* (New York, NY: HarperCollins, 2013), Kindle, 205.

3   Dana L. Robert, *Faithful Friendships: Embracing Diversity in Christian Community* (Grand Rapids, MI: Eerdmans, 2019), Kindle, 1.
4   See quote by Neil deGrasse Tyson, *Geniuses Club*, accessed June 26, 2024, https://geniuses.club/quotes/3946.
5   Wikipedia contributors, "Blood is Thicker Than Water," Wikipedia: The Free Encyclopedia, last modified June 26, 2024, https://en.wikipedia.org/wiki/Blood_is_thicker_than_water.
6   Cultural commentator Stephen Marche notes, "We live in an accelerating contradiction: the more connected we become, the lonelier we are. We were promised a global village; instead we inhabit the drab cul-de-sacs and endless freeways of a vast suburb of information." Stephen Marche, "Is Facebook Making Us Lonely?," *The Atlantic Monthly*, May 2012, https://www.theatlantic.com/magazine/archive/2012/05/is-facebook-making-us-lonely/308930/.
7   "Tackling Loneliness annual report March 2023: the fourth year," Government UK, March 30, 2023, https://www.gov.uk/government/publications/loneliness-annual-report-the-fourth-year/tackling-loneliness-annual-report-march-2023-the-fourth-year.
8   Quoted in Hirsch, *The Forgotten Ways*, Kindle, 244.
9   St. Augustine of Hippo, *The Letters of St. Augustine*, trans., John George Cunningham (Loschberg, DE: Jazzybee Verlag, 2015), 261.
10 C. S. Lewis, *The Four Loves* (New York, NY: HarperOne, 1960), 96.
11 Marsha L. Dutton, *Aelred of Rievaulx: Spiritual Friendship*, trans., Lawrence C. Braceland (Collegeville, MN: Liturgical Press, 2010), 73.
12 Montaigne's exact words are: "So many coincidences are needed to build up such a friendship that it is a lot if fortune can do it once in three centuries." Michel de Montaigne "Of Friendship," *The Complete Essays of Montaigne*, trans., Donald Frame (Stanford, CA: Stanford University Press, 1958), 136.
13 Lee, *Our Unforming*, 129.
14 Robert, *Faithful Friendships*, 8.
15 Emmanuel M. Katongole, *Mirror to the Church: Resurrecting Faith after Genocide in Rwanda* (Grand Rapids, MI: Zondervan, 2009), 156.
16 S. E. Taylor, L. C. Klein, B. P. Lewis, T. L. Gruenewald, R. A. Gurung, and J. A. Updegraff, "Biobehavioral responses to stress in females: tend-and-befriend, not fight-or-flight," *Psychological Review* 107, no. 3 (2000): 411–429, https://pubmed.ncbi.nlm.nih.gov/10941275/.
17 "The tend and befriend theory says that humans, particularly females, often respond to stress by tending to young ones and by seeking connection or befriending one another. When social interactions are comforting, stress levels decrease. A woman who feels threatened at work might reach out to her husband or attempt to develop deeper friendships with her co-workers. A child who is bullied at school might ask for help from his teacher or parents. There is evidence that tend and befriend also has an instinctive basis. In a study of 237 young men and women, researchers found evidence to suggest that men tended to respond to threats by fighting, while women preferred fleeing or tending and befriending." Nora Nickels, Konrad Kubicki, and Dario Maestripieri, "Sex Differences in the Effects of Psychosocial Stress on Cooperative and Prosocial Behavior: Evidence for 'Flight or Fight' in Males and 'Tend and Befriend' in Females," *Adaptive Human Behavior and Physiology* 3, no. 2 (2017): 171–183.

18   See John 3:3–8, which describes what it means to be "born of the Spirit." Whereas Hebrews 10:19 states "Therefore, brothers and sisters, since we have confidence to enter the Most Holy Place by the blood of Jesus," in this verse "brothers and sisters" is the Greek *adelphos*, which comes from *"a"* (denoting unity) and *"delphus"* (denoting womb). It points to physical or spiritual siblings. See also Beth M. Stovell's discussion in "The Birthing Spirit, the Childbearing God," *Priscilla Papers*, 24, no. 4 (Autumn 2021), https://www.cbeinternational.org/resource/birthing-spirit-childbearing-god/. The only reproductive organ God is specifically associated with throughout Scripture is a womb.
19   Cone, *God of the Oppressed*, 60.
20   On May 22, 2017, Salman Abedi detonated an improvised explosive device in the Manchester Arena, resulting in twenty-three deaths (including the attacker). This was the deadliest terrorist attack on UK soil since the 2005 London bombings. See Wikipedia contributors, "Manchester Arena Bombing," Wikipedia, The Free Encyclopedia, July 3, 2024, https://en.wikipedia.org/wiki/Manchester_Arena_bombing.
21   The term "Palestine" has a long history as a region between Phoenicia and Egypt before becoming an official Roman province "Syria Palaestina" in c. 135 BCE in an attempt to suppress Jewish identity with the land. Prior to this and from the fifth century BCE Herodotus and other Greek writers such as Ptolemon and Pausanias, used the term "Palestine" to describe the region and were later followed by Roman writers such as Ovid, Pliny, and Plutarch, as well as Jewish writers such as Philo and Josephus.

6   THE APOSTLES

1   Ashley Quarcoo and Medina Husaković, "Racial Reckoning in the United States: Expanding and Innovating on the Global Transitional Justice Experience," *Carnegie Endowment for International Peace*, paper, October 26, 2021, https://carnegieendowment.org/2021/10/26/racial-reckoning-in-united-states-expanding-and-innovating-on-global-transitional-justice-experience-pub-85638.
2   Kairos is a Greek word that refers to a time when conditions are right for the accomplishment of a crucial action: the opportune, critical, and decisive moment.
3   Rather than simply referring to the presence of distinctives, here diversity is defined as having *mutual respect and appreciation* for people of different races, cultures, ethnicities, sex, abilities, talents, skills, insights, and approach.
4   Martin Luther King Jr., *Stride Toward Freedom: The Montgomery Story* (New York, NY: Harper & Brothers, 1958), 119.
5   "Inter" conveys the idea of sharing, reciprocity, and equality. In these churches, there is robust contact between cultures and a deep understanding and respect for all cultures. Intercultural communication focuses on the mutual exchange of ideas and cultural norms and the development of deep relationships. In an intercultural church, no one is left unchanged because everyone learns from one another and grows together. However, it is also possible for injustice to exist in intercultural contexts. Diversity and inclusion measures do not necessarily create equity and belonging without a proactive commitment to justice.
6   They included: PepsiCo, who announced a commitment of $400 million over five years to "lift up Black communities and increase Black representation at PepsiCo." PayPal's

president and CEO Dan Schulman unequivocally stated, "It is not enough for us to condemn racism. We must be anti-racist." See Gayle Markovitz and Samantha Sault, "What companies are doing to fight systemic racism," *World Economic Forum*, June 24, 2020, https://www.weforum.org/agenda/2020/06/companies-fighting-systemic-racism-business-community-black-lives-matter/.

7   Harriet Sherwood, "Justin Welby says he is 'sorry and ashamed' over church's racism," *The Guardian*, February 11, 2020, https://www.theguardian.com/world/2020/feb/11/justin-welby-tells-synod-he-is-sorry-and-ashamed-over-churchs-racism.

8   *The Guinness effect* is at the very least an indication that all is not well in multicultural churches and that new approaches are needed to develop truly intercultural congregations and leadership structures. See Ben Lindsay, *We Need To Talk About Race: Understanding the Black Experience in White Majority Churches* (London, UK: SPCK, 2019).

9   Jim Memory, "Europe 2021: A Missiological Report," European Christian Mission, 29. The missionary historian Andrew Walls has observed that "the movement of Christianity is one of serial, not progressive expansion," that is a decline in the heartlands but rapid growth at the periphery. Andrew Walls, "The Expansion of Christianity: An Interview with Andrew Walls," Religion Online, August 2000, https://www.religion-online.org/article/the-expansion-of-christianity-an-interview-with-andrew-walls/.

10 Memory appeals to the term "diaspora churches" rather than "ethnic churches" or "migrant churches," stating that he believes that is "the best term to describe the complex phenomena of churches in Europe that have resulted from the migration of Christians from other locations, whether in this generation or generations past. A diaspora is, strictly speaking, a population that has been dispersed but that retains linguistic, cultural, and other connections with its homeland." Memory, "Europe 2021: A Missiological Report," 29.

11 Memory, "Europe 2021: A Missiological Report," 47.

12 Pastor Rick Warren, "Racism is a sin problem, not a skin problem. This is not some minor issue to God. It's at the heart of the Gospel. Learn how to see people as God sees them in," Facebook, June 15, 2020, https://www.facebook.com/pastorrickwarren/photos/a.414149010902/10158492478790903/?type=3.

13 See David Roach, "Most US Pastors Speak Out in Response to George Floyd's Death," *Christianity Today*, June 16, 2020, https://www.christianitytoday.com/news/2020/june/pastors-george-floyd-racism-church-barna-research.html.

14 The original phrase, "When all is said and done, more is said than done" is often attributed to Aesop, the ancient Greek fabulist and storyteller, known for his collection of fables. However, variations of this sentiment, including the one cited here, have been expressed by many throughout history, including with regard to the fight against racism. See Kira Hudson Banks and Richard Harvey, "Is Your Company Actually Fighting Racism, or Just Talking About It?" *Harvard Business Review*, June 11, 2020, https://hbr.org/2020/06/is-your-company-actually-fighting-racism-or-just-talking-about-it.

15 In her 2017 book *Why I'm No Longer Talking to White People About Race*, Reni Eddo-Lodge quotes from a blog post that inspired her book, written on February 22, 2014: "I can no longer engage with the gulf of an emotional disconnect that white people display when a person of colour articulates their experience." You can see their eyes shut down and harden. It's like treacle is poured into their ears, blocking up their ear canals. It's like they can no

longer hear us." Reni Eddo-Lodge, *Why I'm No Longer Talking to White People About Race* (New York, NY: Bloomsbury Publishing, 2017), 26–28.

16. In the UK, according to the Equality Act 2010, it is against the law to discriminate against anyone on the basis of the following nine "protected characteristics": age, disability, gender reassignment, marriage and civil partnership, pregnancy and maternity, race, religion or belief, sex, and sexual orientation.

17. Kelly McDonald, *It's Time to Talk about Race at Work: Every Leader's Guide to Making Progress on Diversity, Equity, and Inclusion* (Hoboken, NJ: Wiley, 2021), Kindle, 67.

18. Ben Lindsay says of the church context, "Talking about race isn't easy. Some of the barriers I have faced in talking to white people about race are defensiveness and dismissiveness." Lindsay, *We Need To Talk*, 20.

19. This is sometimes described as a kind of spiritual bypassing or the tendency to use spiritual ideas and spiritual practices to sidestep or avoid facing unresolved emotional issues, psychological wounds, and unfinished developmental tasks. It is based on ideas developed by Robert Augustus Masters in *Spiritual Bypassing: When Spirituality Disconnects Us from What Really Matters* (Berkeley, CA: North Atlantic Books, 2010).

20. See German Lopez, "There are huge racial disparities in how US police use force," *Vox*, November 14, 2018, https://www.vox.com/identities/2016/8/13/17938186/police-shootings-killings-racism-racial-disparities.

21. Ahmed Olayinka Sule, "Racism harms black people most. It's time to recognise 'anti-blackness,'" *The Guardian*, August 9, 2019, https://www.theguardian.com/commentisfree/2019/aug/09/black-people-racism-anti-blackness-discrimination-minorities. See also Rudroneel Ghosh, "Bridge the Gap: Attacks on Africans in India highlight a glaring lack of people-to-people connect," *The Times of India*, November 24, 2018, https://timesofindia.indiatimes.com/blogs/talkingturkey/bridge-the-gap-attacks-on-africans-in-india-highlight-a-glaring-lack-of-people-to-people-connect/; and Samantha Libreri, "'Let us share the land' – land ownership dominates South African election debate," *RTE*, March 19, 2019, https://www.rte.ie/news/world/2019/0319/1037200-south-africa/.

22. Wikipedia contributors, "Shooting of Chris Kaba," Wikipedia, The Free Encyclopedia, last modified July 8, 2024, https://en.wikipedia.org/wiki/Shooting_of_Chris_Kaba.

23. Islamophobia is the irrational and unjustified fear of, hatred of, or prejudice against the religion of Islam or Muslims in general, especially when seen as a geopolitical force or a source of terrorism.

24. Xenophobia, or fear of strangers, is the fear or hatred of people who are perceived as being different from oneself. This can be based on a person's race, ethnicity, nationality, religion, or other distinguishing characteristics. Xenophobia and racism are similar as both have roots in discrimination. However, xenophobia usually refers to a person's nationality and culture rather than exclusively their race or ethnicity. People can be both xenophobic and racist. See "What is Xenophobia?" Report + Support, University of Edinburgh, accessed May 30, 2024, https://reportandsupport.ed.ac.uk/pages/what-is-xenophobia.

25. Ellen E. Jones, *Screen Deep: How Film and TV Can Solve Racism and Save the World* (London, England: Faber & Faber, 2022), 7.

26. In her defining work, *Legacy of Violence*, Caroline Elkins writes of nineteenth-century British imperialism and of how "Britain 'racialized' the Irish and Afrikaners, equating their

cultures to those of brown and Black subjects, sometimes using dehumanizing language to describe their physical appearances and living conditions, and believing that, just like the Xhosa of South Africa or the Chinese in Malaya, the Irish and Afrikaners were "backward" populations that needed to be civilized." Caroline Elkins, *Legacy of Violence: A History of the British Empire* (New York, NY: Random House, 2022), Kindle, 12. In addition, Noel Ignatiev's seminal work from 1995 describes how the Irish left for America in the eighteenth century, fleeing a homeland under foreign occupation and a caste system that regarded them as the lowest form of humanity. The book delves into the transformation of Irish immigrants in America from a marginalized group to one that participated in the oppression of African Americans. His historical account explores how the Irish, initially facing racialized hostility, sought acceptance by adopting and often exceeding the nativist population's brutal tactics against African Americans. Noel Ignatiev, *How the Irish Became White* (New York, NY: Routledge Classics, 2008). Today, the UK Equality and Human Rights Commission defines race as "your color, or your nationality (including your citizenship). It can also mean your ethnic or national origins, which may not be the same as your current nationality.... A racial group can be made up of two or more distinct racial group, for example black Britons, British Asians, British Sikhs, British Jews, Romany Gypsies and Irish Travellers." See "Race discrimination," *Equality and Human Rights Commission*, February 20, 2020, https://www.equalityhumanrights.com/equality/equality-act-2010/your-rights-under-equality-act-2010/race-discrimination.

27 "Recalling Africa's harrowing tale of its first slavers – The Arabs – as UK Slave Trade Abolition is commemorated," *New African Magazine*, March 27, 2018, https://newafricanmagazine.com/16616/; Thomas Lewis, "Transatlantic Slave Trade," Britannica, updated December 29, 2023, https://www.britannica.com/money/topic/transatlantic-slave-trade; In June 2023, the Brattle Group, a respected global financial consultancy, produced a landmark report that represented the most comprehensive financial analysis of transatlantic slavery ever, that attempted to quantify the amount of reparations that should be payable for the violations of international law arising from and caused by transatlantic chattel slavery. They describe transatlantic slavery as being "without parallel for its brutality, without parallel for its length over 400 years, without parallel for its profitability." Coleman Bazelon, Alberto Vargas, Rohan Janakiraman, and Mary M. Olson, "Quantification of Reparations for Transatlantic Chattel Slavery," Brattle, June 8, 2023, https://www.brattle.com/wp-content/uploads/2023/07/Quantification-of-Reparations-for-Transatlantic-Chattel-Slavery.pdf. See also Aamna Mohdin, "UK cannot ignore calls for slavery reparations, says leading UN judge," *The Guardian*, August 22, 2023, https://www.theguardian.com/world/2023/aug/22/uk-cannot-ignore-calls-for-slavery-reparations-says-leading-un-judge-patrick-robinson.

28 Ahmed Olayinka Sule, "Racism Harms Black People Most. It's Time to Recognise 'Anti-Blackness,'" *The Guardian*, August 9, 2019, https://www.theguardian.com/commentisfree/2019/aug/09/black-people-racism-anti-blackness-discrimination-minorities. Here she references *White Fragility* by Robin DiAngelo.

29 "The classification of human populations into discrete races was formally denounced ... with the 1950 publication of UNESCO's 'The Race Question', in response to Second World War Nazi racism. This stated that, 'For all practical social purposes, "race" is not so much

a biological phenomenon as a social myth. The myth of "race" has created an enormous amount of human and social damage.'" See Jones, *Screen Deep*, 8.

30 "Race is a cultural invention, largely originating during Europe's Age of Exploration (approx. 1400–1650), and has never had a clear definition. Sometimes it has referred to physical appearance (caucasian, negro) and at other times to continent of origin (Asians, Africans, Indians), language (Greeks, Arabs), religion (Jews, Muslims), or even nationality or ethnicity (Irish, Koreans, Hispanics)." See "Most Racially Diverse Countries," World Population Review, accessed May 13, 2024, https://worldpopulationreview.com/country-rankings/most-racially-diverse-countries.

31 See Angela Saini, *Superior: The Return of Race Science* (New York, NY: HarperCollins Publishers, 2019). The word "racialized" carries with it an understanding of the constructed nature of race, which is itself socially, politically, and historically constructed.

32 These nations rank highly in studies that measure ethnic, linguistic, and religions diversity because of their many tribal groups and languages. This is confirmed by Fearon's Diversity Index, Harvard's studies based on 165 countries, and Erkan Goren's study of "How Ethnic Diversity Affects Economic Development." See Wikipedia contributors, "List of Countries Ranked by Ethnic and Cultural Diversity Level," Wikipedia, accessed May 13, 2024, https://en.wikipedia.org/wiki/List_of_countries_ranked_by_ethnic_and_cultural_diversity_level; "Most Racially Diverse Countries," World Population Review, accessed May 13, 2024, https://worldpopulationreview.com/country-rankings/most-racially-diverse-countries; "The Most (and Least) Culturally Diverse Countries in the World," Pew Research Center, accessed May 13, 2024, https://www.pewresearch.org/short-reads/2013/07/18/the-most-and-least-culturally-diverse-countries-in-the-world/; "Open Humanities Data," Journal of Open Humanities Data, accessed May 13, 2024, https://openhumanitiesdata.metajnl.com/articles/10.5334/johd.16.

33 See "Most Diverse Countries," World Population Review, accessed May 13, 2024, https://worldpopulationreview.com/country-rankings/most-diverse-countries; "Canada Population," World Population Review, accessed May 13, 2024, https://worldpopulationreview.com/countries/canada-population.

34 Wisevoter ranks the US at number 68 and the UK at number 82 out of 165 countries. See "Most Racially Diverse Countries," WiseVoter, accessed May 13, 2024, https://wisevoter.com/country-rankings/most-racially-diverse-countries; "The Most (and Least) Culturally Diverse Countries in the World," Pew Research Center, accessed May 13, 2024, https://www.pewresearch.org/short-reads/2013/07/18/the-most-and-least-culturally-diverse-countries-in-the-world/.

35 Ros Taylor, "What the UK Population Will Look Like by 2061 Under Hard, Soft, or No-Brexit Scenarios," July 1, 2019, LSE Brexit Blog, accessed May 13, 2024, https://blogs.lse.ac.uk/brexit/2019/07/01/what-the-uk-population-will-look-like-by-2061-under-hard-soft-or-no-brexit-scenarios/.

36 See Jennifer M. Ortman and Christine E. Guarneri, "United States Population Projections: 2000 to 2050," accessed May 30, 2024, https://www.census.gov/content/dam/Census/library/working-papers/2009/demo/us-pop-proj-2000-2050/analytical-document09.pdf; Jeffrey S. Passel, "U.S. Population Projections: 2005-2050," Pew Research Center,

accessed May 30, 2024, https://www.pewresearch.org/hispanic/2008/02/11/us-population-projections-2005-2050/.

37 Between 2006 and 2019, the diversity of Catholic congregations in the US rose from 17 percent to 24 percent; mainline Protestant congregations rose from 1 percent to 11 percent, and evangelical churches rose from 7 percent to 23 percent. See "Racially Diverse Congregations in U.S. Have Nearly Tripled in Past 20 Years," *Baylor University News*, November 11, 2020, https://news.web.baylor.edu/news/story/2020/racially-diverse-congregations-us-have-nearly-tripled-past-20-years-baylor; and PRRI Staff, "2020 Census of American Religion: County-Level Data on Religious Identity and Diversity," Public Religion Research Institute, July 8, 2021, https://www.prri.org/research/2020-census-of-american-religion/. There are comparable changes taking place in UK and European churches.

38 Journalist, broadcaster, and author Ellen E. Jones helpfully describes colorism as follows: "White supremacy ... often functions as a hierarchy, with whiteness at its apex. Within that hierarchy people of colour with lighter skin, straighter hair or other European-proximate features can be privileged in relation to people with darker skin tones or less European features. Colourism describes this type of discrimination, which often exists within communities of colour." Jones, *Screen Deep*, 15.

39 "Another umbrella term which is sometimes preferred to alternatives such as BAME (Black, Asian and minority ethnic), the North America-specific BIPOC (Black, Indigenous and people of colour) and POC (people of colour). This is because the word 'racialised' carries with it an understanding of the constructed nature of race, and the social process through which some groups of people are considered to have a race or ethnicity, and other people – white people – are considered to be racially neutral." See Jones, *Screen Deep*, 18.

40 Myriam Callegarin, "Why Developing Intercultural Management Skills Is Essential in Today's Complex World," CUOA Business School, February 2018, https://www.cuoaspace.it/2018/02/why-developing-intercultural-management-skills-is-essential-in-todays-complex-world.html.

41 Terri E. Givens, *Radical Empathy: Finding a Path to Bridging Racial Divides* (University of Bristol, England: Policy Press, 2021), Kindle, 1.

42 Julia Middleton, *If That's Leading, I'm In: Women Redefining Leadership* (Julia Middleton, 2003), 174.

43 This is sometimes described as "code-switching," which involves adjusting one's style of speech, appearance, behavior, and expression in ways that will optimize the comfort of others in exchange for fair treatment, quality service, and employment opportunities.

44 Lee, *Our Unforming*, 266.

45 Reverend Romal J. Tune, "Richard Rohr on White Privilege," interview, Sojourners, January 19, 2016, https://sojo.net/articles/richard-rohr-white-privilege.

46 See Nicholas Wolterstorff, "Why the Quartet of the Vulnerable?" in *Justice: Rights and Wrongs* (Princeton, NJ: Princeton University Press, 2008), 75.

47 See the discussion on "implicated subjects" in chapter three of this book.

48 Simeon was from sub-Saharan West Africa, Lucius from North Africa, Manaen from Palestine, Barnabas from Cyprus, and Saul from Tarsus in Asia Minor.

49 See Acts 13:44–50 and Acts 14:19.

50 Interestingly, converts from Islam, Hinduism, and Buddhism in global Jesus-movements today sometimes prefer to call themselves "disciples" or "followers of Jesus" rather than "Christians" precisely because it is not a name the early followers chose for themselves.

51 See Janet H. Cho, "Diversity is being invited to the party; inclusion is being asked to dance," Cleveland.com, May 25, 2016, https://www.cleveland.com/business/2016/05/diversity_is_being_invited_to.html.

7 ESTHER

1 Susan Beaumont, *How to Lead When You Don't Know Where You're Going: Leading in a Liminal Season* (Lanham, MD: Rowman & Littlefield Publishers, 2019), 114.

2 *Collins English Dictionary*, s.v. "Purpose," accessed May 13, 2024, https://www.collinsdictionary.com/us/dictionary/english/purpose.

3 According to Merriam-Webster, a calling is "a strong inner impulse toward a particular course of action, especially when accompanied by conviction of divine influence." It is also defined as "the vocation or profession in which one customarily engages." Calling can include what you do either professionally or personally. It can be a role or status in society. *Merriam-Webster*, s.v. "Calling," accessed July 12, 2024, https://www.merriam-webster.com/dictionary/calling.

4 Addison, *Movements That Change the World: Five Keys to Spreading the Gospel* (Downers Grove, IL: InterVarsity Press, 2009), 33.

5 Incidentally, Hagar is the only person in the Hebrew Bible who actually gives God a name.

6 The scholar Michael Rothberg argues that almost all of us contribute to or benefit from structural injustice. We may not be direct agents of harm, but we can still contribute to, inhabit, or benefit from regimes of domination that we neither set up nor control. Michael Rothberg, *The Implicated Subject: Beyond Victims and Perpetrators (Cultural Memory in the Present)* (Stanford, CA: Stanford University Press, 2019).

7 Phil Thomas, "Raising Up Godly Leaders Among International Students Around the World," Lausanne Movement, October 2023, https://lausanne.org/content/lga/2023-11/raising-up-godly-leaders-among-international-students-around-the-world.

8 Matthew Baird, "Women Are Still Underrepresented in Leadership and the Technology, Information and Media industry," LinkedIn, March 7, 2023, https://economicgraph.linkedin.com/blog/women-are-still-underrepresented-in-leadership-and-the-technology-information-and-media-industry.

9 Blake A. Allan, Ryan D. Duffy, and Bryan Collisson, "Task significance and performance: Meaningfulness as a mediator," *Journal of Career Assessment* 26, no. 1 (2018): 172–182, https://psycnet.apa.org/record/2018-02934-010.

10 See Barbara Kurshan and Kathy Hurley, *InnovateHERs: Why Purpose-Driven Entrepreneurial Women Rise to the Top* (InnovateHERs Press, 2022).

11 See research from Leadership Circle on female and male leaders. This research was based on assessments with over 84,000 leaders and 1.5 million raters (comprising bosses, bosses' bosses, peers, direct reports, and others) and shows that female leaders show up more effectively than their male counterparts across every management level and age level. Cynthia Adams and Lani Van Dusen, "Understanding the Differences in Reactive and Creative

Orientations Between Female and Male Leaders," Leadership Circle White Paper series, March 17, 2022, https://leadershipcircle.com/whitepapers/.

12 Mark Galli, "Where We Got It Wrong," *Christianity Today*, November 27, 2018, https://www.christianitytoday.com/ct/2018/december/where-we-got-it-wrong-segregation-apology.html.

13 Barbara Dianne Savage, *Your Spirits Walk Beside Us: The Politics of Black Religion* (Cambridge, MA: Harvard University Press, 2008), 203. Also see Samuel G. Freedman, "Gardiner C. Taylor, Righteous Wingman," *New Yorker*, April 14, 2015, https://www.newyorker.com/news/news-desk/gardner-c-taylor-righteous-wingman. Similar observations—or criticisms—that too few Black clergy advocated for Black people's rights predated the civil rights movement. For example, in the first decade of the twentieth century, the journalist and activist Ida B. Wells lamented that no church in Chicago, including her own, would let her use church space to hold a public meeting about a lynching. Besheer Mohamed, Kiana Cox, Jeff Diamant, and Claire Gecewicz, "10. A brief overview of Black religious history in the U.S.," Pew Research, February 16, 2021, https://www.pewresearch.org/religion/2021/02/16/a-brief-overview-of-black-religious-history-in-the-u-s/#fn-34217-37, referencing Barbara Dianne Savage, "W.E.B. DuBois and 'The Negro Church,'" *The Annals of the American Academy of Political and Social Science*, 2000.

14 Next Leadership is the name of the organization I co-lead with my friend and colleague, Cham Kaur-Mann. We are particularly passionate about developing high-capacity, change-making leaders. You can find out more about us and our work on our website: https://www.nextleadership.co.uk/.

15 The young women were given beauty treatments for one whole year. For the first six months, their skin was rubbed with olive oil and myrrh, and for the last six months, it was treated with perfumes and cosmetics. Then each of them spent the night alone with King Xerxes.

16 John C. Maxwell, *The 21 Indispensable Qualities of a Leader: Becoming the Person Others Will Want to Follow* (Nashville, TN: Thomas Nelson Publishers, 1999), 3.

8 THE 120

1 The Global North is defined in a geopolitical sense by five current United Nations regions: Eastern Europe (including Russia), Northern Europe, Southern Europe, Western Europe, and North America. Gina A. Zurlo, *Global Christianity* (Grand Rapids, MI: Zondervan Academic, 2022), xviii.

2 "Revival is usually seen as a time of renewal in devotion among Christians as well as an increased zeal for God's work and His Kingdom. It impacts people in churches, cities, regions, and nations in many ways. One of those ways is social change. Compassion for the sick to be healed, as well as the start of hospitals and clinics is the fruit of revival. Concern for orphans, widows and the poor is a product of revival too, as is ministering freedom and deliverance to those who have been considered alcoholics, drug addicts and homeless. The start of Christian colleges with an education which reflects the values of Christ is also linked to revival. The Holy Spirit has been known to increase all of these

ministries during and after His outpouring." Randy Clarke, "A History of Revival, Part 1," Global Awakening, accessed June 7, 2024, https://globalawakening.com/a-history-of-revival-part-i/; "Evangelicalism and Pentecostal/Charismatic Christianity are considered movements within Catholic, Protestant, Orthodox, and Independent Christianity. The four major traditions are mutually exclusive—a Christian cannot be both a Protestant and a Catholic (unless doubly affiliated). However, movements are found within the major traditions and are not mutually exclusive. For example, a Christian can be an Evangelical Protestant or a Catholic Charismatic or an Evangelical Charismatic Independent." Zurlo, *Global Christianity*, xviii.

3   See Michael McClymond, "What Revivals Can Teach Us," *Christianity Today*, February 24, 2023, https://www.christianitytoday.com/ct/2023/february-web-only/what-revival-history-christian-movements-asbury-university.html.

4   Jürgen Moltmann, *The Church in the Power of the Spirit: A Contribution to Messianic Ecclesiology* (Minneapolis, MN: Fortress Press, 1993), 11.

5   Gerard Kelly, *Church Actually: Rediscovering The Brilliance In God's Plan*, new ed. (Oxford, England: Monarch Books, 2012), 45.

6   Addison, *Movements That Change the World*, 24–25.

7   The Great Commission is recorded in the Gospel of Matthew 28:16–20, where Jesus meets with the eleven disciples on a mountain in Galilee and gives them the directive. Even then we read, "When they saw him, they worshiped him; but some doubted" (v. 17).

8   See David R. Thomas, "How History's Revivals Teach Us to Pray," *Christianity Today*, February 20, 2018, https://www.christianitytoday.com/ct/2018/march/praying-too-casually-travailing-prayer.html.

9   Anne Helmenstine, "Can Lightning Strike the Same Place Twice?" Science Notes, last modified May 16, 2023, https://sciencenotes.org/can-lightning-strike-the-same-place-twice/.

10 Theodor Reik, "Essay 3: The Unreachables: The Repetition Compulsion in Jewish History," in *Curiosities of the Self: Illusions We Have about Ourselves* (New York, NY: Farrar, Straus & Giroux, 1965), 133.

11 See title page together with pages 4, 6, 31, etc., in Allen Yeh, *Polycentric Missiology: 21st-Century Mission from Everyone to Everywhere* (Downers Grove, IL: InterVarsity Press, 2016).

12 The term "Two-Thirds World" is an alternative to the more derogatory term "Third World." It refers to the regions of the world that are considered to be developing or emerging, encompassing approximately two-thirds of the world's population.

13 Yeh, *Polycentric Missiology*, 50.

14 Yeh, *Polycentric Missiology*, 45.

15 See Dr. Eddie Hyatt, foreword to Susan Stubbs Hyatt, *Pandita Ramabai, India's Woman of the Millennium: Pandita Ramabai: Her Story in Her Own Words*, ed. Susan Stubbs Hyatt, Int'l Christian Women's Hall of Fame Series, book 3 (Grapevine, TX: God's Word to Women, 2019). See also Adrian Leak, "Indian Convert Who Thought For Herself," *Church Times*, April 21, 2009, https://www.churchtimes.co.uk/articles/2009/24-april/faith/indian-convert-who-thought-for-herself-1; "Pandita Ramabai," CBE International, accessed June 7, 2024, https://www.cbeinternational.org/resource/women-in-scripture-and-mission-pandita-ramabai-2/; and Canon John, "Heroes of the Faith: Pandita

Ramabai," CanonJ.John.com, January 23, 2021, https://canonjjohn.com/2021/01/23/heroes-of-the-faith-pandita-ramabai/.

16   Mukto Mission US and Pandita Ramabai, *The Pandita Ramabai Story: In Her Own Words* (Mukti Mission US, 2019), Kindle, 20.

17   Harriet Tubman was the conductor of the underground railroad that guided more than one hundred thousand enslaved people to freedom from the southern states of America to Canada.

18   Mukti (means freedom, liberation, salvation).

19   Jeff Oliver, *Pentecost to the Present,* Book Three: Worldwide Revivals and Renewal: The Holy Spirit's Enduring Work in the Church (Alachua, FL: Bridge-Logos Publishers, 2017), 74.

20   Victor John, a leader in the Bhojpuri movement, highlights this contrast in India, where traditional norms often undervalue women. This movement breaks the mold by elevating women, acknowledging their worth, and involving them in leadership roles. He states, "Gender issues are a huge problem in north Indian society. Men and women treat each other very differently after accepting Christ than they did before. They now exhibit love and caring that defies all previous customs and traditions. Men and women share equal responsibility in sharing the good news and carrying it forward. They also share equal responsibility in multiplying disciples, leaders and churches…. We view women and treat women as equal partners in the good news and in the ministry. This is counter cultural and intentional on our part. Our stand from the very beginning has been that men and women are equal. Just as God calls men, he calls women as well. If men can make disciples, women can make disciples. So we have many women who are leaders and church planters in the movement. They have discipled people and won whole households. We have no problem with appointing women as leaders in the church. The head of our organization is a woman, a wonderful servant leader." Warrick Farah, "Bhojpuri Case Study," in *Motus Dei: The Movement of God to Disciple the Nations* (Littleton, CO: William Carey Publishing, 2021), 258–259.

21   Martin Luther King Jr., *Strength to Love* (New York, NY: Harper & Row, 1963), 19.

22   "In the Hebrew Bible, the Spirit of God (and more broadly) is grammatically feminine. This is not easily visible when reading in English…. In Greek, in the Septuagint and Christian Scriptures, the word for "spirit" is neuter, meaning that in the breadth of the Scriptures the spirit is anything and everything but masculine. The deliberate choice to render the spirit in masculine terms in Latin texts such as the Vulgate reflects theological commitments apart from the grammar of the texts." Wilda Gafney, *A Women's Lectionary For The Whole Church* (New York, NY: Church Publishing, 2021), 195.

23   Mookgo Solomon Kgatla, "The Influence of Azusa Street Revival in the Early Developments of the Apostolic Faith Mission of South Africa," *Missionalia* 44, no. 3 (2016): 321–335, accessed June 14, 2024, https://scielo.org.za/scielo.php?script=sci_arttext&pid=S0256-95072016000300006&lng=en&nrm=iso.

24   "The 19th Amendment, ratified a century ago on Aug. 18, 1920, is often hailed for granting American women the right to vote. And yet most Black women would wait nearly five decades more to actually exercise that right." In a decidedly calculated move, campaigning in the US was carried out along racial lines and specifically intended to enfranchise white

women. Subsequently, women of colour were largely barred from access. Olivia B. Waxman, "'It's a Struggle They Will Wage Alone.' How Black Women Won the Right to Vote," *Time*, August 17, 2020, https://time.com/5876456/black-women-right-to-vote/. Since Native Americans weren't allowed to be United States citizens in 1920, the federal amendment did not give them the right to vote. They had to wait until as late as 1962. It took a 1975 extension of the Voting Rights Act of 1965 before *all* women were permitted to vote. See "Not All Women Gained the Vote in 1920," *PSB*, July 6, 2020, https://www.pbs.org/wgbh/americanexperience/features/vote-not-all-women-gained-right-to-vote-in-1920/.

25 The civil rights movement in the United States was a social movement and campaign from 1954 to 1968 that existed to abolish legalized racial segregation, discrimination, and disenfranchisement in the country. Its roots emerge far earlier in the nineteenth century.

26 Elmer L. Towns and Douglas Porter, *The Ten Greatest Revivals Ever: From Pentecost to the Present* (Ann Arbor, MI: Servant Publications, 2000), accessed June 14, 2024, https://digitalcommons.liberty.edu/cgi/viewcontent.cgi?article=1192&context=towns_books.

27 Michael McClymond, "What Revivals Can Teach Us," *Christianity Today*, February 24, 2023, https://www.christianitytoday.com/ct/2023/february-web-only/what-revival-history-christian-movements-asbury-university.html.

28 Mitri Raheb, *Faith in the Face of Empire: The Bible through Palestinian Eyes* (Maryknoll, NY: Orbis Books, 2014), 113.

29 Towns and Porter, *The Ten Greatest Revivals Ever*, 28.

30 Pentecostal and charismatic Christianity is the fastest-growing segment of world Christianity today. This group of churches, denominations, and networks grew at an astounding 6.3 percent per year on average between 1900 and 2000—four times as fast as both Christianity as a whole and the world's population. Growth has slowed considerably since then, but this tradition is still growing faster than any other. (From 2020–2050, it is expected to grow twice as fast as both.) According to Zurlo, these groups share an interest in Spirit baptism, spiritual gifts, and spiritual experiences. Most of the growth over the past century took place in the Global South. Africans now constitute 35.7 percent of all Spirit-filled Christians, Latin Americans 30.3 percent, and Asians 19.5 percent. Zurlo, *Global Christianity*, 30.

31 Addison, *Movements That Change the World*, 33.

32 Zurlo, *Global Christianity*, 30.

33 Towns and Porter, *The Ten Greatest Revivals Ever*, 1.

ABOUT THE AUTHOR

KATE COLEMAN was the first Black woman Baptist minister in the UK and previously served as president of the UK Baptist Union and chair of the UK Evangelical Alliance Council. A popular speaker, lecturer, and author, Kate has been recognized as one of the twenty most influential Black Christian women leaders in the UK and has gained a reputation as a pioneer, visionary, and an inspiration to many. She now serves as a strategic advisor, mentoring, coaching, and supporting leaders and organizations in the UK and globally, with a network that spans all sectors and church denominations.